Praise for YOU TALK, WE DIE

'In the competitive world of federal politics, working as an independent member of parliament, I often felt my competitive advantage was that I was a country woman. Grounded in the wisdom of our communities, country women get things done, with low fuss, strategic intent, respect, and persistence. I think there's no greater compliment than to acknowledge Judy Ryan as a wonderful country woman, and this book is a testament to her heritage and skills.'

Cathy McGowan AO,
independent federal member for Indi, 2013–2019

'That smile, those red lips. Judy Ryan's magnetic energy and compassion brought a community together to help some of the most stigmatised and ostracised people in the village of North Richmond. *You Talk, We Die* is captivating and takes you on the extraordinary ride of Judy's grassroots campaign for life-saving law reform.'

Fiona Patten,
Victorian MP, leader of the Reason Party

'*You Talk, We Die* tells the important story of how community action changes lives and changes policy. This book is a blueprint for people who are experiencing this epidemic in their communities. It's a classic example of citizens changing minds — and laws — to protect and support their communities, including its marginalised, stigmatised members.'

Larry Campbell,
Canadian senator and former mayor of Vancouver

'If you want a rip-roaring yarn that illustrates the nitty-gritty of community-led organising, look no further. Read this book and you'll see, firsthand, the reality of working at the coalface of community. You'll understand why no one need ever die of a heroin overdose and why stigma is such a barrier to care. You'll see how a caring and connected local community took on those in power — and won.'

Dr Marianne Jauncey,
medical director of the Uniting Medically Supervised Injecting Centre, Kings Cross, Sydney

'The story of a compassionate woman, a community mobilising against preventable deaths from drug overdose, and the ridiculously Herculean efforts required to eventually achieve Victoria's first drug consumption room — still way short of what's needed for the state, but a magnificent achievement and a worthwhile start. The marathon struggle continues.'

Dr Alex Wodak AM,
emeritus consultant, Drug and Alcohol Service,
St Vincent's Hospital, Sydney

'*You Talk, We Die* is a moving account of the importance of compassion and human dignity. This is a "must read" for all those that aspire to change our community for the better.'

Demos Krouskos,
retired CEO of North Richmond Community Health

'*You Talk, We Die* is essential reading for policymakers, public-health practitioners, and importantly, activists seeking to reduce harms associated with drug use. It highlights the importance of the voice of local citizens in any policy and law-changing endeavour. They brought compassion to their streets.'

Robert Richter KC and David Stanley,
Australian Drug Law Reform Foundation

YOU TALK, WE DIE

Judy Ryan was born and raised in Wangaratta, in north-east Victoria. She has worked in communications for BHP, secondary and tertiary education institutions, and the health sector. Her small business, the Women Love Moving Relocation Service, assists women to transition into new accommodation and new phases of their life. Since 2012, she has lived in Abbotsford, where she has stood as a political candidate in local, state, and federal elections in support of the campaign, led by her, for a safe injecting facility in inner-city Melbourne. In the Queen's Birthday 2022 Honours, Judy was awarded the Medal of the Order of Australia (OAM) 'for service to community health through a range of programs'.

JUDY RYAN

YOU TALK, WE DIE

THE BATTLE FOR VICTORIA'S FIRST SAFE INJECTING FACILITY

SCRIBE
Melbourne • London

Scribe Publications
18–20 Edward St, Brunswick, Victoria 3056, Australia

First published by Scribe 2023

Typeset in Bembo by the publishers

Printed and bound in Australia by Griffin Press

Scribe is committed to the sustainable use of natural resources and the use of paper products made responsibly from those resources.

Scribe acknowledges Australia's First Nations peoples as the traditional owners and custodians of this country. We recognise that sovereignty was never ceded, and we pay our respects to their elders, past and present.

978 1 922585 85 1 (Australian edition)
978 1 922586 91 9 (ebook)

Catalogue records for this book are available from the National Library of Australia.

scribepublications.com.au

To my inspirational mother,
Mary Ryan (nee O'Dwyer)
Who confronted life's challenges with
determination, courage, and dignity,
For the inspiration she is to her loving family,
And for her practical contribution
to her country community.

Contents

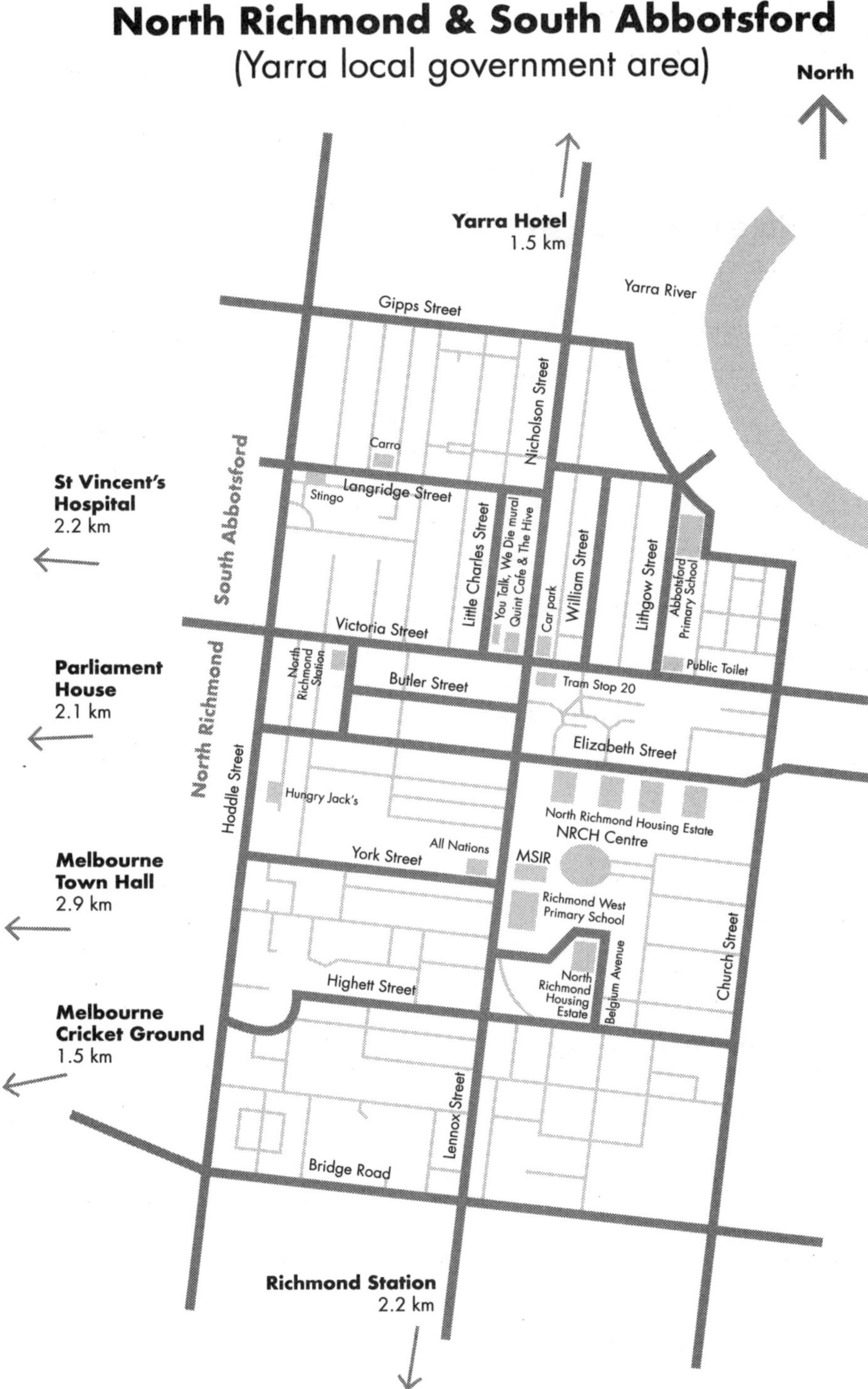

*Distances from the MSIR, 23 Lennox Street, North Richmond

Key abbreviations

AOD	alcohol and other drugs
DHHS	Department of Health and Human Services
MSIC	medically supervised injecting centre (a SIF)
MSIR	medically supervised injecting room (a SIF)
NRCH	North Richmond Community Health
RVSDS	Residents for Victoria Street Drug Solutions
SIF	safe injecting facility

Introduction

'Final question.'

> Do you think politicians would change their minds if their kids had overdosed — or died — in your laneway? I mean, would something bad like that make them change their mind and support a safe injecting place where their kids — or siblings — could go and wouldn't die, where they could get support from other health services?

I was giving a guest talk at the school where I also worked in a communications role three days a week. The class of 16-year-old students had been peppering me with questions as part of their Year 10 'Law and Order: Law Reform' subject. Their thoughtful queries revealed a deep level of engagement with the Victorian legislation that currently required drug addiction to be managed as a criminal rather than a health issue. This lively conversation in 2017 is the reason I enjoy working at schools. The musings of adolescents are unfiltered when social-justice issues are under the microscope.

This was my answer to the final question:

> Yes, I believe they would change their minds and support safe

injecting facilities. I have been told by a veteran Australian politician — whose sibling sadly died from a heroin overdose — that an experience like the one you mention would be a game changer for sure.

It's often stated that 'politics is personal'. Politicians' views are influenced by their lived experiences and their careers before entering politics. There are many examples of politicians who have crossed the floor of parliament to vote against their party's policy if it conflicted with those experiences and their values. A politician who had experienced life with a child or sibling with drug addiction — or dying from an overdose — would bring an authentic voice and empathy to a debate about this controversial issue.

Remember that stigma is a big problem for families managing a loved one with addiction regardless of who they are. Unfair and brutal judgements are made by outsiders, forcing people to manage the problem alone, due to shame. Politicians are the same as everyone else, hiding personal issues that may present them in a bad light.

Getting off the train at Richmond station that sunny but cool afternoon in May 2017, I was unprepared for the trauma that lay ahead of me. I love returning to my inner-city refuge of Richmond and Abbotsford in Wurundjeri Woi Wurrung country.[1] The school I worked at was in an affluent suburb that I found unsettling in its leafy perfection. Richmond and Abbotsford are more my style: historic, cosmopolitan, colourful, and edgy.

Heading north from the station, I took my usual journey home, meandering through narrow streets featuring stately period homes, converted warehouse apartments, restored Victorian and Edwardian houses, and 'renovators' delights'. Michael Cannon records in *Old Melbourne Town Before the Gold Rush*:

> A crazy pattern of alleyways and dead-end lanes began to emerge as the portions [of land] were subdivided [from 1839] without interference from government or council. Richmond was not so badly affected as the Collingwood [Abbotsford] area, but even today it remains a patchwork of crowded little streets, divided by narrow main roads ...[2]

Posters in windows show a roaring tiger. Fences and gates are painted yellow and black. A mural of superstar footballer Dustin Martin features on a shop wall. There is no doubting that you are in Tigerland. The Richmond Football Club headquarters are only a stone's throw — a drop punt — from here, and its supporters are 'Strong and Bold'. The Melbourne Cricket Ground, bordered by expansive parkland, is just as close.

Once I veered onto narrow Lennox Street, I passed the Epworth private hospital, the All Nations Hotel, the North Richmond Community Health centre, and multicultural Richmond West Primary School: 'Australia's leading Chinese immersion bilingual primary school', according to its website. The fact was reported by BBC News Melbourne in 2013[3] and celebrated by Frances Adamson, the Australian ambassador to the People's Republic of China, in 2012:

> Richmond West Primary School … has been running a genuinely bi-lingual program in English and Mandarin since 1982. The teachers are impressive and the students are making excellent progress with their Chinese language proficiency. They will be the next generation of young Australians to engage with China.[4]

Parents travel from across Melbourne, eager for their children to benefit from the taxpayer-funded Mandarin-immersion program that runs across seven years, from preparatory to sixth grade.

Conspicuous on the landscape are five high-rise residential towers, built circa 1964. Janet McCalman notes the controversy regarding the construction of 'huge beehives', and the arrival of 'New Australians', in her award-winning book *Struggletown: private and public life in Richmond 1900–1965*:

> The coming of the post-war immigrants from Europe, then South-East Asia and South America, has constituted the most significant demographic transformation since the gold rushes … As the Italians increased, they began to leave their mark on food and leisure … Then came the Greeks, intensely proud of their culture and identity.[5]

Vietnamese immigrants began to live in Richmond around 1976, soon after arriving as refugees from South Vietnam, escaping a prolonged and deadly war. In the early 1980s, Vietnamese Australians started to establish small businesses on Victoria Street, introducing the community to cheap, exotic delights such as pho, banh mi, and noodles. The laid-back eateries are adorned with golden, glistening roast ducks hanging in windows, attracting patrons from across Melbourne and regional Victoria. There is no shortage of devotees of the Vietnamese dishes in this famous foodie strip affectionately known as Little Saigon.

In the 1980s, the busyness of Victoria Street and the surrounding precinct was amplified by the burgeoning illicit drug market — mainly heroin. Dealing and injecting became a regular occurrence behind shops, between parked cars, in laneways, and near the community health centre and primary school. It is a deadly scene for people with addiction: 34 people had lost their lives in 2016, fatally overdosing in Richmond and Abbotsford. Two Victorian coroners — Jacqui Hawkins and Audrey Jamieson — had recommended in February and May 2017, respectively, that the state government should 'establish a safe injecting facility in North Richmond' to manage the crisis.[6]

It was around 3.00 pm that day in May when my walk came to the bustling, charming, and somewhat grungy Victoria Street, the main thoroughfare that delineates Richmond on the south side from Abbotsford on the north. Warmed by the autumnal sun, I relished the mouth-watering aromas coming from the Vietnamese restaurants, which were interspersed with vacant shops plastered with For Lease signs. I prefer Victoria Street in the cooler months. On scorching summer days, the combined stench of melting bitumen and acrid sparks from hot metal on metal as trams hurtle along their tracks completely overwhelms the smell of food.

I was lost in my thoughts about what we would cook for dinner and other inconsequential matters when a commotion arose on the Abbotsford side of the street. A visibly distressed young man was calling desperately from outside the notorious public toilet block on the Lithgow Street corner, known to locals as the 'unsupervised injecting centre'. This ugly, cold, utilitarian building was regularly flanked by ambulances, fire trucks, and occasionally police cars when drug overdoses were reported to 000, the emergency-services number.

After quickly checking for trams, cars, and bikes, I ran across the street to help. The distressed man's partner, a young woman in her twenties, was lying motionless on her back on the asphalt footpath beside the toilet block. She was wearing jeans, a jumper, and solid hiking boots, and had dark hair and fair skin. She looked familiar. Maybe it was a family resemblance — I had a daughter and nieces about her age, with the same hair colour and complexion — or maybe I had seen her in the area before. Her breathing was shallow, and her lips were bluish. I felt for a pulse, which was very weak. Her eyes were closed, so I couldn't check her pupils. Her legs were spread slightly apart, and her arms were at her side.

Heart racing, I fumbled for my phone and dialled 000 for an ambulance. I was organising my thoughts and words so that I could provide a clear assessment to the operator of the woman's precarious situation, while simultaneously calming her partner. The noisy combination of his distress and the passing traffic made it almost impossible to hear the telephone prompts. Somehow, I managed to calmly advise the operator of the woman's condition from my basic observations. Shutting the phone, I continued calling the woman's name, which her partner had told me, while gently patting her cold face, pleading with her to 'stay with me, help is coming'. She remained unresponsive. I tried to make her as comfortable as I could, putting my coat over her torso for warmth and to protect her privacy.

Having come across drug-affected people over the years, it never ceases to shock me. They are very quiet when overdosed, so it's hard to tell what's going on. It's always traumatic for a non-medical resident, thinking that the person may be dead. No one that I had come across had ever looked — or felt — like this woman did that afternoon. I had heard of naloxone (Narcan), which is easy to use — like an EpiPen — and reverses an overdose. I cursed that I didn't have any with me. I felt desperate. There was nothing more I could do. I could hear my heart thumping.

The young man, too, was ashen-faced, muttering incoherently and calling her name. He was in a dreadful state, unsteady on his feet. I was certain that he would fall out onto busy Victoria Street, risking being hit by a car, so I clung onto his jacket for dear life to try and keep him safe. It was an exhausting experience, managing this situation on my own. The footpath was a tight space. I didn't have time to leave either of them to call out for assistance from passers-by. On a Wednesday afternoon, that section of Victoria Street was bereft of restaurant patrons. I yearned for the relief that would come from the sound of an emergency siren.

After what may have been only a few minutes, but which felt like an eternity, the wail of sirens heralded the arrival of a fire truck and an ambulance. The paramedics relieved me of what had been my responsibility for the woman's welfare — and gave me back my coat. I was shivering. I thought it was a visceral response to this calamity before noticing that the sun had slid behind the clouds, throwing a sullen mood and grey chill over the street. It was probably both.

While the paramedics attended to the woman, I was able to give my full attention to the young man. I told him that I was a local resident and thought that I recognised his partner. He mumbled that 'we always come here for heroin, so that would be right'. As I tried to comfort him, it became apparent from the paramedics' commentary that the woman was dead. This is how Dr Nico Clark describes it: 'Overdose death is quiet. One moment somebody is living and breathing, the next they have stopped breathing ... There's no loud bang. There's no fanfare.'[7] I was numb. A young woman with a medical condition had died needlessly on our main street. *She is dead.* Writing about it years later doesn't diminish the trauma.

The attending paramedics muttered to me that 'the overdoses on these streets are insane'. Later that evening as I tried to process what had happened, this comment took me back to when I was growing up in country Victoria in the 1960s: the 'old days', before the compulsory wearing of seatbelts and 0.05 blood-alcohol level for drivers. As a kid, I learnt of too many locals who lost their lives on our country roads — people we knew, my family's friends. An exasperated anaesthetist from the local hospital expressed his frustration, claiming to my older sisters, who were nurses, that those senseless deaths were 'insane'.

I had been living in Abbotsford near Victoria Street for five years. I was accustomed to finding people injecting, 'on the nod', or overdosed as I moved around the community. I had rung 000 countless times, waiting with drug-affected people until help arrived. But today was the first time that I had witnessed a fatality. Collapsed beside a dirty public toilet block was a dismal, sad, cold place for this young woman to take her last breath.

There was nothing more I could do. As I prepared to leave the scene, I heard the benign sound of a school bell. It was 3.30 pm and Abbotsford Primary School was farewelling its pupils for the day. Within minutes, schoolkids were coming past on their way home, unable to avoid this busy scene. I couldn't look at their faces but could imagine their chatter when they arrived home:

'I saw a dead lady lying on the footpath near school today.'

I pulled myself together as best I could and, in a numbed state, resumed my walk home. The calmness that I had felt when I left Richmond station 40 minutes earlier had been shattered by witnessing a preventable, needless death on a street in an affluent, sophisticated city — only eight tram stops from Parliament House. I was exhausted by the shock and trauma of it all. My husband, John, had been out shopping for dinner and, surprisingly, somehow appeared in front of me on Victoria Street. What a relief it was! I collapsed into his arms; tears held back until I was safely at home.

In the following hours and days, it was impossible to not think about what I had experienced that afternoon. I sympathised with those who mourned the deceased woman, shocked by her premature death. While I knew nothing about her apart from how she had died, she was someone's daughter, sister, granddaughter, aunt, niece, friend — and a mother of two little children, according to her partner. What also bothered me — and there was a lot that bothered me — was that this tragedy had been witnessed by schoolchildren. I worried about their parents having to manage the impact of what their child had seen as they walked home from school that day. And I was deeply concerned about the unrelenting pressure these incidents place on our emergency services, who manage hundreds of callouts to overdoses every year. I determined that I would urgently arrange training in the use of naloxone, which I could have administered that day.

As I reflected on this incident, and on residents managing drug-affected people as part of their daily lives, I was convinced that the growing call from the local community for a better solution

— a trial of a safe injecting facility, as recommended by two coroners — was, absolutely, the right thing to do. Premier Daniel Andrews had emphatically rejected those recommendations: 'I have been very, very clear prior to the election [in 2014] and since. We have no plans to introduce a facility like that.'[8]

I was exasperated, angry, and determined to do what I could to secure parliamentary support for a trial. The enthusiastic engagement of many residents, with the backing of the coroners, gave cause for some optimism.

—

This book came about because of my accidental immersion in one of Victoria's public-health crises — and the fanatical keeping of a diary and archival material. It is a personal story, not a work of scholarship: I do not have any academic or specialist qualifications on the subject. It is about my country woman's eyes on a harrowing inner-city tragedy, years in the making. I knew something had to be done about an issue that, to be honest, I didn't really know much about other than it needed to be addressed — urgently. It has been difficult to write some of these pages, as it required reliving traumatic experiences that form the backdrop of the narrative.

I had a lot to learn about issues that I had never really considered. I have addressed some basic questions that will be in the reader's mind, as they were in mine. What is heroin? What is overdose? What does 'on the nod' mean? What is a safe injecting facility, a medically supervised injecting centre, a drug-consumption room? What is a 'mobile' injecting facility? Do police support safe injecting facilities? What is the 'honeypot effect'? Where should a facility be located? What is harm reduction? What makes a drug-market hotspot? Why North Richmond? Why the reference to AOD (alcohol and other drugs)? Why are fire crews first responders to drug-overdose callouts? What is pharmacotherapy, and does it work? Can people be rehabilitated? Do CCTVs stop drug dealing? The questions are endless.

The international evidence has been emerging clearly over many years about the benefits of safe injecting facilities for people with drug addiction and for impacted communities. The case was prosecuted in both Sydney and Melbourne in the 1990s by myriad experts, law-reform activists, and health advocates. New South Wales led the way in Australia in May 2001 with the opening of the Uniting medically supervised injecting centre in Kings Cross.[9] The Melbourne campaign in the late 1990s failed due to local political opposition, despite Wesley Mission spending $400,000 on an unopened injecting facility in its Lonsdale Street church grounds.[10] In 2016, the time had come — again — to up the ante on this important issue.

I have been hugely supported on the journey by veterans of the drug law–reform sector and by harm-reduction warriors. These people have campaigned for decades, arguing that a shift from law enforcement to the health system has better outcomes for managing people who use illicit drugs. It has been humbling to learn from these experienced professionals, to be reminded of their tireless efforts to bring about practical and compassionate support for marginalised and stigmatised members of our community.

While my initial response to our health crisis was intuitive and emotional, once I learnt the facts I became even more convinced about what must be done. I urge the reader to ponder what they might have done had they confronted a similar crisis in their community. The reader may also be interested in our experience of building a grassroots movement to lobby for an issue of concern in their community.

Finally, I am in awe of the committed doctors, nurses, and allied-health and social-welfare professionals who work in this demanding health sector, in safe injecting facilities and other harm-reduction services. I acknowledge the people who live every day with drug addiction, some of whom take a leap of faith to cross the threshold into a supportive harm-reduction environment like a safe injecting facility. I empathise with their families and friends who provide practical and emotional support while holding out hope for a life that could be re-imagined. They are all burdened by stigma and understand how that can be fatal.

This one's for all of you.

1

They should do something

JULY 2016

Daniel Andrews, Nick Cave, and I share something special: we all grew up in Wang (Wangaratta to outsiders). I have not met either of these blokes, but from what I have read, both share my fond memories of the place. Nick has mused:

> So, like I say, Wang represents a childhood ideal — the river, the ghost gums, magpies, the ranges, the swimming pool, the paper run, my bike, the mighty trees we would climb, the footpaths that would fry our bare feet hard, storm drains, yabbie dams, the high bridges we jumped off, swim holes, vast star-filled skies, the living moon, the smell of a storm coming in the dust, the stench of the abattoir as you came into town from the Glenrowan end, the nests of red-backs [spiders] out in the compost, snakes, the wool mills — they're *all* symbols of my childhood that come up repeatedly in my songwriting …[1]

I could identify with all of Nick's reflections except 'the high bridges we jumped off'. I know those bridges, but never desired to take that leap of faith. The Ovens River was a long drop from the train bridge — and too snag-filled — to make that an attractive pursuit for me.

Daniel's reflection is prosaic but heartfelt nevertheless: 'I'm from this local community — not pretending, I'm just being me. I love this place.'[2]

Nick left Wang and became an international singer, songwriter, author, screenwriter, composer, and occasional actor. Daniel left Wang and became premier of Victoria. I left Wang and became a campaigner for Australia's second safe injecting facility (SIF): not quite as sexy as Nick's and Daniel's achievements, but it has certainly kept me occupied.

It wasn't what I set out to do.

I was born in Wangaratta, and I went to primary school and secondary school there. In the late 1970s, I moved to Melbourne, to 88 Elizabeth Street, North Richmond — near Victoria Street — to attend university. I completed a Bachelor of Business at the Royal Melbourne Institute of Technology in 1982 and worked for nine years at BHP's head office in Melbourne in government relations, marketing, and publications. During these years, I met and married John and we had three children: Daniel, Louise, and Charlie. In 1999, I returned with my family to my country roots, moving to Wodonga, on the Victoria–NSW border, where I worked in marketing and communications at Charles Sturt University in Albury.

In 2006, I started my own business, the You're Welcome Relocation Service, to assist new residents moving to the region, with a focus on belonging and retention. It was the most enjoyable job I had ever done, connecting people to services, schools, jobs, and, importantly, personal networks.

Then in 2012, our three children grown and gone, John and I relocated ourselves, to South Abbotsford to be closer to his elderly mother in Melbourne.

—

On a Sunday afternoon in July 2016, I was heading home along a cobblestone thoroughfare, heaving my canvas shopping bags while chatting with one of my sisters on the phone. As I rounded the corner into the secondary, dead-end laneway that provides pedestrian access to our property, I found a young man slumped, still and quiet, next to our gate. I recognised him as one of 'my regulars'. This spot is 200 metres from Victoria Street and is tucked away, making it a dangerous place for people injecting alone. Branches from neighbours' trees cascade over the fences, providing the perfect screen for visitors seeking privacy — hiding from police and others who may report or interrupt their illegal activity. Locals are familiar with the 'regulars': their appearance, voice, gait, duration of visit, and sometimes their names. From the northern side of my house, and from my garden, I hear them as they arrive, setting up to combine their bottled water with powders that they have purchased nearby, ready to inject. This activity is methodical but with a sense of urgency, usually followed by unnerving silence, and then, hopefully, quiet movement as they sneak away. It is a stressful 20 or so minutes for a concerned resident, ready to intervene at a moment's notice.

Dumping the shopping bags that afternoon, I rushed to check the young man's breathing. He was sleepy, and his breath was shallow. Another call to 000, another stressful wait until the emergency crew arrived. Drug-overdose symptoms can be frightening for someone who finds an affected person. The adrenaline kicks in, enabling you to do what needs to be done, then once the ambulance arrives, there is a feeling of relief — and exhaustion. Fortunately, on that occasion, the young man responded to the paramedics' naloxone and remained under observation for some time in the back of the ambulance. I always think of the family of the overdosed person when I ring 000. Who are they? What would they do if they knew about this current crisis next to my back gate?

Fire crews are dispatched as 'first responders' to drug-overdose cases where the patient is in cardiac or respiratory arrest because they often have a faster response time than an ambulance crew. They are also very valuable at a scene in assisting paramedics with cardiopulmonary resuscitation (CPR) and treatment of the patient.[3] A fire truck, one or two ambulances, and a police car can block traffic flow in our major laneway — and access to our homes — for up to 90 minutes, depending on the number of people who need attention.

To minimise this disruption, residents take proactive measures to prevent people from hiding, injecting, and overdosing on their properties. They park their car as close as possible to the corner of their garage, or right next to an adjacent car, to stop people injecting in the spaces between — making it impossible to know if someone has squeezed into the resultant tight space and to provide emergency access if required.

Residents remove handles off taps in their front gardens to stop people using the water to make the powder injectable. Previously, residents would find people overdosed in their gardens, with the tap still running.

Neighbours in a block of townhouses installed a security gate to their rubbish bins' enclosure to prevent people injecting in that perfect hiding spot. Disused properties or enclosures provide convenient hideaways for people injecting, requiring vigilance and action from locals, who demand that owners and the relevant authorities secure access points.

Some people are very creative when concealing their injecting. Such was the need for privacy for one of the 'regulars' in my laneway that he turned his old bike upside down, so it stood on its handlebars, and draped it with a poncho. It provided the perfect screen behind which he could inject, except that it was very conspicuous.

We urge people who are injecting alone to find an injecting 'buddy' who can raise the alarm if necessary. Whenever I am at home, I am mindful of activity on the other side of the fence, especially when I know someone is on their own.

These realities make our neighbourhood a deadly place for people with addiction, requiring us to remain on full alert when at home, going shopping, or just out and about, living our lives. This heightened awareness is stressful and exhausting, and the disruption is very real and constant.

When John and I moved into the area in 2012, we knew it was a drug-dealing and injecting hotspot. There had been drug activity when I lived there in the 1970s, and it had spiralled across the decades. A retired police officer explained to me why this was the case:

> Three reasons: the extensive public transport network of trains, trams, and buses makes it very accessible for people selling

> and buying drugs; the busy restaurant strip ensures people in possession of illicit substances blend in with the throng; and the old laneways offVictoria Street provide perfect hiding spots for immediate injecting. If you wanted to plan an inner-city drug distribution set-up, you would design North Richmond/South Abbotsford.

From day one, John and I were confronted with the consequences of drug injecting. People slumped motionless in laneways or staggering in Victoria Street. The constant sirens evoked the sense of living in a 'war zone'. We had a hotline to the City of Yarra council's syringe-disposal and street-cleaning teams, who removed bloodstained swabs, spoons, water bottles, litter, and human waste. My doctor recommended that I get a hepatitis vaccination.

My sister Helen and I experienced a particularly post-apocalyptic vision while shopping on Victoria Street in 2015. We felt like we were moving slowly underwater as we watched drug-affected people trying to function in public. Some were moving like every step was their last. Others were in freefall, bent in half and swaying precariously close to the roadway with their arms hanging loose. At one point, I pathetically bent down and asked one man if he needed me to call an ambulance. His eyes were translucent. I looked up and met the gaze of a man passing by — a stranger — and his look mirrored my own sense of shock and horror, like we were extras on a weird movie set.

The drug-using activity escalated to the extent where, on that afternoon in July 2016, I had reached breaking point. Our laneway was filthy and treacherous. Seeing that young man slumped against the wall prompted a familiar response: another son, brother, father, nephew, grandson, friend. My own family had experienced the tragedy of the drug crisis with the premature deaths of my nephews Ewen — in Brisbane in 1996, aged 21 — and Richard — in North Richmond in 2003, aged 28.

Enough was enough!

'They should do something,' I groaned to John.

I emailed the three councillors in my local electorate, Langridge Ward: Amanda Stone (Greens), Geoff Barbour (Labor) and Stephen Jolly (Socialists). I described the scene in my laneway, indicating my support for a safe injecting facility (SIF) in the City of Yarra. I received an emailed reply from each of them, expressing their support for the SIF. I noted with concern that Stephen Jolly had copied *The Age* newspaper reporter Clay Lucas into his response to my private email.

I mulled the question 'who's they?' and recalled the history of failed attempts to establish SIFs in Victoria over the decades. In opposition, Victorian Labor leader Steve Bracks had promised to establish five SIFs if he won the September 1999 state election. Melbourne suburbs with high levels of injecting heroin use were proposed locations: Springvale, St Kilda, Footscray, Fitzroy/Collingwood, and the CBD. In November 1999, newly elected as premier, Bracks established the Drug Policy Expert Committee, chaired by Dr David Penington AC. Its purpose was to review existing illicit-drug policies and report on a SIF trial. In April 2000, the Drug Policy Expert Committee's stage-one report — *Drugs: responding to the issues, engaging the community* — recommended an 18-month trial for the SIFs.[4]

The Bracks government introduced the Drugs, Poisons and Controlled Substances (Safe Injecting Facilities Trial) Bill 2000 into parliament in June that year. It was rejected in the upper house following vociferous local opposition. The government subsequently dumped its SIF policy before the state election in November 2002.[5] 'In 2006, 2010, and 2011 attempts were made by health policy advocates to ignite policy debate about the introduction of supervised injecting facilities in Melbourne, Australia.'[6] Clearly those attempts were unsuccessful, unlike in NSW, where the trial of Australia's first medically supervised injecting centre opened in Sydney's Kings Cross in May 2001.[7]

Mindful of this dismal history in our state, 'they should do something' looked like a grim proposition.

Then a frightening prospect — they might be *me*!

What the hell could *I* do?

What would Mum do?

—

Mary Ryan (nee O'Dwyer, 1924–2003), my mother, was a tour de force. She and my father, Maurice Ryan (1922–1966), both came from large families. Mum was the eldest of seven children; Dad was the fifth of seven boys. They had six kids in nine years — Rosemary, Helen, David, Michael, Mark, and Louise — before calling it quits. Baby gear was offloaded to equally fecund relatives and neighbours. I arrived five years later, in 1961, promptly followed by Gabrielle in 1962.

My O'Dwyer and Ryan ancestors arrived in Australia from County Tipperary, Ireland, in 1850 and 1865, respectively.

> [Both families] took an active interest in the public affairs of their adopted country — local government and the community in general. Perhaps it was the history of the Irish famine (1845–

> 1852) and the ineptitude of both national and local authorities to alleviate the problem that drove them to seek some sort of control of their destiny by seeking public office.[8]

An exemplar of community pro-action was my gentle, determined grandfather Ray O'Dwyer (1897–1979). Using a horse-drawn sledge, he spearheaded the installation of the first district schoolhouse in the early 1930s, and was a pioneer in irrigation, providing a reliable source of water for the farming families in the drought-ravaged NSW Riverina area from 1969.[9]

Dad grew up on a farm at Burramine, near Yarrawonga, in north-east Victoria. Both his parents were deceased by the time he was aged 19. He studied for a bachelor of engineering science before voluntarily enlisting in the Australian army as a lieutenant in 1944. He served in Lae and Rabaul, Papua New Guinea, overseeing the rebuilding of war-damaged bridges and roads. After marrying Mum in 1946, he was the engineer for Oxley Shire (now part of the rural city of Wangaratta) before joining an earthmoving and civil-construction firm based in Wangaratta. He was the breadwinner. But Dad collapsed and died from a heart attack at home in 1966: he was 43. While I have no memory of him, I know that he volunteered his engineering skills and what limited time he had to improve green spaces in Wangaratta, as well as surveying the land and designing a gravity-fed irrigation system in the Burramine region, providing much-needed stock water to farmers in times of drought.

Mum also grew up on a farm — in Savernake, in the Riverina. She attended boarding school in Yarrawonga, where she completed her 'intermediate' certificate: the current Year 10 equivalent. With zero opportunity for tertiary education and no official qualification or training herself, Mum made sure that her children would not experience the same deficiency. Widowed at the age of 42, Mum raised and educated eight kids, ranging in age from three to 18. *When the going gets tough, the tough get going* epitomised Mum's approach to life, post-1966. *Never die wondering* was a personal mantra of hers, underpinning the need to take calculated risks and *just get on with it.*

In 1964, Mum and Dad had joined a small group of residents to form a credit cooperative in their neighbourhood in Wangaratta. As directors, they serviced the financial needs of the members of the predominantly working-class community every Sunday out of a small shed in the local church grounds. Their credit union merged with another local credit union in 1969, after Dad's death, forming the Wangaratta Credit Union.[10]

Mum was invited to become a director of the larger co-operative. She drove to the first evening meeting and saw the lights on in the local hall. She was overwhelmed by her perceived inadequacy in both qualification and experience, and terrified at the prospect of being involved in this new organisation. She drove around town before summoning the courage to finally attend the meeting — a godsend for the new credit union and the community in general. Mum served nine years as a director, spending many weeknights visiting families 'struggling to make ends meet'. She used her natural ability to manage finances, developed since Dad's death, to help them organise their financial affairs. She would work out a budget with them or help them access appropriate loans from the credit union.[11]

At the same time as she was keeping her own kids housed, fed, clothed, and educated, Mum maintained a significant involvement in social-justice issues within the community. She supported regional families whose kids wished to complete secondary schooling or apprenticeships in Wangaratta by providing boarding facilities at our home. 'Unmarried' mothers, orphans, the bereaved, women and children experiencing family violence, and those who had 'fallen on hard times' also benefited from Mum's practical compassion.

Her death certificate in 2003 records her usual occupation as Home Duties. If Home Duties included all the complexities of nurturing and educating children for years, becoming a small-business owner employing local people, providing meals and accommodation for myriad country kids, providing financial and other essential voluntary services to the broader community, then it was an appropriate title. To me, it was demeaning. Mum was a mover and shaker in our country community. She was intelligent, well respected, and an inspiration to many, not the least her grateful offspring. Community Champion is the accurate description of Mum's 'occupation'.

The challenges I faced as the seventh of eight children in a cash-strapped, single-parent family ensured that I could stand up for myself from an early age. The argy-bargy of negotiating life in a large family with significant age and 'power' differences developed a strong sense of self. Often accused of being 'too outspoken', I proudly explain that 'I was taught by experts'. I also learnt to 'pick my battles': some things you just have to let go. Fiercely protective of her brood, Mum had a highly tuned bullshit detector (she would abhor such a description) and had no fear speaking truth to power. I channel her tenacity whenever I have to deal with big, confident personalities who are used to getting their own way.

As an adult, I have enjoyed active participation in the regional community in north-east Victoria. I know that community well, and my clients at the You're Welcome Relocation Service benefited from my contacts. I have often wondered, what if 34 people had fatally overdosed from heroin in one year in Wangaratta or Wodonga — as had happened in Richmond and Abbotsford in 2016? How would those rural communities have reacted? Tolerated the horror and done nothing, or known that it was unacceptable and demanded action? I knew in my heart that the latter would have been the only option.

I had only lived in South Abbotsford for four years in 2016, and I worked on the other side of the city. I knew people who lived on both sides of Victoria Street but was still in the process of finding my local tribe. I had joined a community choir (being unable to sing was no deterrent) and the Yarra Community Friends' program. I mentored an Indigenous girl whose family lived in the nearby public-housing towers. I was developing my networks.

If *they* was me, I knew that I couldn't do it on my own. It had to be *we* and *us*. Support from the ground up, rather than top down, would be essential in establishing a SIF with solid community support. I needed to determine if other residents felt as strongly about the local drug-injecting crisis as I did. If they did, would they support a campaign for a SIF in our community? I needed to do some market research urgently, but was busy with my job, had limited surplus funds, and few local connections.

Invoking Mum's spirit for inspiration and guidance, which mantra would it be? *Never die wondering* or *Just get on with it*? Maybe it was both.

2

There's only one poll that counts

AUGUST–OCTOBER 2016

'There's only one poll that counts' is the predictable response to a published newspaper poll by all politicians whose fortunes have bombed. They shrug off behavioural shortcomings and policy deficiencies by referencing the only poll they respect: an official election result.

I had busily spent July and August on the search engine, learning about SIFs, the Sydney medically supervised injecting centre (MSIC), illicit-drug addiction, and harm reduction. I had much to learn. 'MSIC', it turned out, was just another name for a SIF. The Sydney MSIC website was a treasure trove of information for this novice:

> The first 'official' supervised injecting facility in the world began in Switzerland in 1986 … there are more than 120 supervised injecting facilities operating around the world, in Switzerland,

> Germany, Spain, The Netherlands, Norway, Luxembourg, Denmark, Canada, Portugal, Iceland and France, amongst others ... all supervised injecting facilities aim to improve public health and public amenity by reducing drug use in public places. They are often established in areas where there is a high concentration of people injecting drugs on the street in full view of others. The centres vary depending on what is happening in the local area ... The skills and qualifications of staff may vary too, but supervised injecting facilities all have common goals: To improve health and wellbeing; To reduce the number of deaths from overdose; To reduce public drug use.[1]

SIFs are health centres where registered nurses and health-education officers supervise drug injecting that would otherwise happen elsewhere — often in public and under dangerous conditions. People can inject illicit drugs in a SIF without fear of legal consequences. In the event of an overdose or other health issue, a SIF provides immediate access to emergency medical care. SIF staff connect with clients and offer them referrals to a variety of services, including specialist addiction treatment. SIFs around the world have been found to reduce the number of fatal and non-fatal drug overdoses and the spread of bloodborne viral infections (including HIV and hepatitis B and C) both among people who inject drugs and in the wider community.

Melbourne's journalists sought the views of local traders whenever there was a flare-up of drug issues in our area: increased drug dealing, fatal and non-fatal overdoses, and associated activities. Traders predictably responded with a demand for a greater police presence and the installation of more video surveillance in Victoria Street. I already knew from my own experience that CCTVs don't deter drug activity. Drug dealers simply relocate their business to other spaces, away from the camera's eye. Residents' views were missing in this conversation with the media. How could I possibly address that imbalance?

A friend posted on Facebook that she was nominating as a regional candidate in the Victorian local council elections scheduled for Saturday 22 October 2016. It was a light-bulb moment for me: I would run as an independent, single-policy candidate for Langridge Ward in the City of Yarra council election — 'supporting a trial of a medically supervised injecting centre in Victoria Street'. I would keep it simple: a vote for me (an unknown, unaffiliated resident) was a vote for an MSIC trial in the North Richmond and South Abbotsford environs.

One real barrier to this cunning plan was that I had recently rebranded the You're Welcome Relocation Service to suit an urban setting, and I was excited about promoting my new relocation service, Women Love Moving. This crazy election idea would impact my future income, as I had planned to leave my school job so I could focus on developing the new business. I was torn. My head was telling me to defer my candidacy by four years and run in the 2020 council election, while my heart affirmed my instinct: you must do something — now. I equivocated about my decision to the extent that my appointment to register as a candidate with the Victorian Electoral Commission's Returning Officer occurred only 15 minutes before the deadline. I was taken aback when that officer wished me 'all the best, campaigning on this important issue'. I had tremors all the way home on the tram, overcome by a sense of terror about what I had just done. Who the hell did I think I was to be doing this? I was putting myself 'out there' with what would be (given Victoria's history) a controversial policy, a personal budget of $1,000, a campaign team of two supporters — John and my neighbour Loraine Little — and the likelihood of attracting a handful of votes if I was lucky. Trumping the fear were those words in my head: *never die wondering*.

My frugal promotional material comprised three white T-shirts with 'Vote 1 independent Judy Ryan' for us to wear, 1,000 red-and-white flyers to use when doorknocking and letterboxing in North Richmond and South Abbotsford, and eight posters to attach to friends' and supportive neighbours' gates and fences. My independent 'brand' colour was red: I am a red-lippy and red-glasses woman. The campaign team's doorknocking experience on both sides of Victoria Street was more positive than I had anticipated: many residents were desperate for practical action on the local drug crisis and were supportive of the idea of an MSIC trial. One concerned voter focused on the dominance of the colour red on my flyers: 'What does it mean?' she asked with furrowed brow. 'It means that I really like red,' I reassured her.

I received unsolicited advice on two campaign staples: that I must have a strong presence on Facebook and Twitter, and that I must not campaign with a single policy. On the first point, I was concerned about receiving abusive comments and dealing with trolls, and so I decided not to bother with online platforms. On the second point, while I remained steadfast on my decision to campaign for an MSIC, I did get the wobbles on the single-policy principle and so, for a short time, included extra items in my repertoire. In the end, however, I trusted my heart and dumped the extras. The management of rampant drug injecting and overdosing in my community was the issue that had got me out of my armchair. I was an independent candidate, answerable to no one. I had to back myself. The purpose of the exercise was to determine if other residents were supportive of an MSIC trial. We regularly heard what the traders wanted. It was time for our voice to be heard, and I wanted that voice to be clear, not sullied by other distractions.

In the four weeks prior to the council election, I was bombarded with questionnaires from local interest groups, each one warning that 'your response will inform our advice to members when it comes to voting preferences'. Only one questionnaire piqued my interest. The William Street Residents Group had distributed a small leaflet into our letterboxes.

Victoria Street Drug Solutions

> Public drug use and dealing is at a twenty-year high. The time has come for a compassionate approach to a community problem. We are a group of residents that believe the way to address the high levels of public drug taking, dealing and the associated crime and risk to public health and safety is to trial a medically supervised injecting facility, with support services, within the Victoria Street precinct.
>
> Council elections are on Saturday, 22 October. We urge residents to use their vote to elect councillors that will fight for a compassionate solution to the drug epidemic on Victoria Street.
>
> A document outlining our proposed solution to the worsening drug use along Victoria Street and the surrounding residential streets can be found on Facebook, alongside our personal stories and experiences.
>
> We are not affiliated with any candidates or political parties.

I responded immediately through Facebook to let them know of my support for their solutions and of my motivation for nominating as an independent candidate. Margot Foster was co-author of the leaflet; she responded, enquiring if I supported a 'fixed-position' SIF, which I had read about. The alternative is a 'mobile' SIF, a specially fitted-out van with three injection booths — these operate in cities such as Barcelona and Berlin. They work in addition to fixed sites, as they can't provide the capacity or additional services of a fixed site.[2] I believed that our community needed a 'fixed-position' SIF due to the enormity of the drug-injecting problem. Three injection booths in a 'mobile' SIF would be totally inadequate.

I met with Margot to discuss my candidacy and to share our lived experiences. Margot had lived in South Abbotsford for over two decades. Years prior, her son had been accidentally pricked with a used drug-injecting needle that had been left in the grounds of his preschool centre. The months-long wait for test results had been excruciating. She wanted action so that others would be spared the worry she had endured. Her William Street neighbour Kylie Troy-West was the other co-author of the leaflet, and the mother of a toddler.

I also spoke with fellow candidates and renominating councillors who had unanimously supported an MSIC trial in the previous council term. As there had been no appetite at the state-government level for a SIF, nothing had eventuated. Veteran independent councillor and former mayor Jackie Fristacky explained the history surrounding the issue in the City of Yarra. She wished me luck, cautioning that I shouldn't anticipate much support: 'it's an ugly issue for many'. I appreciated her candour, and her assessment did not surprise me at all.

Two weeks before the election, I participated in a candidates' forum at Fitzroy Town Hall, facilitated by resident and radio 3AW broadcaster Tom Elliott. Loraine Little accompanied me, for which I was truly grateful. I was nervous at the prospect of being pilloried, and had a sense of foreboding as I took my seat at the front of that historic hall. The crowd was at capacity, bursting with engaged, vocal residents. It was the perfect setting for a public shellacking of an up-herself country woman.

I had prepared the mandatory three-minute introductory blurb. As I got up to speak, I heard Mum's voice: *just get on with it*. 'Politics is personal,' I said. I spoke from the heart about my experience of living in our local 'war zone', and about the impact on my family of the deaths of my two nephews. 'Evidence from overseas — and Sydney — suggests that both young men would have lived had they had injected in a SIF. That's what is needed right now in our community.' I sat down. Prompted by Tom Elliott for a show of hands for my single policy, there was unanimous support — not only from the audience, but from the candidates sharing the stage with me. I was stunned, as was Elliott, judging by the look on his face and his incredulous response: 'What? All of you?'

Mingling in the hall afterwards, I talked to Margot and Kylie from William Street. I was approached by constituents who supported my policy. Some were quite emotional as they spoke of their own experiences as residents. I felt empowered by their warmth and support. One resident, Liz, emailed me her story the following day:

> One morning recently, I noticed a car with a young man sitting rather awkwardly in the driver's seat. Concerned that something was amiss, I went outside to the open passenger window to

> ask him if he was ok. I saw that he was trying to inject himself in his arm. What struck me was not that he was injecting but, that on hearing my question, he looked up and immediately apologised for what he was doing: 'I'm so sorry; I will only be a minute'. As soon as he had injected himself, he took off accelerating into traffic. I don't know what upset me the most: that this well-mannered young man was shooting up alone at 9am or that he drove off into traffic with who-knows-what capability of driving while under the influence. I learned that day that drug users are people who should not die on our streets from overdoses. We all need to be protected from unintended consequences of drug use.

I was grateful for the help of family and friends who distributed my how-to-vote cards on election day. We could cover three out of five booths in Langridge Ward and focused our efforts on the booths that were in the vicinity of the drug hotspot around Victoria Street.

Election day in October was typical Melbourne — four seasons in one day — with the dominant season being winter, featuring arctic blasts of horizontal sleet. The concept of the 'democracy sausage' was particularly seductive that day, mainly thanks to the warmth provided by those fatty snags in white bread, dripping in salty tomato and mustard sauce. I had voted at the early voting centre the previous week. Placing '1' in the square next to 'Judy Ryan' was a bucket-list experience, and doing so ahead of time gave me the freedom to chat with voters on election day about my support for an MSIC trial.

People felt strongly about my policy, both positive and negative, and were keen to engage. Irene came from both a health and legal background, had lived in the area for a long time, and supported a SIF: 'It should've happened years ago.' Bill had lived in Kings Cross in Sydney for years before arriving in North Richmond in 2013. He made an impromptu speech at the entry to the polling booth: 'Judy is on the money with this issue. North Richmond is worse than Kings Cross was when overdosing was at its peak there. I was against a SIF until I attended an open day at the Kings Cross MSIC. It changed how I think about drug use as a health issue.' Bill committed his support to an ongoing campaign for an MSIC after the election 'regardless of the outcome'.

One woman told me that she wasn't voting for me, because her father had recently had a heart attack. 'He had a long wait for an ambulance because of the drug users overdosing in our area.' I suggested that was why she should vote for me. 'An MSIC trial will free up ambulances for people like your father.' She returned 20 minutes later and said that she had voted for me.

On the other hand, I also heard people say, 'Who's Judy Ryan? I'm not voting for her.' It was the response that I had expected from the outset!

At the end of an exhausting day, my small, quality team defrosted in the warmth of my home with pizzas and wine. We picked over the conversations we'd had with voters across the day. Our anecdotal 'market research' was unequivocal: many residents, who were immediately impacted by the drug-dealing and injecting crisis, supported an MSIC trial. There was widespread public concern and an appetite for the resolution of this decades-old health issue.

I hadn't bothered organising scrutineers to attend the official vote count. I knew that I wouldn't get enough votes to win a council spot, and it wasn't the purpose of my candidacy anyway. Throughout the evening, my niece kept her eye on the progress of the count online. She excitedly announced that I had polled 400 primary votes. I was in disbelief! Never in my wildest dreams …

I finished up with 579 primary votes (including the third-highest vote out of 11 candidates in the Abbotsford voting centre, which I had specifically targeted) and 791 second preferences across all five polling booths.[3] After voting for their rusted-on candidate, many people gave their second vote to an unknown candidate and an MSIC trial. I include this information for the reader as it indicates the huge support in the community for a much-needed health facility, and vindicates my decision to run on a single issue. (Indeed, the number of second-preference votes for me must have been higher than 791. The last candidate elected was the Labor Party's Danae Bosler. Some of Danae's 1,604 first-preference votes would have been second-preference votes for me, but we don't know how many, because Danae's preferences were never distributed. If the reader is a budding psephologist, the Victorian Electoral Commission website includes a *Distribution Report* and a *Results by Voting Centre Report*.)

Returning councillor Amanda Stone rang the following morning to congratulate me: 'You nearly got over the line. We were all surprised that you didn't have scrutineers at the count. You obviously thought that you wouldn't win.'

I ended up with 4.63 per cent of the primary vote, which meant that I would be reimbursed my $250 nomination fee. That was a real bonus!

Never die wondering had proven itself as a strategy on this occasion. Mum would be pleased! If it really was true that 'there's only one poll that counts', it would be possible to build an authentic community campaign for an MSIC trial with this level of support. As I wasn't successful in being elected to council, I wouldn't be distracted by important but time-consuming municipal responsibilities. But what about the impact on my new relocation business? That would have to wait.

My mind was racing. *Just get on with it* was going around and around in my head.

3

Getting on with it, starting in Sydney

NOVEMBER 2016

The day after the local council election, I was still overwhelmed by the positive response to my single-policy campaign. The personal stories and conversations with voters had translated into a 'mandate' for an MSIC trial in our community. Paradoxically, I felt like a winner even though, on the results, I was a loser!

Margot Foster, Kylie Troy-West, and Bill wanted to form a residents' group to advocate for a SIF. Virginia Dods, another long-term resident whom I'd met on election day, invited me to attend the upcoming meeting of the Collingwood and Abbotsford Residents' Association to outline my plans. This community engagement was exactly the outcome I had hoped for: to join forces with like-minded residents who understood the need to urgently address the drug-injecting crisis. Exciting times indeed!

I continued to frequent the Sydney MSIC website. If the

website administrators had checked their analytics, they would have been justified in notifying the authorities about a stalker. My election campaign had been based entirely around the idea of this life-saving facility. I needed to immerse myself in its physical space and speak with its experts. I sent an email to introduce myself and request a tour of the centre.

On Friday 4 November, my sister Gabrielle and I flew to Sydney, where we were met by cousin Kate McNamara, who drove us to 66 Darlinghurst Road, Kings Cross. I appreciated their support and company that day. The MSIC had just marked its 15th year of operation. Its trial — or temporary — status had ended in 2010, when Kristina Keneally's Labor government passed legislation to permit the Uniting Church to operate the centre on a permanent basis: hence its official name — Uniting MSIC.

Its operations manager, Miranda St Hill, met us at 4.00 pm in the reception area (Stage 1 of the facility). People entered discretely. No fuss. No chaos. Apart from the security officer outside the front door — which matched the large frosted windows below a conspicuous '66' — we could have been in a suburban accountant's office: light-filled, plastic chairs, posters on the wall, and a young man sitting at a computer behind the counter. That was it.

> When a person comes to the MSIC for the first time, they go through a 10–20 minute registration and interview process with a nurse or counsellor. This helps staff get to know the person and their needs, and also checks that they meet the criteria for using the service. People under the age of 18, pregnant women and first time injecting drug users are excluded.[1]

A client followed us into the service that afternoon and approached the counter, providing the young man with his password. 'What are you injecting today?' 'Heroin.' 'When did you last inject?' 'Yesterday.' 'Okay. Take a seat. You should have a booth shortly.' This experience was surreal for me. The calm, respectful manner with which the client was treated was memorable. Tours of the MSIC normally happen when the service is briefly closed for staff training, so that visitors can walk through without interrupting client care. But given the pressing need for a facility in Melbourne — and my specific advocacy efforts — I had been given the rare opportunity to come through during operational hours, to get a feel for how it really worked. I appreciated this thoughtful consideration.

From what I had read on its website before the visit, the MSIC's 'record of success' was impressive:

> Approximate number of clients since Uniting MSIC opened in 2001: 16,500.
>
> About 70% of the people registered with Uniting MSIC have never accessed any local health service before coming to us. This shows that Uniting MSIC provides a unique and important entry point for access to health and social welfare services in Kings Cross.
>
> Since opening we have supervised more than one million injections.
>
> Number of injections a day: Ranges from 150–200.
>
> Number of overdoses successfully managed: More than 8,500.
>
> Number of fatalities: Zero.
>
> We've taken the pressure off emergency services with an

early study showing the number of ambulance call-outs to Kings Cross dropping by 80%.

70% of local businesses and 78% of residents support the centre.

More than 14,500 referrals have been accepted by our clients, connecting them to health, drug treatment and social welfare services.

Among our frequently attending clients, 80% have ultimately accepted a referral for addiction treatment.

The other 20% of frequently attending clients have had a referral offered to them but not accepted yet. Most have agreed to talk about their situation with a team member, who outlines the benefits of treatment. Importantly, we continue to work with everyone we see.

The service has been independently evaluated multiple times. All results show it to be a successful and cost-effective program. There are over 220 peer-reviewed research papers that show that facilities like this work.[2]

Clients take their own supply of drugs to the MSIC, for personal use only. Upon entering an injecting room (Stage 2), they are provided with clean syringes and safe disposal bins. Their injecting is overseen by emergency nurses, discretely positioned behind a counter.

The drugs may be illicit, such as cocaine or methamphetamine (aka ice or crystal meth), or they may be prescription pain medications, such as benzodiazepine, morphine, or oxycodone. The most commonly injected drug at the MSIC and the reason for the centre's existence is heroin.

Heroin is a highly addictive drug made from morphine, a

psychoactive (mind-altering) substance taken from the resin of the seed pod of the opium poppy plant. Heroin is mixed with water and injected with a needle. It can also be sniffed, smoked, or snorted.[3]

The key issue with heroin is that the difference in dose between a 'therapeutic level' — one that gives people the high they want — and a 'lethal level' is very small. Heroin crosses the blood–brain barrier quite quickly, so the onset of action is rapid. People are less tolerant of the effects of heroin if they have had a recent period of no use, or less use — however, higher tolerance can lead to people taking larger amounts to get the same high. Changing purity levels of street heroin can also lead to an overdose.[4]

A short-term effect of heroin is being 'on the nod', the person's head nodding as they get sleepy, then jerking when, or if, they regain consciousness.[5] When a person overdoses on heroin or another opioid — morphine, oxycodone, or even codeine — breathing can slow down or stop, and it can be very hard to wake them from this state.

> When staff first notice a client showing signs of any trouble after injecting, they quickly assess their oxygen levels and levels of consciousness. If oxygen levels are low and the client is unresponsive, staff will use an oxygen mask or bag to assist clients with their breathing. When people die from overdose, it's because they have stopped breathing and their brain lacks oxygen, making oxygen equipment so vital in the treatment of any overdose.
>
> In serious cases, Narcan [naloxone] can be used to reverse the effect of an opioid drug and is given by nursing staff at the MSIC …

> Having skilled staff and equipment onsite to intervene immediately when a client shows signs of an overdose has meant that not only has there never been a death at the MSIC but also that many brain injuries have been prevented.[6]

After injecting, clients move into the after-care area (Stage 3). They interact in an informal way, with staff offering counselling support, referrals, health education, and medical treatment by means of drugs such as methadone.

I clearly remember the calm, professional atmosphere of the centre. Miranda explained that they rarely experienced problems with clients' behaviour, thanks to the skill of the staff: in de-escalating issues before they develop, in treating everyone with dignity and respect, and in being truly 'person centred'. Miranda showed us a powerful and poignant 14-minute film about the MSIC, featuring the distressing reflection of a mother whose son had died alone from overdose. Miranda kindly answered our questions without hesitation, concluding: 'The unfortunate reality is that a person with power may have to experience a family tragedy to appreciate the importance of an MSIC — and then do something about it, usually in the face of prejudiced opposition.'

Bob Carr had done just that when he became premier of NSW in 1998. His Labor government had held a review into drug use in the state, and the MSIC was the result of that review. Fifteen years earlier, his younger brother, Greg, had died from a heroin overdose, aged 28.[7]

My visit to the MSIC was affirming and proved the adage *where there's life, there's hope*. I was determined to get a similar facility established in our community. It would be life-changing for people injecting illicit drugs in the area. It would also enable residents and traders to start addressing longstanding public-amenity issues. I asked Miranda if I could use their MSIC film to show to residents at proposed community education forums. She regretted to advise that, as it was an in-house resource, it couldn't be shown outside the facility. Fair enough.

We thanked Miranda for her time and headed out into Darlinghurst Road. At 5.00 pm on a Friday afternoon, it was busy in the street. There was lots of foot traffic, bars operating, and older kids carrying schoolbags. I was keen to speak with residents and traders who had lived and worked in the area before and after the MSIC opened. According to the MSIC website, 'In 1997–1998, random telephone surveys of more than 300 Kings Cross residents showed majority support for the establishment of a supervised injecting centre.'[8]

I later talked to two women who had experienced life near the MSIC location, pre– and post–the 2001 opening. Margaret Harvie, from the residents' group, reflected: 'People have forgotten how bad the area was before it opened. New residents don't know what it was like. Residents who were here in the 1990s will never forget. They are the ones who can truly appreciate the contribution that it has made. I am very grateful that this facility will continue to operate just down the road from where I live. Long may it continue.'

Jen Manning is a pharmacist in Darlinghurst Road, Potts Point, situated close to the MSIC. She went to school nearby and remembered being scared seeing syringes everywhere. She was happy to list the positives of the MSIC: 'No one is dying. Fewer people are overdosing in the street. The centre is not having a negative impact. Users are not asleep in our backyard, and there are no break-ins at the pharmacy.'

—

On 16 November, I met with Margot, Kylie, and Bill for the first time to analyse the election outcome and plan our future campaign. I reported on my visit to the MSIC and gave them a copy of its publication, *Cross Currents*.[9] The first order of business was to instil community values into 'Victoria Street Drug Solutions', the name that Margot and Kylie had used on their William Street Residents Group election-campaign leaflet. We added the prefix 'Residents for' to clearly state our purpose, identify our membership, and differentiate us from the local traders' group, the Victoria Street Business Association.

The new Residents for Victoria Street Drug Solutions (RVSDS) established four key objectives:

- provide a representative voice for residents in the City of Yarra — specifically North Richmond and South Abbotsford — regarding the impacts of public drug dealing, using, and overdosing on the community
- educate the community on the benefits of and facts about MSICs
- advocate for the health, welfare, and wellbeing of our community, including people who take drugs, with regards to improved public amenity
- advocate for an MSIC in the Victoria Street precinct where people determined to inject illegal drugs could do so safely.

We also discussed the development of a website, a social-media plan, a petition, and, of course, fundraising.

The following week, Jeremy Dwyer from the Coroners Prevention Unit contacted me. He had heard about my candidacy in the recent election campaign and had a request: 'Coroner Jacqui Hawkins is heading an inquest on 14 December into an overdose death in North Richmond. She is keen to hear from residents who may be regularly exposed to heroin-related harms in the City of Yarra and particularly around North Richmond. The deadline for submissions has been extended to ensure the missing voices of residents were considered.'

Margot and I agreed to submit individual reports to the Coroners Court by 24 November. RVSDS had hit the ground running!

Kylie reflected on the impact the drug crisis was having on her Abbotsford neighbours, and the genesis of RVSDS.

> I lived in quite a few places [before] moving to Abbotsford … over the three years that I have been here I watched neighbours, especially people that have been in the area for a long time, just retreat because they have reached breaking point. People's goodwill and concern for the wider community's wellbeing is wearing really thin now … twenty-five years of pretty consistent drug use in the area really does wear you down.
>
> In September last year in the lead-up to the council elections, my neighbour (Margot) and I were having dinner … we were pretty much at the point of despair when we decided we would band together and start a campaign to see if we could encourage the local community to vote for candidates to support a MSIC. Twenty years earlier my neighbour's son had a needlestick injury … the fact was nothing had moved along in that time — nothing meaningful had happened — and that my child was at

the same risk as her child had been. That was the motivation for us to get going. We headed up to the candidates' Q and A where we met Judy. We questioned all the candidates. We printed flyers, started a Facebook page, launched a website, and off we went. A few weeks after the election, we banded together with Judy.[10]

4

The coronial inquest

DECEMBER 2016

I received an email from Greg Denham, executive officer of the Yarra Drug and Health Forum, inviting me to discuss the issues with him, Hieng Lim from the Neighbourhood Justice Centre, and Meca Ho, long-time president of the Victoria Street Business Association.

Meca was direct when the four of us met in his restaurant on Victoria Street. He spoke with conviction that the 'solution' to the local drug issues continued to be a greater police presence and more CCTVs in the street, and he spoke about his strong, enduring relationship with Richard Wynne, state Labor MP for Richmond since 1999. He finished by expressing his obvious annoyance at my recent election campaign, suggesting that it had 'created a problem in Victoria Street'.

I had listened patiently, but it was time to speak up: 'Residents share Victoria Street with the traders. They are the bread and butter of your businesses. Our voices aren't being heard. We want to work with traders to improve the precinct for everyone.' We clearly had our work cut out.

That was enough conversation for our first meeting. We shook hands, promising to meet again in the new year.

The following day, residents received a letter from Richard Wynne: 'CCTV to boost public safety in the heart of Richmond':

> I recently joined traders and police to announce a $250,000 funding package for a pilot CCTV project in the heart of Richmond.
>
> CCTV cameras will be installed on Victoria Street, an area which has become known for drug use and dealing.
>
> Criminal behaviour ... will be caught on CCTV cameras as part of a new project to improve safety. We know CCTV deters crime ... that's why we are investing in crime prevention and boosting police resources ...
>
> I applaud the residents [sic] and traders for their work on this CCTV project. The cameras are to be installed in the first quarter of 2017.[1]

It had been a hectic time with the campaign, the election, and establishing RVSDS, as well as working at the school and promoting my new relocation business, which I feared would disappear into the ether. I was feeling run down and needed a break. I had been diagnosed with breast cancer in June 2012, and following surgery and radiation therapy, I was now in the fourth year of remission and was mindful of taking care of my physical and mental health. John booked a house in Lorne, on Victoria's Surf Coast, for a mini holiday. Our daughter, Louise, and her partner, Tom, took a four-day break and came from Sydney to join us, along with Daniel, our oldest son, who was living in Melbourne.

The holiday would be 12–15 December. Coroner Hawkins' inquest was scheduled for 9.00 am on 14 December. I was determined to attend the city location, especially as the coroner had specifically requested input from RVSDS after submissions had closed. The inquest subject was the drug-overdose death of 'Ms A' in the toilet of the Hungry Jack's restaurant in Hoddle Street, North Richmond.

A young mother with small children, Ms A had been well known by the outreach workers from North Richmond Community Health (NRCH). They had become increasingly alarmed at the number of their clients who had died from drug overdose. Ms A's death was one of 34 fatal overdoses in 2016.[2] Kasey Elmore and Penny Francis from NRCH's AOD program had contacted the Coroners Court about their concerns. The public inquest relating to Ms A followed soon afterwards.

Waking in Lorne to my 5.00 am alarm on 14 December, I seriously considered not driving two hours to Melbourne, preferring lunch with my family and a walk along the beach. However, *Never die wondering* kicked in — again. I arrived at the court at 9.00 am, having stopped en route at the Anglesea newsagent to buy the biggest Spirax notebook available. It would be filled by day's end with expert information and evidence, statistics and quotes, and names and contact details.

Robert Richter QC cross-examined five expert witnesses: Greg Denham, Professor Paul Dietze (AOD researcher, Burnet Institute), Demos Krouskos (CEO, NRCH), Dr Marianne Jauncey (medical director, Sydney MSIC), and Judith Abbott

(Victorian Department of Health and Human Services). Abbott was responsible for assisting the government in its drug policy development and implementation. 'Asked what international evidence ministers had been given about the efficacy of MSICs, [Abbott] was forced to admit that none had been provided, despite the fact the department's role was to offer whole, unbiased and complete evidence to ministers.'[3]

Attending the inquest was a powerful and educational experience for me. The unequivocal view of the other four witnesses was that an MSIC would make a significant contribution 'to reducing heroin-related harms including overdose deaths, based on national and international evidence'. Margot and Kylie were unable to attend the hearing. Bill popped in briefly, as he was working nearby.

Another benefit of attending the inquest was the important networking opportunity. Speaking with witnesses and other key people was illuminating. I met Fiona Patten MP from the Sex Party (later renamed the Reason Party),[4] who was preparing a private member's bill for an MSIC trial in North Richmond; Robert Richter and David Stanley (the Victorian president and the national treasurer of the Australian Drug Law Reform Foundation); Jen Black (principal solicitor, Fitzroy Legal Service); and Penny Francis from NRCH. I was surprised to learn that these people knew about the voter support for the MSIC at the recent election. To my astonishment, Demos Krouskos mentioned the fact in his evidence to the coroner: 'To give you an indication of the level of interest and support from the community, a candidate at the recent council election received over 400 votes, on the basis of her single policy to establish a safe injecting facility.'

I hadn't appreciated the impact that the election result had on committed harm-reduction activists. The support of residents for an MSIC had sparked a renewed sense of hope in long-time campaigners, who had been lobbying for a SIF in Melbourne for decades. Many had skin in the game prior to the Bracks government's unsuccessful efforts in 2000. A quick lunch at a nearby coffee shop between the morning and afternoon sessions provided the opportunity to meet with Demos, who kindly paid for my sandwich and coffee: 'It's the least I can do to thank you for your election efforts.'

I also met Marianne Jauncey and Paul Dietze. I queried Paul about the honeypot effect, referring to the copious notes that I had taken in the morning session. A 'honeypot' is a location that attracts crowds of people, who put pressure on the area and its residents. One of the most common concerns, historically, for SIFs is that they will attract people who inject drugs to an area they otherwise would not have visited. Paul said, 'Victoria Street is clearly an established drug market. It's been highly active since the late 1990s. The honeypot effect is about the purchase location [of drugs] rather than a service location [of a SIF]. Most SIFs are set up in places that are already honeypots.'

I also asked Paul about 'mobile' SIFs — a van or a bus — as he was co-author of the research paper that I had read in October. A 'mobile' SIF was not a solution for North Richmond:

> The problem with most 'mobile' SIFs that I've seen is that they are relatively limited in size in comparison to the fixed-site facilities that are around. They are only generally used as an adjunct to the fixed sites. To rely entirely on a 'mobile' SIF, you would need something very, very big — much bigger than the

> ones that are in Europe. However, if it was something that was in addition to a fixed-site location, there would be some merit in that.

As I walked back to the court for the afternoon session, I felt energised by the approachability of these experts. Their years of experience was just what I needed.

I had much to think about as I drove two hours back to Lorne to join my family for our last evening away together.

It was time to write to Richard Wynne about the formation of RVSDS, the growing support for an MSIC trial in his electorate, and our disagreement that simply installing more CCTVs was a solution. I hand-delivered the letter to his electoral office in Smith Street, Collingwood, on 20 December.

I also thought about the death of Ms A in Hungry Jack's and the effect of that tragedy on her two little kids, her family, and the young employee who found her overdosed in a toilet cubicle. Surely an MSIC would reduce that extensive trauma?

The year ended on a sad note — literally. I was deeply moved when I read a letter to *The Age* signed 'names withheld, Ocean Grove', under the heading 'Cutting the Drug Toll':

> We recently lost a grandson by heroin overdose — in North Richmond. We wonder whether a supervised injecting room might have saved his life. Last year, 172 people died from heroin overdose in Victoria (*The Age*, 16/12). We wonder at the incalculable number of families who have been — and

> will be — devastated by addiction. Just as the road toll with its connection to alcohol was taken seriously and effectively minimised, our thinking and strategies against the scourge of drug addiction should be re-evaluated. A start would be for society and government to lift addiction out of the 'taboo' category and recognise it for what it is: a disease which needs medical treatment. It is time to cut the 'drug toll'.

On Christmas morning as I prepared for a busy, joyful family gathering, tears flowed as I thought of the grieving family from Ocean Grove and others like them. That they felt the need to write anonymously said a lot about the stigma that's associated with the death of a loved one by drug overdose. The stigma adds to the pain. A grieving mother confided that she told people that her child had died in a car accident and not from a drug overdose: 'There is sympathy for the car-accident scenario. I wasn't judged as being a bad parent.'

I sent my love and sympathy out into the universe, hoping the family from Ocean Grove would know that strangers could feel their pain. I wondered: would I meet the authors one day to express my sympathy in person? You never know. Life's a funny thing.

5

If not us, who? If not now, when?

JANUARY–FEBRUARY 2017

I read three influential books over the summer. Each had a significant impact on my understanding of the catastrophic failure of the 'war on drugs', offered an international perspective on the management of drug supply and addiction, and detailed the practicalities of establishing a SIF.

Johann Hari's *Chasing the Scream*[1] is a compelling and hard-hitting examination of the comprehensive failure of the 'war on drugs'. It is a brutal read in many instances, providing the important international context and referencing SIFs in various cities.

Matt Noffs' *Breaking the Ice*[2] is another important analysis of the 'war on drugs' — this time from a national and regional perspective — specifically relating to methamphetamine use. It compares Australian and New Zealand strategic management plans. The book concludes with 'If not us, who? If not now, when?' It was the perfect motto for our campaign, summing up the feelings of the members of the embryonic group. It was henceforth included in our 'official' RVSDS email signatures.

In the Eye of the Needle: diary of a medically supervised injecting centre[3] documents the establishment of the Sydney facility's first 30 months of operation — and the battles to keep it open — from the perspective of its inaugural medical director, Dr Ingrid van Beek AM.

> Van Beek [includes] the mechanics of opening and running the centre; the emotional toll it takes on staff; the humanity of the drug users the centre serves; the needs of the clients; and the scrutiny that an institution comes under for being deemed 'controversial'. Ultimately this book is about how compassion, health care, dignity and human rights can be obtained for drug users.[4]

My copy of the book came from the source. In early January, my new 'besties' from the Sydney MSIC had thoughtfully sent me a package of their publications for distribution at proposed community forums. They included *In the Eye of the Needle* in the package. I felt hugely empowered by these wonderful people. My gratitude is eternal. Reading Ingrid's book inspired me to religiously diarise everything that would happen in the campaign over the next few years — however long it would take.

A formal objective of RVSDS was 'to educate the community on the benefits and facts about MSICs'. Like me in July 2016, many thought these facilities sounded like a good way forward for our community without fully understanding the specifics of a SIF. I thought that a pamphlet targeting non-medical supporters of an MSIC trial would enhance their general knowledge, empowering them to discuss the issue with others. Using the Sydney MSIC resources, along with the copious notes that I'd taken at the coronial inquest in December, I created a flyer for supporters:

Ten Facts You Must Know About MSICs — They ...

1. save lives — greatly reduce the overdose deaths in our streets, lanes & gardens
2. reduce public injecting & discarded syringes in our streets and laneways
3. reduce callouts to emergency services — 80 per cent drop in ambulance callouts when Sydney MSIC opened, reducing demand on hospitals' emergency beds & personnel
4. work well as a discreet clinic-like building in the middle of the drug hotspot
5. provide counselling & referrals for a range of rehabilitation & health services
6. reduce the spread of blood-borne diseases — HIV infection and Hepatitis C
7. are legal — legislation permits users to inject their own drugs in a safer space — dealing in the MSIC is prohibited
8. are not open 24/7 — Sydney MSIC is open during extended business hours each day
9. do not have a 'honeypot effect' — no increased drug using & crime in the area
10. may be funded by the confiscated proceeds of crime — no impact on health budget

[Information from *Cross Currents*, a publication of Sydney MSIC 2014, and evidence from 100+ MSICs operating in sixty-eight cities in eleven countries: Canada, Switzerland, Germany, Netherlands, Norway, Luxembourg, Spain, Denmark, Scotland, France & Australia.]

I used the time away from my school job in January to ramp up my networking. I visited Fiona Patten in her electorate office in suburban Brunswick. It was the first time we had spoken since meeting at the inquest. Personable and professional, Fiona briefed me on her private member's bill supporting an 18-month trial of an MSIC in North Richmond, which was to be tabled in parliament in February. She also arranged an invitation for me and other RVSDS members to give evidence at the Law Reform Committee's parliamentary inquiry into drug-law reform in June.

I caught up with the new City of Yarra councillors, who I had met as candidates during the election campaign, including Danae Bosler, Mi-Lin Chen Yi Mei, and Daniel Nguyen. I also met with Greens politicians Richard Di Natale (federal senator for Victoria, and former AOD doctor), Adam Bandt (federal member for Melbourne), and Colleen Hartland (Victorian upper-house MP for the Western Metropolitan Region).

I arranged a meeting with NRCH CEO Demos Krouskos, along with neighbours and new RVSDS members Loraine Little and Greg Hordacre. There had been increased drug activity in our laneways and carports due to an undercover police blitz in Victoria Street. Residents knew when police ramped up activity in the strip — drug dealing and injecting were displaced into side streets. These 'solutions' don't address drug activity; they relocate it. I knew Demos was the 'go-to' person for both local and historical information, having heard his evidence at the inquest.

He is a lifelong resident and had been CEO of our community health centre for many years.

Demos clearly enjoyed discussing public-health issues associated with living and working in a drug market. Displacement of drug activity was a major concern for him. Life was more treacherous for people injecting drugs when they were running and hiding. He employed two outreach workers to watch out for people injecting in North Richmond hideaways; his service could not extend its reach north of Victoria Street into South Abbotsford.

Another important activity in January was to formalise the use of respectful language when discussing people with addiction and proven harm-reduction measures. This was key to setting the tone of our campaign and the presentation of information at our community forums. Educating the community in the use of appropriate language also highlighted the stigma experienced by some of our most vulnerable citizens. Pejoratives such as 'junkie' and 'shooting galleries' are all too familiar in the community and in the media. Such loaded words diminish the seriousness of addiction and affect the provision of services to assist 'real people who are judged' and in need of health and allied services.[5]

ABC Melbourne's morning radio broadcaster, Jon Faine, hosted a panel discussion on Melbourne's drug crisis. I rang in to provide a resident's perspective on our local situation, assuring the panellists that 'this will be an issue at the 2018 state election'. Later that day when I was walking home with my shopping, I came across a man injecting in the low-rise public-housing estate just off the main laneway. I walked past to give him some privacy, returning when he was packing up his gear. I introduced myself and asked if he was okay. He was ready to chat with me:

> About five years ago, I had a workplace accident. I broke a bone in my neck. I was a forklift driver and was paid out by WorkCover insurance. I haven't been able to work since. I've been to so many doctors and specialists for medication, and nothing has worked — nothing. I'm in total agony, so I've started using heroin to get relief. I use it here every morning. Then I go and walk along the Yarra [River — 500 metres from this spot]. I can do that for about two hours, pain-free. It's worth it.

—

RVSDS met twice at my home in February. Both meetings were attended by ten residents, including new neighbour Ciska Burrie. We outlined our four key objectives as established in November and gave out copies of *Cross Currents* along with my 'Ten Facts' flyer. People felt refreshed and energised after the summer break, ready to start campaigning. Many had contacted relevant state-government ministers about our campaign and the need for an MSIC. Local resident and Fitzroy Legal Service lawyer Jen Black, whom I had met at the inquest in December, assisted us with the development of a petition to parliament.

Opportunities to promote RVSDS in the media came thick and fast. Greg Denham invited RVSDS to be a signatory to an open letter to the Victorian parliament from 48 key public-health organisations urging the introduction of an MSIC trial in North Richmond. Organised by the Alcohol and Drug Foundation, 'Let's Start Saving Lives' was published in the *Herald Sun* on 9 February. Other signatories included the Salvation Army, Anglicare, the United Firefighters Union, Ambulance Employees Australia, the Australian Medical Association, the Royal Australian

College of General Practitioners, Victorian Trades Hall Council, Yarra City Council, Drug and Alcohol Nurses of Australasia, a variety of youth and health services, and leading drug agencies.

David Stanley from the Australian Drug Law Reform Foundation invited me to participate in a *Herald Sun* photo shoot outside the NRCH centre on 13 February. Fiona Patten, Greg Denham, and Mi-Lin Chen Yi Mei were promoting the introduction of Fiona's private member's bill for an MSIC trial. Complementing this promotion was a massive mobile billboard, erected on 17 February in the carpark on the north-east corner of the intersection of Victoria and Nicholson Streets. The billboard proclaimed: '60,000 in Richmond streets — end the needle nightmare'.[6] Across the road, on the north-west corner of the intersection, was Quint Cafe, an eclectic hangout from which you could see everything that went on in the shopping strip, including drug dealing, overdosing, and emergency vehicles blocking the traffic. We often went there to debrief, and it was becoming the unofficial RVSDS headquarters.

Jon Faine and veteran Channel 7 political reporter Brendan Donohoe requested interviews. I suggested the syringe-littered dead-end laneway next to my house for the television interview. Brendan's response to our campaign for an MSIC trial was telling: 'I can't believe we are still talking about this issue. I've been in the game since [Victorian premier Jeff] Kennett's time [in the 1990s], and it was an issue then. It needs to get sorted.'

Brendan contacted me again the following week. Coroner Hawkins' report into the death of Ms A was released on 20 February with the recommendation 'That the Honourable Martin Foley MP as Minister for Mental Health take the necessary steps to establish a safe injecting facility trial in North Richmond'.[7]

This was the first of three coroner's reports to be released in 2017, all containing the same key recommendation.

Now Jon Faine and Claire Slattery from ABC radio's *AM* program contacted me to arrange interviews with residents. Claire met with us that evening at Margot Foster's home, where RVSDS had gathered to discuss the coroner's recommendations. Afterwards, I walked Claire through the neighbourhood to provide context to the interviews. I pointed out drug-dealing hotspots and unsupervised injecting areas: carparks, public toilets, laneways, gardens. It was the first of many walking tours that I would provide MPs, reporters, academics, and students seeking a greater understanding of the scale of the crisis. I always encouraged them to talk with other residents: 'Don't just take my word for it.' The tours became an important plank of RVSDS community education policy.

Kylie Troy-West described her life in this street:

> I have neighbours that have performed CPR on people that have overdosed, some of whom have died, which is an awful fact. All houses on my street have removable tap heads … that was a decision that was taken nine years ago as a preventative measure … if you cannot access any water on the street, then your ability to inject on the street is reduced … neighbours banded together to tackle that problem.
>
> On my street I cannot pick up a piece of litter from the gutter because I might get a needlestick injury. And every time my son wants to go and draw chalk animals on the footpath, I have to go out before him, check up and down. Is there anyone injecting? Are there any dealers? Are there any syringes?[8]

Fiona Patten invited Margot and me to join her at Parliament House on 22 February to witness the introduction of her private member's bill: the Drugs, Poisons and Controlled Substances Amendment (Pilot Medically Supervised Injecting Centre) Bill 2017.[9] The bill was immediately referred to the Legal and Social Issues Committee for investigation, to report back to the parliament in mid-September. We had drinks in the members' dining room afterwards with Fiona and her chief adviser, Andrew Shears.

As I extended my network of experienced and knowledgeable practitioners, one name on my radar was Bob Carr, the longest-serving NSW premier and former Australian foreign minister. How could I have a conversation with this veteran Australian politician? At that time, he was head of the Australia-China Relations Institute at University of Technology Sydney. My daughter's friend also worked at that organisation and referred me to Bob's office manager. Bob agreed to a 15-minute telephone conversation with me, Margot, and Kylie on 24 February. A real coup!

Bob was congenial and affirming of our early campaign strategy. He provided a confidence boost, especially as our efforts to connect with relevant Victorian government ministers continued to be futile. He had three parting recommendations:

> Have a strong advocate in the parliament. [Done — Fiona Patten.]
>
> Visit the Sydney MSIC. [Done.]
>
> Hope that a state politician who may have had a personal connection to someone with addiction, or a fatal overdose, may empathise with the issue.

February ended with the retirement of the influential head of Victoria's powerful police union, Ron Iddles. The outgoing officer publicly indicated his support for Coroner Hawkins' recommendation of a trial SIF for heroin users in Richmond to help curb drug overdose deaths: 'In relation to heroin, where there have been so many deaths, I support a trial. It is a trial, so why shouldn't we support it?'[10]

Iddles' position was at odds with Premier Daniel Andrews, who had rejected the coroner's recommendation for a SIF trial that same week.

6

It's a marathon, not a sprint

MARCH–APRIL 2017

The campaign cranked up in March.

RVSDS became an incorporated association to assist with grant applications, to receive discounted hire rates on public venues, and to secure public liability insurance. Adopting the *Model Rules of an Incorporated Association*, I was appointed 'secretary', the only official position of the association. We kept the administration simple and clearly stated the four key objectives that were developed in November.[1]

On 15 March, I was invited to an Alcohol and Drug Foundation meeting with CEO John Rogerson, David Stanley, Greg Denham, and Fiona Patten, among others. I attended these monthly meetings to keep abreast of what other organisations were planning. I also kept them informed of RVSDS campaign efforts and events.

Following our telephone meeting with Bob Carr, I received

an invitation to the launch of a report commissioned by Australia21, an independent, not-for-profit policy think tank: *Can Australia Respond to Drugs More Effectively and Safely?*[2] The launch was to take place on 20 March at Parliament House in Sydney, with Bob and former Liberal premier of Victoria Jeff Kennett co-launching the report. Australia21 chair Paul Barratt, Dr Alex Wodak AM (president, Australian Drug Law Reform Foundation), Mick Palmer (former commissioner, Australian Federal Police), Nicholas Cowdery QC, Marianne Jauncey, David Stanley, Rebecca Bunn (Australia21 volunteer), and staff from the Sydney MSIC were also in attendance.

Mick Palmer spoke passionately about the failed 'war on drugs' and the urgent need to focus on a health-strategy approach: 'We have to stop locking up our kids.' Mick was the second retired senior police officer in three weeks who had put his weight behind taking a different approach to tackling the country's illicit drug problem. It was humbling to attend this stellar event, which was, once again, an excellent networking opportunity for this newbie.

I caught up again with Rebecca Bunn later that week in Melbourne. She was coordinating Australia21's Smarter About Drugs program, encouraging young people's input into the national drug conversation. Inspired by what I had learnt at the Sydney launch, I discussed the possibility of the school where I worked participating in the program. Peter Farrar, the Year 12 legal-studies teacher, jumped at the opportunity for his switched-on students to be involved. It was a trailblazing project for both organisations.

The Yarra Hotel in Abbotsford was the venue for the Harm Reduction Saves Lives forum on 22 March. I had met the organiser,

Councillor Stephen Jolly, during the election campaign. He had a reputation for using publicity stunts to highlight controversial issues, as per his statement in the promotional flyer: 'At this meeting, we will vote on direct action including a mobile safe injecting facility (SIF).'

Anticipating an approach from the councillor to support his plan, I had raised the proposal with Alex Wodak at the Australia21 launch. Alex is a physician and had been director of the AOD service at St Vincent's Hospital in Sydney. A giant in drug law–reform advocacy and activism, his advice was unequivocal: 'Civil disobedience or stunts should only be contemplated when you have no other options. There is a huge cost to the people involved.'

I relayed Alex's sage advice to the councillor when we caught up at the forum, and I took the opportunity to spruik the RVSDS campaign for the MSIC to others at the pub that night. I was approached afterwards by supportive residents Michelle Zwagerman, Tony Worsteling, Melody Patterson, and Frank and Dianne McCulloch. They were keen to get involved in our growing team. More hands to the pump!

I reflected on another huge month and was glad that I was keeping a record of all the names, meetings, activities, and media reports. It's easy to forget everything that happens when there's so much going on. Our campaign was gaining momentum. Well-credentialed people were coming out of the woodwork to assist us. Their knowledge and experience were significant. These interactions upped my energy and enthusiasm for our endeavours. The downer was our frustration that we hadn't received any response to our correspondence to state-government ministers. I had heard nothing from Richard Wynne after hand-delivering my letter in December. At the very least, an acknowledgement of receipt would have been appreciated.

—

It was an action-packed RVSDS meeting at my home on 12 April, with attendance from many new recruits. Marianne Jauncey had approved our use of the Sydney MSIC educational video that I'd seen when I visited the facility in November. It included comments from staff, people who were involved in the establishment of the MSIC in 2001, and a mother who grieved the death of her son. The parts filmed inside the facility itself included MSIC staff playing the role of clients.[3] I was excited about showing the video at our meeting. I knew that it would inspire and invigorate this burgeoning group of residents.

The video would become a staple at our public presentations and was a game changer as far as our community education was concerned. It was key to helping hundreds of residents understand what an MSIC was, and how it saved lives and a community. Marianne concludes the film with a powerful piece to camera: 'Tell me: when will the next one open in Australia?' That rhetorical question was always greeted at our forums with hoots, cheers, and punching the air.

It was at that 12 April meeting that the team made a prudent ideological decision. We vowed not to accept funding from any political or similar organisation, to remain 100 per cent independent. Accordingly, we declined an offer made by the Victorian Greens to fund the printing of RVSDS flyers, which was conditional upon featuring their branding. Michelle Zwagerman later wrote:

> The event that had the biggest impact was my very first RVSDS meeting. I was impressed that so many skilled people had gathered and were working together for the good of others and our community. It inspired me, and subsequent meetings kept me motivated. I thought it fantastic that we had the confidence that we could make a difference, with our collective sense of purpose, justice, compassion, and empathy! We stayed true to the single goal, in a positive, constructive way.

In the wake of that meeting, and in desperate need of funds for the printing of 20,000 flyers, I sought and received an unconditional donation of $950 from a friend who was happy to help — and to remain anonymous. I will be forever grateful for his generosity and confidence in our campaign in those early days.

The RVSDS team discussed future events, including community forums, which would start in early May. We would provide authentic engagement with a structured format featuring the MSIC film, a guest speaker, a Q&A session, and advice about 'friendraising' activities. A social gathering would conclude each event. We would precede each community forum with a meeting of the key RVSDS members, to discuss campaign planning, fundraising, and potential guest speakers.

We also planned the March to Save Lives, a community rally to coincide with International Overdose Awareness Day on 31 August. Kylie Troy-West was a professional event coordinator, employed by a metropolitan council. Having organised many community events in public places, she was experienced in liaising with relevant authorities, managing public-liability issues, booking street spaces, talking with local Indigenous groups about a Welcome to Country smoking ceremony, organising volunteers … whatever it would take to make our March to Save Lives an event that could actually save lives. We farewelled Margot, who headed overseas for a few months.

There was continuing and increasing interest in RVSDS. I was interviewed by many people throughout our campaign: students from RMIT, Deakin, Melbourne, La Trobe, Monash, and Griffith universities, as well as community and online journalists. I always took interviewers on a neighbourhood tour to provide greater context to their articles and reports. While it was tricky fitting these in with my paid work and RVSDS schedule, it was always enjoyable. Spreading our message about an MSIC trial, courtesy of enthusiastic journalism students, was another key plank of RVSDS community education. We wanted a shift in thinking from a law-and-order frame to a health and harm-reduction one.

I had read up on the theory, to move beyond what was for me an instinctual desire to reduce harm. According to Harm Reduction International:

> Harm reduction refers to policies, programmes and practices that aim to minimise negative health, social and legal impacts associated with drug use, drug policies and drug laws.
>
> Harm reduction is grounded in justice and human rights. It focuses on positive change and on working with people without judgement, coercion, discrimination, or requiring that they stop using drugs as a precondition of support.
>
> Harm reduction encompasses a range of health and social services and practices that apply to illicit and licit drugs. These include, but are not limited to, drug consumption rooms, needle and syringe programmes, non-abstinence-based housing and

> employment initiatives, drug checking, overdose prevention and reversal, psychosocial support, and the provision of information on safer drug use. Approaches such as these are cost-effective, evidence-based and have a positive impact on individual and community health.[4]

Master of Journalism student Charlotte Grieve interviewed me for an article for the University of Melbourne publication *The Citizen*. Liam Mannix from *The Age* booked an interview and a tour of the 'notorious street with topless taps'. I gave them both a 'show bag' containing everything they needed — RVSDS flyer, 'Ten Facts' pamphlet, *Cross Currents*, and a copy of Coroner Hawkins' report.

RVSDS member Greg Hordacre reported on an unexpected community-engagement opportunity in late April:

> After living seven years in the area and regularly frequenting Victoria Street for meals and supermarket shopping, I was thrilled to find my ideal property and move into the 'hood in 2016. I was aware of the injecting drug culture and homelessness. What I wasn't ready for was the high level of compassion shared by residents for those on the street and experiencing addiction. Shortly after moving in, my partner and I held a garage sale. I was blown away meeting my neighbours and hearing their stories. I fully expected negativity but was struck by the shared openness and desire to do something together: something that would effectively help those that used our streets, back lanes, and doorways as their home.
>
> It also struck me that the voices of those living in North Richmond and South Abbotsford, regardless of whether they

were in a dwelling or on the street, had been stifled. Years of institutional and government neglect had created a ghetto where this problem could be conveniently corralled. This neglect had impacted everyone, shutting down all voices, creating an impression that no-one cared. That couldn't have been further from the truth.

At our garage sale that sunny afternoon, we met many locals who wanted genuine solutions. The only contrary voice was a former senior police officer. He said the need to effectively address the situation would never progress until drugs were decriminalised and those addicted were treated for their health issues. My mind was blown. I lived among people who had a strong vision for social justice and understanding. Buoyed by these new friends, I knew we had every chance to make an impact to improve safety and amenity in our neighbourhood.

Greg Denham constantly reiterated that our campaign was 'a marathon, not a sprint'. While he intended no offence, this mantra was anathema to me. The frequency of people injecting and overdosing — and the screaming of sirens — added to the sense of urgency surrounding our efforts. From our perspective, there wasn't a minute to waste.

7

Location, location, location

MAY–JUNE 2017

Jeremy Dwyer from the Coroners Prevention Unit was the keynote speaker at the Yarra Drug and Health Forum meeting at Richmond Town Hall on 1 May. Armed with graphs and statistics, he talked about the 'tsunami of fentanyl' — an opioid pain medication — impacting the international drug scene. I propped myself at the back of the meeting room with a wad of newly minted RVSDS flyers. I handed them to people as they departed the meeting.

The first RVSDS community forum was held in a local warehouse on 4 May. We welcomed and registered residents and gave each person a package of our flyers and the 'Ten Facts' pamphlets for distribution to their neighbours. They viewed the Sydney MSIC film. There wasn't a dry eye when Judy Smith spoke about her only child, Daniel.

> My son — only child — Daniel died from heroin overdose [last year]. He was 28 years old. He died alone, in my car. Daniel was an intelligent young man. He hated what it did to him, but he was gripped with addiction. People say to us — simply tell [him] to stop. If only it was that easy.
>
> If he didn't have clean needles, I felt that he was going to be facing major health issues down the track. Daniel taught me tolerance that I never, ever thought I would have … and he taught me that my love for him was unconditional. There was nothing I wouldn't have done to keep him alive.
>
> I have kept quiet for so long. We have lost everything. It's time to speak out.

People asked questions and heard the plans for our friend-raising events in June. As planned, the forum concluded with a social event, with residents mingling and sharing experiences and thoughts about the drug-injecting crisis. There was a positive buzz in the room. We were thrilled with the inaugural event and recruited many new supporters to our campaign. Kylie Troy-West reflected: 'The working group has grown to about fifteen people. The broader group, as well the Facebook community, is almost at 500. It is baby steps, but everyone that we talk to locally is really supportive of what we are doing, and that is really what is motivating us to keep going.'[1]

Coroner Audrey Jamieson reiterated Coroner Hawkins' recommendation for a trial MSIC in North Richmond in a report on 8 May: 'If a safe injecting facility can shift drug injecting from public locations to a clinically supervised environment, this would be hoped to lessen the traumatic impact of injecting drug use and overdose and death on local residents who are exposed to these activities in their everyday life.'[2] I was surprised to read that 'Ms Judy Ryan, Residents for Victoria Street Drug Solutions' had been included in the distribution of Coroner Jamieson's report — along with Mental Health Minister Martin Foley, Department of Health and Human Services secretary Kym Peake, and other officials.

While a response from government MPs to RVSDS correspondence had not been forthcoming, members of the Richmond branch of the Labor Party voted unanimously in support of an MSIC. It was good to know that someone was hearing the message. Branch member and RVSDS supporter Tony Worsteling made an inspired suggestion that we attend the upcoming two-day Labor Party annual conference. He reserved a table from which we displayed banners, distributed flyers, encouraged petition signing, and engaged with delegates. Special Minister of State Gavin Jennings was very hospitable, as was Pete Steedman, the former federal member for Casey, in Melbourne's eastern rural fringe. Emma Greeney, adviser to Minister Foley, was very engaging. Richard Wynne was in attendance but didn't acknowledge our presence, despite most of the group being members of Labor's Richmond branch.

It was another hectic month with the media. Claire Slattery interviewed me for *The World Today*. Laura Turner from Channel 9's *A Current Affair* requested an interview for a report on the heroin crisis. Anxious about a sensationalist interpretation of this issue, I was hesitant but agreed to meet with her. I was unaware that Laura's sister, Skye, had fatally overdosed two months earlier. The interview and neighbourhood tour with Laura were difficult for both of us. Her courage in telling a personal story on this program, intertwined with the escalating overdosing crisis in our community, was extraordinary. I don't know how she did it.

Securing public wall space for proposed RVSDS billboards featuring two ambulances in Victoria Street — with the tag 'Medically Supervised Injecting Centres Save Taxpayers' Dollars' — proved futile: 'Too confronting,' cried property owners. I had thought that drug injecting and overdosing next to the walls were confronting, not a photo of two ambulances.

Happily, the energy that had been expended on the failed billboard endeavour was recaptured with the prospect of a street-art installation to amplify our message. Thanks to the fancy footwork of David Stanley, key RVSDS supporter and 'international man of mystery' (he had the knack of popping up 'out of nowhere'), I met dynamic street-art curator Dean Sunshine. With new focus, we honed our message to suit an enduring, contemporary medium. All we had to do was secure an appropriate wall with the agreement of a congenial owner, and the services of inspired artists. How hard could that possibly be?

May ended tragically. I attended a fatal overdose of a young woman on Victoria Street outside the 'unsupervised injecting centre' on my way home from work. It still haunts me.

—

In June, the second RVSDS community forum was well attended. Our letterboxing and word of mouth had kicked in. We used the same format as the May meeting, and once again people responded with compassion — and a sense of hope — to the Sydney MSIC film. Our numbers grew with residents from a diverse range of backgrounds, which was pleasing. Having an inclusive membership was a key RVSDS objective. We discussed plans for the March to Save Lives in late August and asked attendees to inform their families, friends, and neighbours.

We hosted two friendraising events that month: a sausage sizzle at Bunnings in Collingwood, and an auction and film night at the RVSDS warehouse, featuring the 2006 Australian film about addiction, *Candy*. Both events were hugely successful. Hundreds of people chatted about the MSIC and signed our petitions. I particularly noticed when older residents, many using walking aids, pushed through the queues to sign our petition: 'It should've happened years ago.'

Kylie Troy-West reflected:

> Across 2016, seven people died of heroin overdose only a few hundred metres from my home. In April 2017, a young woman, a mother, aged twenty-one, died out the front of the pub on the corner of my street. By this point, RVSDS was starting to put serious pressure on the government to act. For me, this death [of] someone so young, a mother like me, so close to home, affected me deeply. It motivated me to do everything I could to get an MSIC opened in our community.

June was a big month for interaction with state politicians. There were two simultaneous Victorian parliamentary inquiries into an MSIC.

On 5 June, Kylie and I gave both public and in camera evidence to the Drug Law Reform Committee inquiry.[3] The proposed location of an MSIC was a key focus of the committee. My notes from December's coronial inquest informed my response whenever people asked me about proposed locations. Marianne Jauncey's evidence to the inquest was unequivocal:

> We know from all over the world that people use drugs where they buy drugs. The link between the sale, purchase, and use of drugs is place based. When considering the position of the Sydney MSIC at 66 Darlinghurst Road, we knew that an MSIC located 600 metres up the road near St Vincent's Hospital was too far from where ambulance callouts to heroin overdoses occurred. That's why our physical building is placed right in the middle of the hotspot. You need to put an MSIC where the issue is. Page 21 of *Cross Currents* features a stylised map of Kings Cross, 'splattered' with pink dots pinpointing the location of the MSIC. Each pink dot represents one of the 677 ambulance callouts to heroin overdoses that occurred in the area in 1999. There were 335 that occurred in Darlinghurst Road alone. You locate the solution where the problem is.

The distance from the overdose hotspot in Richmond to our own St Vincent's Hospital, in Fitzroy, is 2.2 kilometres. Based on Marianne's evidence, an MSIC located within that hospital precinct, as proposed by some, would fail because it was too far away. Marianne had also reflected on issues associated with a standalone MSIC such as the Sydney facility:

> You need to have a number of integrated, holistic primary-care services in close vicinity to the MSIC. It generally works to create a 'one-stop shop' that ensures clients have easy access to other services. It's important to lower the threshold and barriers for people to be able to take that next step. Having an integrated service would be beneficial.

This would be achieved in our community if an MSIC was

co-located with a general healthcare facility, such as the NRCH centre.

I responded to the location question at the Drug Law Reform Committee's inquiry:

> Ms PATTEN: … we have asked other people who have come today where they think the facility should be established … Other people have said the North Richmond health centre …
> Ms RYAN: … [the location should] be based on the evidence of the ambulance service in terms of where the majority of their call-outs are. I think that is where we should focus.
> Ms TROY-WEST: … North Richmond health would be a really easy place to put it, but I do not think that the easy solution is necessarily the best solution, because we want something that will be effective … I think we need to follow the evidence as to where a centre should be located instead of opting for the easy choice.[4]

Committee member and Liberal MP Murray Thompson questioned the source of RVSDS funds, perhaps worried that I was speaking for a left-wing political organisation. I confirmed our policy of financial independence and invited him to contribute to our cause at the RVSDS sausage sizzle at Bunnings the following Saturday.

Most members of this parliamentary committee visited South Abbotsford and North Richmond the week after the hearings. I introduced them to the 'topless taps' street among other drug-using locations. I encouraged them to chat to residents as we walked around the area. At one point, committee chair and Labor MP Geoff Howard gently tapped my arm to indicate an open drug deal taking place a few metres ahead of us. I responded knowingly, noticing the shocked look on his pale face.

On the evening of 7 June, I was an observer at the Legal and Social Issues Committee inquiry into the Drugs, Poisons and Controlled Substances Amendment (Pilot Medically Supervised Injecting Centre) Bill 2017.[5] Other people in the gallery included Demos Krouskos and Penny Francis from NRCH and Emma Greeney from Minister Foley's office. Expert evidence was presented by Jeremy Dwyer, Robert Richter, David Stanley, and the Alcohol and Drug Foundation's Geoff Munro. Dan Flynn, Victorian director of the Australian Christian Lobby, which was opposed to an MSIC, was also presenting.

Committee member and ultra-conservative Liberal MP Inga Peulich attended for only one presentation: that of the Australian Christian Lobby. Inga was standing outside the committee room when I headed home. I quietly asked if she had known anyone with drug addiction. She retorted, 'I could have you kicked out of the parliament for daring to speak to me.'

Members of this committee toured our drug hotspot the following week. Greg Denham and I were invited by the committee's staff to lead the tour. MPs witnessed the usual sights: open drug dealing, discarded syringes, people who were drug-affected, and ambulances blocking laneways. As usual, I advised the MPs to speak with residents about their experiences. As we walked along one laneway, we noticed a liquid dribbling, blood-like, into the gutter before we came across a knocked-over bottle of red wine and a man slumped in a carport. We rushed to him, and he responded to our efforts, but it was another heart-stopping moment, witnessed on this occasion by our parliamentary representatives.

At the conclusion of the tour, there was a roundtable discussion at NRCH with the politicians, local drug experts, outreach workers, and council employees: 25 attendees in total. Committee chair and Liberal MP Margaret Fitzherbert co-hosted the meeting with CEO Demos Krouskos. Inga Peulich, who had been absent from the morning's tour, joined us just in time for lunch. When Fiona Patten reported to the group that we had witnessed an overdose in a carport, Inga demanded to know who had led the tour. When Fiona let her know it was Greg and me, Inga retorted: 'Of course you would've seen an overdose.' While others were shocked by this absurd response, I wasn't at all surprised, having experienced her rudeness the previous week.

Laura Turner's courageous report on her sister's fatal overdose and the escalating drug-injecting crisis in North Richmond aired on *A Current Affair* on 19 June. Our tour of the area formed the basis of the report, and Alex Wodak provided expert commentary. This mini-documentary triggered yet more media interest in the RVSDS campaign.

I enjoyed a long conversation with a local resident and supporter of SIFs, Tony Parsons. Tony had been a magistrate of the Dandenong drug court since 2008 and supervising magistrate of the Victorian drug courts since 2012. He was a member of the premier's Ice Action Task Force.

Another enjoyable feature of the campaign was participating in community-radio interviews in Collingwood. 3CR host Bill Pitt invited Yarra Drug and Health Forum chair Peter Wearne and me to appear together on the *Living Free* program, addressing drug, alcohol, gambling, and other addictions. Chatting with new comrades from the drug-education sector was always energising, educational — and fun.

8

The 'military wing'

JULY 2017

On 6 July, Danny Hill, assistant secretary of Victoria's ambulance-employees union, was guest speaker at our third community forum. As frontline emergency workers, paramedics were appreciative of residents' response to the health crisis in the neighbourhood. Danny answered our questions, reinforcing his members' solid support for an MSIC in our area. We also viewed the Sydney MSIC film. Colin and Liz Gomm attended the forum that night, responding to our flyer in their letterbox. They were clearly impressed with the experience and became key supporters of RVSDS.

I was pleased to announce to the forum that, according to a recent article in the Ballarat *Courier* newspaper, the chair of the Drug Law Reform Committee, Geoff Howard, had voiced his support for SIFs, contradicting current Labor policy.[1] Hearing evidence at the recent inquiry and witnessing drug dealing in a local laneway during the pollie tour had clearly had an impact on Geoff. This public support bolstered RVSDS confidence, as did the admission on 22 July that former police commissioner Ken Lay also supported SIFs: 'We probably weren't brave enough to go into the safe injection rooms but, speaking as an individual, there is a real attraction to harm reduction for me. Forget about trying to arrest your way out of this.'[2] Lay was the third top cop in Australia to — once retired — declare his support for drug harm-reduction measures and SIFs.

The receipt of a $1,000 community grant from the City of Yarra and an anonymous donation of $3,000 were a welcome boost to our coffers, especially with the arrangements for the March to Save Lives ramping up. The City of Yarra, Victoria Police, the Victoria Street Business Association, Ambulance Victoria, and Public Transport Victoria were cooperative regarding access to the Victoria Street precinct for the event. Kylie Troy-West requested permission to use North Richmond station as a gathering place for the march and a park in Lennox Street for the rally afterwards. She discussed road closures, traffic management, public transport, and safety. Event promotion, placards, banners, crowd management, marshalling, first aid, and a quality sound system for guest speakers and musicians were high priorities. Andy Simpson from the company Sound Experience offered pro bono support to Kylie. We were in good hands. They were a formidable team.

Thoughtful discussion took place regarding the purpose and structure of the event, with a decided focus on bereaved families and friends. They would lead the march, each carrying a photo of the deceased. For the rally, we would invite speakers who had experienced the loss of a loved one through overdose. Politicians were welcome to attend but not to participate in the formalities.

We acknowledged that the taking of country from Indigenous

people has created untold suffering and disadvantage, resulting in pain and despair in their communities. Inequities, neglect, and marginalisation expose them to a range of licit and illicit drugs tacitly sanctioned by our culture. While these substances provide short-term relief from the pain, they cause long-term grief as communities face the challenge of dispossession and inequality. Decades of failed government policy has enabled heroin to become a crutch for too many people. Recognising this, we reached out to Wurundjeri elder Aunty Di Kerr to speak first at the rally.

A search for musicians to perform at the conclusion of proceedings was underway. We finalised the design and printing of RVSDS T-shirts: purple, orange, and white was a combination that was distinctly different to the colours of any local political party. The purple T-shirts would feature the words 'Medically Supervised Injecting Centres' in white — with a big orange tick — on the front, with 'Save Lives' on the back. It was my job to order a large purple-and-orange vinyl banner from a Victoria Street printer, to mobilise the media, and to organise the meeting of bereaved families at Quint Cafe on the morning before the march.

The Bank of Melbourne — next to Quint Cafe — was selected to manage our RVSDS account. The Abbotsford-branch customer-service officer, David Yang, did exactly what his title promised by simplifying account management for three co-signatories. When he discovered that we used Quint Cafe as our unofficial headquarters for meetings and interviews, he donated food and drink vouchers. His generosity was an unexpected but welcome bonus. Hosting journalists, students, and other interest groups was costing me a small fortune.

Quint Cafe manager Lily and her staff were also kind and generous. They regularly witnessed overdoses and rang 000, and wanted to play their part in our campaign. They stepped up their support ahead of the rally, displaying promotional posters in their windows, placing petitions and flyers on their tables, and offering free coffees and pastries for the day itself. This was one of many times when I was overwhelmed by the love and support of this extraordinary inner-city community.

Herald Sun reporter Ian Royall toured the 'topless taps' street with Kylie's husband, Derek, who invited me to join them. I was expecting Ian to be an opponent of the MSIC, with a fixed mindset about people with addiction. In fact, the reverse was true, and he became a solid supporter of our campaign. I gave him the usual showbag of information, which now included the second coroner's report. The tour of that street had become an effective tool in changing hearts and minds. I could tell from Ian's feedback that he had been affected by the experience.

Ian was asked by journalist Jenny Valentish in an interview in January 2018, 'Why was your coverage of the campaign for a safe-injecting centre so nuanced, as opposed to the usual NIMBY (Not In My Back Yard) stories we find in newspapers?'

> I went over there to Richmond a few times and spent a fair bit of time talking to people, experiencing what life was like in the neighbourhood. It's not like I had to do weeks of undercover investigation, but it's not till you go there that you actually see what people are living with. I spoke to [residents] Judy Ryan and Derek Troy-West. They were basically saying, 'Build a safe-injecting centre at the bottom of my street. I don't care — it's got to be better than what's happening now.'

> A few key things they said to me really struck home. Judy said, 'What we're doing is not working' and 'We all make bad decisions in life ... but most people get away with it.' That's true. When you're in primary school and you're thinking about what you want to be when you grow up, no one thinks: 'a heroin addict'. It's just through circumstance and dumb shit and mental health issues that they become stuck. Who are we to judge?
>
> I just reported what I saw and what people said to me — journalism 101. I did make an effort to not use the word 'junkie' — I used the words 'addict' or 'user' because I felt we needed to change the conversation a little bit. The focus was how cheap heroin had become and how people were dying, and what it was doing to residents. I know we're not supposed to take an angle — just put both sides of the story — but I had trouble finding people who opposed a safe-injecting centre. You get the state opposition [Liberal–National coalition], saying this would be state-sanctioned drug use, or creating drug ghettos, but I'm thinking, 'how can it be worse than what it is now?'[3]

On Friday 7 July, Coroner Gregory McNamara reported on the overdose death of 27-year-old 'SO' in a laneway near Victoria Street on 11 August 2016. The coroner also supported 'the recommendations made by Coroner Hawkins in her finding following an inquest into the death of Ms A'. His report was harrowing reading. SO was one month younger than my oldest son. He had died two streets from my home in the month that I'd started researching SIFs. Coroner McNamara commented:

> I ... note that SO travelled from Greater Geelong to the City of Yarra on the day of his death, and that he was found deceased

> in a non-residential location … Coroner Audrey Jamieson addressed several distinctive features of fatal heroin overdose in the City of Yarra: 'Compared to other Victorian LGAs [local government areas] examined, over the past five years a much greater proportion of fatal heroin overdoses in the City of Yarra involved people who travelled there from other areas; and a much greater proportion occurred in non-residential locations such as parks, carparks, public toilets, restaurant toilets, cars, and on streets.'
>
> SO's death is another example of the pattern of heroin-related deaths in the City of Yarra. In addition, his death exhibits characteristics which are unusually pronounced in the City of Yarra compared to other parts of Victoria with high rates of heroin-related deaths.[4]

My heart ached for SO's family.

Early on Sunday 9 July, I heard my phone pinging relentlessly in the kitchen. Thinking the worst, I got poor John to check it. He returned with a cuppa: 'I think you're in the newspaper.' Sure enough, journalism student Charlotte Grieve's investigative article had appeared in *The Sunday Age*.[5] Following months of painstaking interviews with stakeholders, 'New Richmond alliance pushes for safe injecting room' packed a punch. It triggered an astonishing response, not the least being the following email, forwarded to me from the RVSDS website administrator, Kylie: 'This has come through addressed to you. Pretty powerful stuff. We are going to do this …'

> Hi Judy, I just read your article in *The Age*. My twenty-seven-year-old son, Sam, died in Little Lithgow Lane, Abbotsford/

North Richmond on August 11, 2016. He was one of the seven who died in the street, every mother's worst nightmare. The coroner's office contacted me on Friday and said that his report was closing that day and that the findings would be made public, but his details would be deidentified to protect certain parties. I support what you are doing and trying to achieve. His loving brother, grandparents and I want to use Sam's death to help bring about the implementation of safe injecting rooms. Please let me know how I can help in any way.

Yours sincerely, Loretta Gabriel

I was gobsmacked. Later that afternoon, after I pulled myself together, I emailed Loretta, thanking her, and sending our condolences. Two days later, I followed up with an invitation to meet with her. She was keen, but as she lived near Geelong, it would have to be by phone. We booked in a call on Thursday morning. The night before, I had a light-bulb moment. I emailed Loretta:

A random question, Loretta. Do Sam's grandparents live in Ocean Grove? I read a letter in *The Age* last December from 'names withheld' from Ocean Grove. Their grandson died in North Richmond during the year from a heroin overdose. I still have that letter. It was so tragic. I thought about them and the boy's family at Christmas.

Loretta replied:

Yes, Judy. That letter was written by my father. [My parents] were very close to Sam. My father very much wants to help bring about safe injecting rooms so if he can help, just let me know.

I responded:

OMG Loretta. Please tell him that his letter made me cry. I kept it and see it every time I open my folder. When politicians ignore us and we feel like giving up, I read that letter and it has kept me going. You were in my thoughts on Christmas morning and now I have found you … amazing!

A tearful 90-minute telephone conversation took place the following day. I followed up the call with the following email:

I am so pleased we have found each other. You have been on my mind since December. I am humbled that you, Damian, Jack, and your dad will be at our rally on Sunday 27 August. If you are happy with this, we want the four of you to be in the front row of the walk from North Richmond station. I will be with you along with others who have lost sons, daughters, brothers, and sisters to the heroin crisis.

Ian Royall's investigative report, 'Heroin Scourge: $17 a hit', had appeared in the *Herald Sun* on Wednesday.[6] He organised for my opinion piece — 'How injecting rooms will save lives in Richmond and Abbotsford' — to be published the following day.[7] This prompted interviews with radio stations Triple M, ABC, 3AW, 3CR, and Triple R.

Ian told me that he was writing an article on Coroner McNamara's report on SO. I told him about my correspondence with SO's mother. He was stunned. I contacted Loretta, and she agreed to speak with Ian for the article, providing details and a photo of Sam. Ian reflected on that conversation in the January 2018 interview with Jenny Valentish:

> I spoke to Loretta Gabriel, whose son Sam O'Donnell died of an overdose. She's very articulate and normal, a good woman. I later realised that Sam used to briefly go out with my daughter, at the point that he was just getting into drugs. So then there was this strange personal connection, and you think, well, sliding doors — that could have been my daughter. I didn't include that in my reporting, but I did think that could have been my family dealing with that, like Loretta, for ten years. It's a cliché, but this can happen to anyone.[8]

Loretta was invited to speak on ABC Melbourne with Jon Faine on the day the article appeared in the *Herald Sun*. She was determined to use the release of the coroner's report to destigmatise death by overdose. Sam would have been proud of her. We were proud of her.

The National Party federal senator for Victoria Bridget McKenzie also appeared on Jon Faine's radio program that week. What a contrast she was to Loretta. An opponent of SIFs, she exposed her lack of knowledge about the facilities. Encouraged by the positive response from politicians who had participated in my tours of our area, I immediately rang her office to invite her on a private tour. 'Senator McKenzie would definitely be interested,' I was told.

A date was made, then rescheduled … and repeat. She never appeared. I also rang the office of National Party state MP and shadow health minister Emma Kealy, inviting her to join me on a private tour. I had a referral from retired National Party MP Hugh Delahunty, from Kealy's hometown of Horsham. I didn't hear back from her, either.

Street-art curator Dean Sunshine secured the perfect space for our installation: the rear wall of The Hive shopping centre, in Little Charles Street, Abbotsford — corner of Victoria Street. The timing was perfect: 20 August — one week before the rally, which would stir up media interest. He had contracted the services of renowned Melbourne street artists Ling and Mayonaize (aka Matt Thompson and Caleb Walmsley). Ling specialises in stylised, 'blockbuster' lettering.[9] Mayo creates a calligraphic style of lettering.[10] Both artists are key influencers in the industry, and command significant fees. When approached by Dean about commissioning this work, they agreed to undertake the assignment for a significantly reduced fee. They supported our campaign, wanting to honour their peers who had succumbed to drug overdose.

Greg Hordacre and I organised a meeting at the Carringbush Hotel (the Carro) with communications consultant Jayne Dullard, who offered her support to the campaign. We needed to finalise our message for the street-art installation. I had been inspired by an article that I had read about the opening ceremony of the 25th Harm Reduction International conference, in Montreal in May. As Canadian federal health minister Dr Jane Philpott delivered a keynote speech, activists and members of the audience participated in a silent protest organised by the Canadian Association of People Who Use Drugs (CAPUD). In a symbolic gesture to the Canadian government, participants turned their backs to the minister while she spoke. They held placards that exclaimed 'They Talk, We Die'. CAPUD demanded an immediate and adequate response to the overdose epidemic in their community.[11] 'Wow,' I thought. 'That is one powerful message.' It resonated with how I felt as a resident in a drug 'war zone' who had failed to get an adequate response from her state representatives.

Over a wine or two at the Carro, Greg, Jayne, and I flipped the Canadian message: 'They Talk, We Die' became 'We Talk, They Die'. Not totally satisfied with this rearrangement (and after another wine), the message morphed into the more inclusive 'You Talk, We Die'. It was a bingo moment! 'You Talk, We Die' clearly represented the perspectives of both the residents and the people overdosing in the area: 'You' (the parliamentarians with the overseas tours and inquiries) are talking while 'We' (the people overdosing in the laneways and the community) are dying.

As a final gesture, the installation would also acknowledge those who had fatally overdosed in our community across the years by including the first names of 34 people. That was the number of people who had died in 2016, triggering the scrutiny of the Coroners Court.

We told Dean Sunshine and David Stanley that we were ready to go. They loved the message and the significance of including 34 names. A cunning plan was hatched to stencil *#youtalkwedie* on local streets prior to the rally.

Activity accelerated at the end of the month. The campaign gained momentum. I gave a lecture to communications students from Deakin University and met with La Trobe University honours students. They were very engaged with this issue, asking thoughtful questions and submitting impressive assignments in response.

I met with the executive officer of the philanthropic organisation Igniting Change. After giving them a lengthy tour of the area, we received a generous donation to assist with the cost of the street-art installation. The balance was covered by the Alcohol and Drug Foundation and a contribution from a Richmond businessperson who requested anonymity. This all happened in a matter of days, once again demonstrating the groundswell of support.

In view of the regularity and success of my tours of the area, Greg Hordacre had a great idea: he would film one of my tours to upload to our website. After a coffee at Quint Cafe on the last Sunday in July, Greg filmed the tour using a smartphone. We went to the usual places of interest: the 'topless taps' street and dangerous laneways, concluding at the public-housing estate and community health centre in North Richmond. The strident wail of a siren announced the arrival of an ambulance in the centre's carpark to attend another overdose. It was not a set-up for our informal video. It was the reality of our daily lives.

On a lighter note, the *Yarra Reporter* published a lively article about our grassroots campaign, cheekily referring to me as 'North Richmond's Erin Brockovich'.[12] More appropriate was David Stanley's intelligence that RVSDS had become known by long-term campaigners as the 'military wing', due to our on-ground efforts in a 'war zone'.[13]

We didn't argue with that.

9

March to Save Lives

AUGUST 2017

August was another massive month. A presentation to the Richmond branch members of the Labor Party at the Carro, chaired by Labor staffer and local resident Onagh Bishop, kicked off proceedings. The following day, I met with John Ferguson from *The Australian* newspaper and took him on 'the tour'. That night, I met with the Abbotsford Primary School council, to whom I showed the Sydney MSIC film, distributed flyers, and promoted the upcoming March to Save Lives.

The fourth community forum was live-streamed on Facebook for the first time. Guest speaker and Channel 9 reporter Laura Turner had to withdraw due to illness. *Herald Sun* reporter Ian Royall happily stepped into the breach and provided useful tips on interacting with the media at the rally. He was terrific, and enjoyed lots of conversations with residents at the social event afterwards. Andrew Kavanagh, filmmaker from SBS Viceland, recorded the forum and interviewed attendees. RVSDS members were excited to be wearing the new purple T-shirts, which had arrived that day. There was an excited buzz in the air.

In the four weeks leading up to the March to Save Lives, Michelle Zwagerman organised our purple T-shirt brigade to doorknock traders and residents to promote the rally. Posters and flyers were displayed in shop windows in Victoria Street, indicating huge support. Greg Hordacre and volunteer Annie Ryan developed a four-week promotional strategy to guide the rollout of key campaign messages. Annie overhauled our website, which had been set up in November 2016 by the former 'Victoria Street Drug Solutions' duo of Margot Foster and Kylie Troy-West. The revamped look gave focus to our message and resources. Greg renewed our Facebook and Instagram pages to promote compassionate and caring solutions and to highlight the great work our volunteers were doing doorknocking in the area.

Loretta Gabriel and her son Jack marked the first anniversary of Sam O'Donnell's death, on 11 August, with a visit to the little laneway in Abbotsford where he'd died. They displayed a large poster of Sam, a floral wreath, and, written on the ground in chalk, lyrics from one of Sam's songs: 'One long year ... I need you here but you're never coming home ... One long tear.'

Loretta sent me a photo: 'We will never go back to that place again.' I think of Sam, Loretta, Jack, and their family every time I am in the vicinity of that lonely, deadly place. Sam's anniversary, two weeks prior to the rally, rammed home the purpose of what we were doing. It kept us 100 per cent focused on a positive outcome for the rally in the short term and the opening of an MSIC in the long term — or, hopefully, sooner.

—

I had invited Andrew Kavanagh to take a tour of the area when we caught up at the community forum. We met at my home on the morning of 17 August. During the tour, we came across a man — aged in his forties — in a grungy laneway off Victoria Street. I introduced myself and Andrew to him, telling him that I was part of a residents' group campaigning for an MSIC trial in the area. He said his name was Kevin, and he seemed up for a chat. I asked if he would use such a facility. He said 'of course' he would and, having rolled up his sleeves ready for injecting, showed us his scars: 'Who wants to live like this?'

Kevin invited Andrew and me to stay with him while he injected, as he was concerned about the quality of the drugs he'd just bought. He gave unsolicited approval for Andrew to film his actions, provided his face was blurred. Belying Kevin's dishevelled, fatigued appearance was an articulate man with a tragically common story: his drug use helped him escape the memory of abuse he had endured as a child. I recalled the sobering words of an experienced professional in this sector: 'We don't have a drug-abuse problem in this country. We have a child-abuse problem.'

Kevin declared the injection that morning was '$50 worth of shit'. Exasperated, he rolled down his sleeve, grabbed his well-worn backpack and water bottle and hurriedly exited the laneway. I never saw him again. The scene is etched on Andrew's and my memories forever.

When appropriate, residents often interacted with people who preferred secluded and dangerous spots to inject, listening to their stories and offering help if needed. We had all called 000 many times, and had waited with people until professional help arrived. It always felt like the management of the crisis had been outsourced to residents. Those injecting drugs had been part of our community for years. Mostly, they were appreciative of the connection we made, responding with a 'Thanks, love' or 'Sorry, love', depending on where they were in the injecting process. They would assure us that they would 'clean up' before they went on their way. When clients of the needle and syringe exchange at NRCH were consulted about whether they would use an MSIC, the answer was usually in the affirmative.

—

The towering *You Talk, We Die* mural was installed in the week preceding the rally. Across three days, Ling and Mayo created a dynamic tribute, honouring the people who had died in the precinct from overdose, and acknowledging the impact the crisis was having on those who lived and worked there. Ling's electric-blue letters soared two metres high against a solid charcoal background. Mayo elegantly wove the names of 34 people through Ling's imposing letters, giving the message an ethereal quality. It was majestic. Anthony Zielke from the Alcohol and Drug Foundation filmed the entire production, producing a fabulous one-minute time-lapse video.[1] Ling and Mayo thanked us for commissioning their combined artistry: 'It was really nice to produce something that engages people in a different way.'

The artwork triggered an emotional outpouring. Many came to be photographed in front of the mural, paying tribute to their loved ones named on that concrete wall in Little Charles Street. Ling and Mayo's creation remains untouched and well visited to this day.

Dean Sunshine recorded the experience in *Land of Sunshine: documenting street art and graffiti in Melbourne and beyond*:

> I was approached by a local residents' association who were trying to get the government to start a trial for a supervised injecting room to minimise the increasing number of drug overdoses and deaths in the area. They wanted to organise a mural with a goal to raise awareness of the growing community issue while being respectful to the people that had been personally affected. After months of discussions, Matt Thompson and Mayonaize were chosen as the artists. We all agreed on a concept and finally located a wall … [there is] a video of the mural being painted [and] the finished pics with the thirty-four names of the people that unfortunately lost their lives in the area over the last twelve months.[2]

The mural generated a lot of discussion in the media, raising public awareness of the drug-injecting crisis and the March to Save Lives. Ebony Bowden from *The Age* wrote an article that featured a large photograph.[3] There were radio interviews with ABC Melbourne, 3CR, and Ross and John on *The Rumour File* on 3AW: 'A confronting piece of street art has been painted in Richmond ahead of a community rally pushing for a drug-injecting room in the suburb. The March to Save Lives rally is taking place on Sunday. Ross and John found out more from Judy Ryan …'[4]

Ian Royall promoted the rally in the *Herald Sun*. Laura Turner produced an advertisement for Channel 9. David Stanley's production of the *#youtalkwedie* stencil was 'absolute gold'. The hashtag appeared on walls and footpaths the day before the rally, thanks to a huge effort by him, working in the dead of a freezing night, with campaign stalwart Ash Blackwell. Consistent with our values-based approach to the campaign, we opted for a 'reverse graffiti' stencil — environmentally friendly, it creates no residue and fades over time, so there is no need for removal: David and Ash used a power washer, not paint, to clean the letters into dirty walls and footpaths.

We tried in vain to get our rally flyers into the North Richmond public-housing towers. I was advised by departmental officers that they were 'too political'. What rubbish! The public-housing residents were in the hotspot of drug dealing, injecting, and overdosing. They deserved to have their voices heard, not censored. We also knew that Labor and Greens flyers were often distributed in those buildings.

—

At last, it was Sunday 27 August. Arctic temperatures and horizontal sleet plagued preparations in the morning, as did a sense of foreboding that the weather would deter supporters. Also of concern was the discovery the previous day of flyers being distributed in Victoria Street, calling on traders to protest at our march. Kylie Troy-West alerted Senior Sergeant Andrew Brick, the officer in charge of the rally, who reassured us that crowd safety would not be compromised by this distraction. Victoria Street Business Association president Meca Ho was reported by the *Herald Sun* as saying, '[The association] had not been consulted by the traders' protest group … and that we support a safe injecting room but not on Victoria Street.'[5]

There were two gathering places at 9.30 am on that cold, wet Sunday: Quint Cafe for the grieving families who would lead the march, and North Richmond station for the public. The level of anxiety I felt that morning as I prepared to meet with bereaved families before leading the march and rally was extreme but, in hindsight, unnecessary. Months of intense preparation paid off. The mood of the families who met at the cafe was one of poignant anticipation. It was humbling that so many had accepted our invitation, bringing photos of their loved ones. Meeting Loretta, her husband Damian, son Jack, and father Carl that morning was emotional. Introducing family groups was rewarding. They hugged, clasped hands, rubbed arms, and shed tears, acknowledging their membership of an exclusive club that no one wants to join. After we'd enjoyed the warmth of Quint Cafe's hospitality, RVSDS overseer Loraine Little announced that it was time for us to head 400 metres up Victoria Street to join the throng at Aunty Di Kerr's Welcome to Country ceremony.

While I'd been hosting the families at the cafe, there had been huge activity at the warehouse. Kylie and her deputy, Andy, ran a safety briefing session outlining the event plan, the risk-management plan, and the emergency-management plan. Quint's donated coffee and pastries were inhaled by the wonderful RVSDS team: Tony, Melody, Frank, Dianne, John, Greg, Loraine, Colin, Liz, Michelle, Margot, and their neighbours. Photographer Ciska Burrie snapped away, capturing the sense of nervous anticipation.

Carrying safety jackets, water bottles, placards, a loudhailer, trestles, first-aid kits, signs, and flyers, the marshals moved to North Richmond station to prepare for the arrival of the public. Signage was displayed: 'If you're attending in memory of a loved one, we invite you to walk at the front of the march. Please speak to a volunteer at the information table.'

The police had already arrived at the staging point, with approximately 30 officers in attendance. Kylie and Greg reminded them about the traders' protest that had set up at the corner of Lennox and Victoria Streets, aiming to disrupt the march. Senior Sergeant Brick advised that they had seen the gathering and had matters in hand: 'Don't worry; we've got this.'

As the families walked from Quint Cafe towards North Richmond station, we could see and smell the smoke wafting as Aunty Di prepared for her poignant welcoming ritual. We were astonished to see a large crowd gathered with their beanies, scarves, overcoats, umbrellas, placards, and oodles of warmth and compassion, and the determination to be heard. Hundreds continued to pour off buses, trains, and trams. It was an unbelievable vision on that bleak Melbourne morning. I was genuinely touched to spot students and teachers from the school where I worked.

Conspicuous in his official hi-vis gear, Greg Hordacre was approached by a man looking shocked and upset who said, 'Lost my son — can you help?' Thinking a child had wandered off, Greg asked the man for a description of his son, but he soon realised that the man had in fact lost his son to a heroin overdose, and was asking for permission to walk at the front of the rally. Greg clearly recalls the sobering nature of the experience.

Before the hundreds of assembled people, Aunty Di conducted the Welcome to Country, an important acknowledgement of the need to heal and to find ways of living and working together. She invited us to listen to the land that we were on and to open our hearts and walk together, listening with a compassionate ear to all people in our community. A SIF on this land would significantly improve the health outcomes of Indigenous members of the community. We were humbled that she made herself available to welcome us to her country, and are indebted to Aunty Di for her generous support of our seminal event.

Following the Welcome to Country, we gathered behind our newly minted RVSDS banner. Marching along Victoria to Lennox Street, we chanted in thunderous unison: 'Thirty-four — how many more?'

How many more deaths would it take for the government to accept the recommendations of three coroners?

A group of 700-plus people marching and chanting about overdose deaths on a grey morning is seared forever in our community's memory.

The rally took place in a park on the corner of Butler and Lennox Streets, forcing the crowd into all the surrounding nooks and crannies. It was a sight to behold. The rain miraculously ceased as a mother and a grandfather (Loretta Gabriel and Carl Francoli), a sister (Laura Turner), and an aunt (myself) described their personal grief at the loss of loved family members. Robert Richter reflected on the decades-long battle for a SIF in Melbourne. He wondered aloud if he would see one opened in his lifetime. Richmond musician Morgan 'Grace' King played guitar and sang 'From Little Things Big Things Grow'.

At the conclusion of the formalities and media interviews, Loraine escorted Loretta's family back to my home for a cup of tea and to defrost: 'Carl's lips are blue.' A potential client of an MSIC, 'Georgia', introduced herself to me, indicating her support for the facility. The marchers were dispersing onto trams and into cafes along Victoria Street when a flurry of paramedics dramatically interrupted their movement. A young man who had been seen at the rally had overdosed on the corner outside Quint Cafe. He survived.

Veronica was one of the over 700 who attended the march and rally:

> Rain threatened, an icy wind blew but there was no deterring the large gathering of sombre citizens determined to make visible their support for a meaningful response to so many tragic deaths. We curiously asked each other 'Where are you from? What brings you here?' We shared stories of concern, commitment and belonging to a community that extended well beyond our gathering at Richmond. We listened to the heartbreakingly poignant testimonials of the families who shared their lived experience of grief and tragic loss, our anger growing at the blatant failure by those in power to address this issue, our determination growing as we all asked: how many more deaths will it take before they act?

Mainstream media outlets were busy getting interviews and footage for that evening's television news programs and the following day's newspapers. Radio 3AW did a live cross to Loraine while she was marshalling before and after the rally. Ash organised the live stream of the rally, enabling many to tune into proceedings, including my daughter, Louise, and her partner, Tom, now living in Townsville, and my son Charlie and his partner, Katie, in Berlin. Freelance filmmaker Dan Riddiford and Anthony Zielke from the Alcohol and Drug Foundation each filmed the march and rally, producing two short, evocative videos of the entire event.[6]

Our March to Save Lives was all over the Sunday night news bulletins. The minor protest by a handful of local traders, mostly disgruntled about council parking issues, featured prominently, of course: a scuffle at a rally adds colour and movement to any news report. The police had managed the minor hiccup without fuss.

I wondered if Richard Wynne had seen footage of the rally.

I had not heard a peep from his office since the campaign had started, months prior. He could not miss the images of hundreds of people coming out on a miserable Sunday morning in his electorate to support an MSIC. Surely, I thought, this event would trigger a response from him. If the television footage didn't do the trick, maybe the positive coverage in both *The Age* and the *Herald Sun* newspapers the following day would help.[7] Hope springs eternal …

Feedback from bereaved participants was affirming and humbling:

> It was like being at a funeral; the feeling of loss and grief was palpable.
>
> We could publicly grieve without being judged.
>
> We related to each other's raw emotions.
>
> It was a good idea to exclude politicians from the formalities, giving due respect to the solemn occasion that it was and making it very authentic.
>
> It was cathartic.
>
> The collective grief of 'normal' families marching sent a powerful message to the broader community.
>
> Thank you.

The enormity of organising a safe march and rally about such a controversial issue cannot be overstated; neither can the sense of relief when it was over. There were many contributors. Of significance were Kylie, as key coordinator, and Andy, her deputy. Their early engagement with key stakeholders and their organisation of volunteers ensured a safe and successful event. Everyone involved had executed their areas of responsibility with precision, professionalism, and good humour. The feedback from Senior Sergeant Brick: 'It was the best organised rally that I have ever been a part of. All the paperwork, risk assessment, stakeholder engagement … everything was spot on.'

Kylie later reflected:

> As part of our campaign in August 2017, I organised the protest march down Victoria Street with my RVSDS comrades. Watching more than 700 members of our community gather to march together, to support the opening of a life-saving supervised injection centre, was one of the proudest moments of my life. I really felt that day was pivotal in shifting the political tide of resistance against an MSIC.

Loraine's reflection:

> Probably the greatest impact on me was when we started engaging with the families of those with addiction or who had died as a result of addiction. The pain and trauma they lived with, in part heightened due to the stigma of a family member succumbing to addiction, was so palpable, particularly at the rally.

Four years later, a long-term North Richmond resident would contact me:

> I am ashamed to say this but, until that rally, I had become immune to people being overdosed in our area, slumped in the streets. I'd literally step over them because it was so commonplace. I am horrified reflecting on what I had become: a person lacking humanity. That march — and the speeches at the rally — rocked my sense of decency, changing the way I thought about the issue. I was — and remain — a huge supporter of the facility.

I was especially pleased to be interviewed the day after the rally by Jo Lauder from Triple J's *Hack*. Daughter Louise heard the discussion as she was driving home from work in Townsville. It was 'pretty cool' to hear her mum talking about SIFs on the national broadcaster's youth station. Young adults totally get these harm-reduction measures.[8]

—

On 31 August, International Overdose Awareness Day, an official event was held at the Corner Hotel in Richmond. Comedian and heroin-overdose survivor Greg Fleet hosted a panel that included Fiona Patten, Laura Turner, and paramedic Ward Jongebloed. It was a memorable night, and I met many people who had attended the rally, including Jill Mellon-Robertson, whose son, Jahn, had died from an overdose a few years prior. I also met two women who had kids at Richmond West Primary School. They had come along to learn more about the MSIC. I kept in touch with both of them.

I have no memory of attending my paid workplace that August, but presumably I did. Juggling paid work and RVSDS activities was a real challenge.

10

'You better come in'

SEPTEMBER 2017

Following the success of our rally, I wrote a letter to Premier Daniel Andrews, who was continuing to publicly oppose the opening of a SIF. In the letter, I compared our idyllic childhood experiences in Wang (albeit ten years apart) with the realities that the kids living in our inner-city community faced every day, witnessing people injecting and overdosed in the street on their way to school. I thought that acknowledging this anomaly might provide him with a new perspective on trialling a SIF:

> The confronting and traumatic experience of daily life in a drug epicentre has taken its toll. From little kids to the elderly, residents have had enough of the daily misery and chaos that is drug injecting and overdosing. It's about living with dignity — for both residents and for people with addiction.

My letter was personally handed to Andrews at a regional meeting of Labor Party supporters in early September by a friend, Damien Sheehan, who could vouch for my good intentions. Coincidentally, as I was writing that letter, a random email appeared in the RVSDS inbox from a resident who called herself Brenda:

> My six-year-old son and I saw a person who had injected on the street, a syringe hanging out of his leg, mumbling. My son is very upset and traumatised and has repeated memories of it. We'd like to do something to help the SIF proceed. If there's any campaign support required — like boosting the social media presence for example. We can help. Thanks, Brenda (and Bobbie).

There was a flurry of media activity in anticipation of a press conference at Parliament House on 7 September. The Legal and Social Issues Committee was releasing its report on Fiona Patten's private member's bill. Jo Lauder, Claire Slattery, Ian Royall, Ebony Bowden, John Ferguson, and Laura Turner all contacted me for a comment. I quoted key points from my letter to the premier.

Fiona Patten encouraged me to speak at the press conference that day, along with representatives from key health organisations. It was rather intimidating standing in the towering cloisters of Parliament House. A posse of camera operators and reporters with notebooks and furry microphones encroached upon my personal space as I recounted how three coroners had recommended a SIF trial — all in the past five months. These recommendations were clearly supported by the community, as evidenced by the attendance at the recent rally. I concluded: 'The government must establish a SIF trial because it is the right thing to do.'

It was gratifying to have the support of RVSDS members who also attended the press conference, proudly wearing their purple T-shirts while displaying our banner as a backdrop to proceedings.

Our fifth community forum was held that evening at the local warehouse. We debriefed on the rally and reviewed the achievements of ten months of RVSDS activism. The guest speaker, Fiona Patten, explained the contents of the report that had been released that day, and the likely outcome.

John Ferguson's 'Heroin centres "favoured" but MPs neutral'[1] and Ian Royall's 'Bid for safe injection room denied'[2] referred to the fact that the committee's report did not include any recommendations at all. This omission was due to the dissenting opinion of Inga Peulich. The report did, however, include several findings that recognised the harm-reduction potential of SIFs.[3] The bill was to be further debated in the parliament on 20 September.

The determination to get a SIF trial legislated would continue unabated.

I received an unexpected call from the office of Richard Wynne with a rather blunt invitation: 'Richard said you better come in.' In anticipation of an inevitable meeting with Richard, I had studied his inaugural speech to the Victorian parliament, delivered in November 1999. An excerpt from that speech:

> Illicit drugs are a cause of suffering both to those who use them and to the community that bears the brunt of drug activity.

> Honourable members will be aware that my electorate is already grappling with the consequences of drug dealing and drug abuse. As a community, we can no longer stand by as the death toll from drug abuse escalates to a level that may well rival the road toll.
>
> Drug addiction is as much a health issue as a law enforcement issue. With that in mind, the Bracks government has developed a comprehensive response to illicit drug use which strikes a balance between law enforcement, prevention, rehabilitation, and harm minimisation and which includes the piloting of safe injecting facilities.
>
> I am working closely with traders, senior police, drug agencies and the City of Yarra … to develop a consultation program. I expect that the consultation will be broad, and that the government's response will be informed by community input.[4]

Across the months of the campaign, I had considered the items that would be on my agenda when I eventually met with my local MP:

- the harsh reality of his constituents' lives that underpinned their campaign for an MSIC, supported by the recommendations of three coroners
- the urgency surrounding the need for an evidence-based health and harm-reduction approach to rampant drug use, eschewing the failed decades-long criminalisation approach
- the passion and commitment of RVSDS: our door-knocking efforts had enabled contact with myriad

people and perspectives; our forums had engaged and educated hundreds of residents and attracted the support of key organisations

- the respectful relationships that RVSDS had developed with other stakeholders: local businesses, allied-health bodies, receptive politicians, media outlets, and people who used drugs in our laneways
- the coming together of more than 700 people on a bitterly cold morning in support of an MSIC; the prior consultation with relevant authorities to ensure that it was a safe event; the courage of families who smashed the stigma surrounding overdose by publicly sharing their loss and grief
- the creative process — and the donation of labour and funds — that enabled the monumental mural that captured the community's sentiment and acknowledged the loss experienced by grieving families
- our positive engagement with local traders: the generosity of the businesses in Victoria Street that supported our campaign and rally; proof that we had not orchestrated the traders' protest at the rally to boost the media exposure; how residents as regular patrons had a vested interest in improving our iconic shopping strip; and
- how the community had to provide input into the development of a consultation program, as stated in the conclusion to Richard's inaugural speech.

Richard had a solid political curriculum vitae. He'd been a Melbourne city councillor from 1986 to 1991, and lord mayor of

Melbourne in 1991. He had held various ministerial portfolios following his election as member for Richmond in 1999. In 2017, he was a senior member of the Victorian cabinet in his capacity as minister for planning and as minister for housing. For the purposes of our coming meeting, however, he was my influential local MP.

After welcoming me into his electorate office in Collingwood on the morning of 8 September, Richard motioned to the chairs surrounding the coffee table. I sat next to Onagh Bishop, senior adviser to the special minister of state, Gavin Jennings. Onagh, whom I had met at the Richmond branch meeting in August, had been invited as a chaperone, which was intriguing. I was surprised that Richard chose to stand away from the coffee table with his arms crossed, in what felt to me like a rather combative stance. At 1.9 metres tall, he could be physically intimidating. I wasn't fazed, only thinking that it would have been preferable had he sat at the table.

A robust discussion ensued. I got to my feet, too, as our conversation progressed. When our time allocation had expired, we shook hands. I guaranteed RVSDS support in trying to resolve Richmond's drug-injecting and overdose issues, once and for all. I felt a sense of relief as I left Richard's office. He and I had clarified our respective positions, resulting in a mutually respectful understanding. We shared a common purpose.

Richard had secured just over 700 more primary votes than his Greens rival at the 2014 state election,[5] the same number that police estimated had attended our rally.[6] He knew that an MSIC trial would deliver him votes at the 2018 election. In a desperate need of a caffeine hit, Onagh and I talked further over coffee. While I had initially been ambivalent about her attendance at the meeting, I was glad that she had been there as a member of Labor's Richmond branch that officially supported an MSIC trial.

—

Wayne Gatt, the new leader of Victoria's police union, made an official statement on 17 September: 'Our members would not oppose a safe injecting facility in Richmond.'

His statement was pivotal in shifting the government's position on an MSIC. As union secretary, he spoke on behalf of rank-and-file officers in the state. It was refreshing that an influential police officer had voiced support for a SIF before his retirement.

RVSDS held its monthly meeting (between forums) at my home. While we were cautiously optimistic about a change of heart by the premier following Gatt's announcement, we remained focused on our strategic activities. In line with RVSDS community-engagement objectives, two subcommittees were formed. Colin Gomm, Michelle Zwagerman, Greg Hordacre, Loraine Little, and Pat Conway formed the RVSDS/Victoria Street traders' liaison group, which would enhance our united voice. In anticipation of attending parent forums at Abbotsford Primary School in October and Richmond West Primary School in November, Liz Gomm and Virginia Dods planned the translation of our RVSDS flyers into Vietnamese and Mandarin. The wrap-up of the rally was a satisfying exercise, accompanied by celebratory wines and copious amounts of Aldi's excellent blue-vein cheese and crackers.

Stephen Jolly invited me to meet him at Fitzroy Town Hall on 22 September. I arrived at the hall as arranged, but it was empty, except for the Fitzroy Legal Service team setting up for a trivia night. The councillor was nowhere to be seen. It then became clear that he had sent a proxy, Max. A pleasant young man, he seemed nervous meeting me. It was a sunny Friday afternoon, and as we were across the road from the Napier Hotel, I offered to buy him a beer. Over a pleasant chat, Max mentioned the RVSDS rally the previous month, and reported Stephen's flattering praise of RVSDS for 'doing the hard work' in campaigning for a SIF. The penny dropped! Max was sounding me out about supporting direct action — the 'mobile' SIF stunt. It was time to take my leave. I thanked Max for his company and told him to pass on a message to his boss: 'Don't contact me again about this idea. The answer is no.'

At the end of September, the Victorian Alcohol and Drug Association published my article 'Living in a Government-sanctioned Drug Ghetto in 2017' in its quarterly newsletter.[7] Written in early August, before the rally, it was a bleak assessment of life in our area without the hope of an MSIC trial. Gareth Boreham dropped in from SBS Sydney for a tour and an interview. Daniel Piotrowski from the *Daily Mail* rang and asked for 'Erin Brockovich of North Richmond'. Despite my assurance that I wasn't that person, he also travelled from Sydney for a tour and an interview. The resulting article, 'Welcome to Australia's most liveable city: Inside the heroin hellhole behind the trendy cafes', quoted Meca Ho: 'The sad part is it's a choice they make. I kinda see mates I went to uni (with) on the streets taking drugs.' He was in favour of an MSIC — as long as it wasn't on the main thoroughfare. 'I don't mind, we do need a medical facility. But not in Victoria Street …'[8]

John and I headed overseas to visit our son Charlie. I needed a break at the end of a huge twelve months, and was excited about seeing our youngest child, although I was a bit toey about being absent when there was so much going on at home. I wondered what I might miss out on while I was away.

11

The press conference

OCTOBER 2017

Martin Foley, the minister for mental health, assembled key stakeholders in early October to discuss the practicalities of establishing an MSIC in North Richmond. Along with RVSDS acting secretary Greg Hordacre and Fiona Patten, there were representatives from NRCH, the Australian Medical Association, the University of Melbourne, and Ambulance Victoria, as well as ministerial adviser Emma Greeney and Cherie Short, the mother of Aaron, who had died from heroin overdose in 2015. Acknowledging the importance of reducing the stigma and marginalisation of people who take drugs was identified as a key focus of community education. Providing information and seeking community feedback on the issue was critical to changing attitudes.

Comedian Greg Fleet spoke at our sixth community forum on 5 October. Greg had had a long, public battle with heroin addiction, and spoke candidly about his life being saved after overdosing in the Sydney MSIC. If he had overdosed in North

Richmond that day, he likely would have died. His story — and others like his — resonated with residents who knew the scenario all too well.

I regularly walked south along Lennox Street to Richmond station. It was common to see people injecting, 'on the nod', or overdosed in the playground of Richmond West Primary School or next door in the carpark of the NRCH centre. As these incidents had been commonplace in this area for decades, both establishments had well-honed drills for managing evidence of drug use and overdoses in front of schoolkids or NRCH patients.

Kids at the school knew all too well what to do when they found a syringe — or a body — in the playground. A parent at the school in 2013 clearly recalled being with her daughter when they came across a syringe when out walking the dog: 'Mum, Mum, look — it's a syringe. We need to call an adult.' She was left to ponder her child's understanding of her role as a parent!

A past teacher wrote of her experience at the school:

> Teaching involved many and varied challenges, the community drug problem being one of them. It was not uncommon to see needles in the playground and in Lennox Street and beyond ... Every morning we had to sweep the sand pit to extract the syringes that had been left overnight.[1]

Patients at the NRCH centre regularly experienced a mass exodus of doctors, nurses, social workers, and emergency-management officers responding to a Code Blue — an acute medical emergency — when yet another person had overdosed in the adjacent carpark:

> The crack team of a dozen or so people would rush outside with oxygen canisters on wheels and 'toolboxes' filled with medication to resuscitate the person. It was always confronting and sobering for those of us waiting inside, knowing that someone could have died without that medical help. We never felt annoyed at the interruption to our appointment.[2]

—

Upon returning from overseas, I hit the ground running. Greg Hordacre had done a sterling job in my absence. He'd also kept me updated, so I hadn't missed a beat.

We received exciting news that an international drug law–reform advocate, Canadian senator Larry Campbell, would be visiting Australia the following month as a guest of the Australian Drug Law Reform Foundation. Larry has a fascinating CV. In the 1960s, he was an officer with the Royal Canadian Mounted Police, moving to the force's drug squad in 1973. In 1981, he worked for the Vancouver District Coroner's office, and was appointed British Columbia's chief coroner from 1996 until 2000. After becoming mayor of Vancouver in 2002, Larry helped established a SIF in September 2003 to help curb the city's drug-injecting problem, and championed the idea of a 'four pillars' approach to ending drug addiction: prevention, treatment, law enforcement, and harm reduction. He was elected to the Canadian senate in 2005.[3]

Larry's friend and Australian Drug Law Reform Foundation chaperone David Stanley made sure there would be time in Larry's hectic schedule of meeting politicians, drug law–reform activists, and the media for him to meet with RVSDS. We were honoured to be included in the itinerary and to have the opportunity to learn from Larry's huge experience in establishing Vancouver's first SIF. We decided to reschedule our seventh community forum to coincide with Larry's visit on 13 November. Demos Krouskos offered the NRCH community meeting room for this forum. The promotion of our Canadian guest speaker became a major focus for our group. It was a real coup for the community to have a speaker of international renown presenting in our space about our issue.

A by-election for the neighbouring state electorate of Northcote was scheduled for 18 November. This followed the premature death from cancer of Fiona Richardson, a well-regarded Labor politician. A Labor seat since its inception in 1927, environmental issues, rising house prices, and demographic trends guaranteed there would be a fierce battle for Northcote with the Greens. Fiona Patten's new Reason Party also nominated a candidate, Laura Chipp. At Laura's campaign launch on 24 October, Fiona confided in me: 'We are very close [on a decision about an MSIC]. If you can go to work late, next Tuesday [31 October], that would be good.'

On Monday 30 October, Channel 7 political reporter Brendan Donohoe interviewed Greg Denham and me in Victoria Street for that night's news grab, hinting that there was 'movement at the station'. In what was unfortunate timing, I had a severe coughing fit in reaction to the pollen from plane trees in the street. In between gasps of air, I croaked: 'Residents remain hopeful that the government will establish an MSIC to save lives and save our community. It is never the wrong time to do the right thing.'

I gave it my best shot, but I am sure that my hoarse contribution ended up on the cutting-room floor. I didn't get to find out, as Brendan Donohoe rang me at 6.00 pm to say that 'Cabinet has agreed to an MSIC trial.' Ten minutes later, Richard Wynne rang to advise me 'in the strictest confidence — that Cabinet has approved an MSIC'. My delight was genuine, as I was still in the warm glow of Brendan's call. Richard urged me to attend the premier's press conference at NRCH at 10.00 am the following day. Fiona Patten rang immediately after Richard: 'It is very confidential' — not! I checked online media reports to make sure I hadn't misheard the three messages. Sure enough, both Channel 7 and *The Age* were reporting that there would be 'an announcement tomorrow about an MSIC'.

Ignoring confidentiality caveats, as the cat was well and truly out of the media bag, I contacted the RVSDS team to break the news, inviting them to my home for an urgent celebration. Despite it being Monday night, there was 100 per cent attendance. We hugged, chatted, laughed, imbibed, and sang … it was the sweetest few hours. This group of erstwhile strangers had come together across 12 months to achieve something that was nothing more than a pipe dream according to recent history and the naysayers. United in a common goal, we were relentless in our determination, utilising diverse skill sets and taking risks. That alone was worth celebrating. As the team shimmied into the dark at the end of that joyous evening, I was flooded with a deep sense of gratitude for having moved into this community with all its problems and discovering the humanity of so many of its occupants.

I also thought of Mum and her mantra *Never die wondering*. How right she was!

—

The following day, Premier Daniel Andrews stood on a grassy knoll between North Richmond's public-housing towers and its community health centre, and announced the establishment of a two-year trial of a SIF.

Another name for a SIF is a drug-injecting room (DIR). Sydney has its MSIC. Our SIF would be known as a medically supervised injecting room (MSIR).

NRCH would be the licensee. Commencing nine months hence — in July 2018 — the trial would operate for 12 months as an interim facility within the NRCH centre before a permanent building was constructed on the adjacent carpark: the scene of many overdoses over the years. The government's *Drug Rehabilitation Plan* included $87 million for the establishment of 100 new residential rehabilitation beds, a new rapid-withdrawal and rehabilitation model, and a training boost for the AOD workforce. There would also be tougher penalties for heroin trafficking: 'The threshold for commercial trafficking, which has a maximum sentence of twenty-five years' jail, will be lowered from 250g to 50g. For large-scale commercial trafficking, which can be punished with a life sentence, the threshold will be lowered from 750g to 500g.'[4]

In a nod to a bipartisanship, Andrews announced that former Liberal premier Jeff Kennett would head up an expert review panel to oversee and report on the first 18 months of the MSIR trial.[5]

While this was the first time we learnt of the much-anticipated location of the MSIR, a hint had been provided by Richard Wynne as long ago as 10 November 1999, in his contribution to a parliamentary debate regarding the Bracks government's plans:

> The proposed safe injecting facilities should be located in the community. Many community health centres that already address the drug problem — I cite as examples Springvale, Footscray and my electorate of Richmond — are possible locations for the placement of safe injecting rooms. The centres in my electorate already provide support to drug users via needle exchange programs.
>
> The government intends to work with the community, traders, local government, community health centres and health professionals to ensure a result in the City of Yarra that is agreed to by all parties.[6]

We had speculated for months as to the location of a facility. Despite persistent efforts, we'd been unsuccessful in accessing the data relating to ambulance callouts where paramedics administered naloxone, indicating an opioid overdose. That data had obviously persuaded the government that Lennox Street was the preferred location.

Surrounded by Martin Foley, police minister Lisa Neville, Richard Wynne, Fiona Patten, assistant police commissioner Rick Nugent, and Ambulance Victoria's Mick Armstrong, Andrews explained the rationale behind his change of mind:

> To stubbornly continue with a policy that's just not working, then that's the wrong thing to do when there is an alternative — one that can save lives … leadership is about being prepared to say a different way is worth trialling. A jump in the number of overdoses showed the current approach was failing. If you can be supervised — if you can get the urgent health care that saves lives — that surely, on any measure, is a better outcome than

> seeing that death toll go up and up.
>
> There can be no rehabilitation if you are dead. If you are lying in a laneway or in a gutter, there can be no pathway to treatment for you. We have the highest heroin overdose death toll since 2000 … thirty-four people have died lonely, terrible deaths, many — perhaps all — of which could have been prevented. I wouldn't be doing this if I didn't have the complete support of Victoria Police, Ambulance Victoria, as well as support from groups like the Australian Medical Association and others who spend their entire time working to support those who are addicted to heroin and other drugs.[7]

In a bizarre twist — and to highlight the critical nature of the announcement — a woman collapsed from a suspected heroin overdose in Lennox Street, just metres from the premier's press conference. The MSIR couldn't open soon enough.

The huge media contingent in attendance that morning included Brendan Donohoe, who tweeted a photo of the premier congratulating me 'on running a good campaign'. Predictably, however, the announcement was negatively couched by the media in terms of a government 'backflip'. RVSDS disagreed with this assessment — the government had done the right thing after consulting the experts and considering the evidence. We applauded the change of mind and policy.

I was approached by *The Age* and the *Herald Sun* for comment. Jon Faine congratulated me on the campaign, and Jane Lee from *AM* did an on-air interview.[8] There was television interest from Sky, Channels 7, 9, and 10, and from Gareth Boreham at SBS.[9] *Border Mail* newspaper reporter David Johnston rang me about writing an article. I knew David well, having lived in Albury-

Wodonga for 14 years. He said, 'Your advocacy for the MSIR is of huge interest to our community.'[10]

As I drove to work at the school that afternoon, I reflected on Greg Denham's continual reference to the campaign for an MSIC being 'a marathon, not a sprint'. I was deeply grateful for the decades of hard slog by myriad individuals and organisations that had culminated in that day's historic announcement. I hoped that they were satisfied with the recent efforts of the 'military wing'. To persist with the tortured sporting analogy, after months of focused training, we had grabbed the relay baton (three coroner's reports and a private member's bill) at the top of the straight, and raced it across the finishing line.

12

The MSIC Act

NOVEMBER–DECEMBER 2017

Coroner Hawkins' report on Skye Turner's fatal overdose was published at the start of November. The coroner recorded:

> Ms Turner's sister, Laura, advised the Coroners Court that her sister was supportive of a safe injecting facility. It is possible that had Ms Turner used heroin in a safe environment, where medically trained people were supervising her use, they may have been able to prevent her from overdosing. They may also have assisted with providing her with community referral for her accommodation, medical treatment, and safety.[1]

Coroner Hawkins' case for SIFs was unequivocal: they prevent overdoses and refer clients to services, including medical treatment.

'"The loss has been devastating": Labor's case for safe injecting rooms' was the theme of November's episode of *Pod on the Hill*, the Labor Party's weekly podcast. Richard Wynne invited me to join him in recording a discussion about the government's planned trial of the MSIR in North Richmond.[2] As we approached the chairs in his office, he asked me on which side I would prefer to sit: 'On the left, of course,' prompting a guffaw. It was pleasant chatting with Richard — in a seated position — in his ministerial office, overlooking the glorious Carlton Gardens. In the wake of the MSIR announcement (which was still sinking in), it was surreal to be recording a conversation with my local MP and with podcast host Nicola Castleman.

On Friday 10 November, my husband, John, and I were invited to attend the Australian Drug Law Reform Foundation's annual dinner, at the Wayside Chapel in Kings Cross, where Larry Campbell was the keynote speaker. It was an honour to meet Larry, who was engaging in his address and in person. Luminaries of the drug law–reform sector were all there: Ingrid van Beek, Richard Di Natale, Alex Wodak, Marianne Jauncey, Miranda St Hill, and more. I was inspired again to hear from these humanitarians who had worked and campaigned for decades for a compassionate approach to supporting people with addiction.

Three days later, I was delighted to spend two hours with Larry on the afternoon of our forum in Richmond. I arranged to meet him at Quint Cafe. He appreciated the immersion experience in that significant location: they had similar settings in Vancouver. A tall man, he folded himself into the smallish space that I had reserved at the rear of the cafe, next to the window so he could observe the street scene, which included an incident involving police arresting a drug user directly outside.

With good humour, Larry spoke about his interesting career, most notably about being an independent senator. He clearly relished the freedom from party constraints in his participation in Canada's representative democracy.

I was keen to get Larry's advice on what to expect with the opening of our MSIR nine months hence. I'd already read his interview with *The Globe and Mail* after he'd established the first SIF in Vancouver: 'You're not going to see a magical change in the Downtown Eastside, but over time you will see a change. And over time you will see health start to return.'[3]

He told me that the MSIR alone would not solve the drug problems in North Richmond, but it would give medical staff a chance to talk to people with addiction, one on one: 'We are never, ever going to cure drug addiction. Never. But what we can do is help those who have that addiction to stay alive and stay healthy until we can help them get into some sort of treatment.'

'What would you do differently?'

'In hindsight, I should have opened five centres.'

I have recalled that response many times in the years since our MSIR opened.

Larry had heard about our *You Talk, We Die* mural and was keen to see it for himself. It was just around the corner from Quint Cafe. I explained that the inspiration for the message had come from the Canadian Association of People Who Use Drugs and their silent protest in Montreal. He was visibly moved when he saw that impressive artwork, and insisted on a having his photograph taken, with me, in front of it.

As expected, the seventh community forum, live-streamed from the NRCH meeting room, was a cracker. It was well attended by residents and Fiona Patten, David Stanley, and various ministerial advisers. There was also a special guest appearance by Marianne Jauncey from Sydney, which was wonderful. Larry is a raconteur, and people were at ease asking questions. He was thrilled with the extra-large RVSDS T-shirt we gave him, which he happily donned for a group photo.

—

We had two other events in the NRCH meeting room in November before it was transformed into an interim MSIR.

At the first event, RVSDS members were trained in the administration of the opioid antidote naloxone (sold under the brand name Narcan). It attaches to opioid receptors, and reverses and blocks the effects of opioids, quickly restoring normal respiration to a person if their breathing has slowed or stopped because of an overdose. Naloxone should be given to any person who shows signs of an opioid overdose or when an overdose is suspected. It can be given as a nasal spray, or it can be injected into the muscle, under the skin, or into the veins. The latter form works like an EpiPen, making it easy for anyone to use — I have carried it in my backpack ever since.[4]

At the second event, members of the community were hosted by the Department of Health and Human Services (DHHS), with Martin Foley in the chair and Richard Wynne as MC. They presented the government's plan for the interim MSIR that would be operating out of that very room in seven months' time, and answered questions from the audience.

It didn't escape anyone's notice that this was the first government-led community consultation concerning the establishment of a SIF in Richmond in recent times. The monthly RVSDS forums had gone some way to filling the information vacuum and engendering community support, but they were not official events. In the wake of the 2016 Yarra council election — when it was clear that there was an appetite for a SIF in the community — community input should, I believe, have been sought at that time.

▬

RVSDS was nominated for CoHealth's 2017 Frank Fisher Award, for its 'work and commitment toward improving access to community health care'. This citation recognised our team's efforts and validated our approach. We sincerely appreciated the gesture.

Following David Johnston's article in *The Border Mail* in October, I received positive feedback from friends in Albury-Wodonga about our community's response to the drug crisis. Families in regional Victoria understood the need for a medical approach to drug addiction, but had difficulty in getting quality support in remote areas.

Three weeks later, friends alerted me to a gaudy headline in that same newspaper: 'Tilley's fears for smack mums' kids at drug injecting rooms'.[5] Local Liberal MP Bill Tilley had made a speech in parliament on the Drugs, Poisons and Controlled Substances Amendment (Pilot Medically Supervised Injecting Centre) Bill 2017. My former local member speculated on the behaviour of vulnerable people if SIFs were legalised, as recorded in *Hansard*:

> Maybe some bright spark will set up a franchise operation where local addicts can meet with their dealer in the carpark before heading inside McSmack's to minimise the harm they do themselves. Whilst mummy gets high, the kids can play in the adjacent playroom or watch Smacky McSmackFace the clown make animals out of the discarded heroin balloons.[6]

This crass stigmatisation of people with addiction belied Bill's support for a SIF. As a member of the Law Reform, Road, and Community Safety Committee (along with Fiona Patten) and a former police officer, he had visited the Sydney MSIC, where he engaged with the centre's staff and the local police. The view of other committee members had been that he was positive about the facility.

The editor of *The Border Mail* published my response to his speech:

> I was a Benambra constituent for many years. I was shocked to read 'Tilley's fears for smack mums' kids,' trivialising people with serious drug addiction who want to stay alive and seek rehabilitation through a medically supervised injecting centre (MSIC) in North Richmond. Mr Tilley is totally out of step with Victoria Police's support for a MSIC trial. His comments are also misleading.
>
> Mr Tilley actually expressed his support for a MSIC after visiting the Sydney centre this year with his parliamentary colleagues from the Law Reform, Road and Community Safety committee. His offensive comments, reported in *The Border Mail*, would cause huge distress to people with loved family members or friends struggling with the scourge of drug addiction.
>
> Most people who overdose in North Richmond suffer from mental illness. Some of them come from regional Victoria. On a daily basis, I witness the tragedy of drug use and overdose in the laneways in my neighbourhood. I was with a young woman when she died from an overdose.
>
> I often wonder how Wodonga residents (including young children and the elderly) would cope if thirty-four people were

found dead from drug overdose — in a ten-month period — around the High and Stanley Streets precinct. I suspect they — like the residents of North Richmond — would demand that their elected leaders take urgent action, based on the evidence from many cities around the world that have successfully established MSICs.

These centres save lives, they save communities, and they rehabilitate very sick people. They reduce ambulance callouts by 80 per cent, saving tax dollars, and they free up precious resources for other community members.

The North Richmond residents applaud the Andrews' government for listening to Victoria Police, Ambulance Victoria, the AMA, other health experts, grieving families, and our community, and for changing its mind about establishing a trial MSIC in our area. Some Benambra families with Melbourne-based children may, one day, be very glad it did.[7]

—

Rather than an effort to save lives, Andrews' support for the MSIR was seen by commentators as an attempt to save votes at the Northcote by-election. RVSDS was not naive about this reality: that's politics. We believed, however, that had we not demonstrated the community support for the MSIR through our campaign and the March to Save Lives, Andrews would not have been so courageous in making his so-called 'backflip'. Notwithstanding the alleged gymnastics by the premier, the Greens candidate Lidia Thorpe wrested the seat from Labor with a swing of 11.6 per cent. While the Greens were supportive of the MSIR, other issues in the by-election were equally appealing to progressive voters: euthanasia, sustainability, housing, renting, equality, and funding for schools and community groups. The MSIR announcement hadn't been a game changer.

Towards the end of November, I was invited to speak about the RVSDS campaign at the Yarra Drug and Health Forum annual general meeting. I also shared the platform at the Victorian Commercial Teachers Association conference with Fiona Patten and RVSDS member Melody Patterson, who gave a presentation on how much she had learnt from taking part in grassroots organising. She concluded: 'I am feeling proud and grateful to have participated in this group assignment.'

But the most important activity at the end of the month was organising a December gathering to officially celebrate the MSIR announcement and the great work our supporters had done in 2017.

—

December started joyously! RVSDS co-founder Kylie Troy-West gave birth to Ada: a healthy baby was the perfect exclamation mark to our year. Everything went according to plan, as would be expected of our experienced event manager.

RVSDS met at the Aviary Hotel in Victoria Street to discuss our contribution to the forthcoming annual Lunar Festival. Meca Ho had secured us pole position at this iconic celebration of the Vietnamese new year. We decided we would refresh our message to the community regarding the benefits the MSIR would bring, focusing on improved public amenity.

It was humbling and thrilling to be in the parliamentary gallery on 14 December to witness the debate and the passing of the *Drugs, Poisons and Controlled Substances Amendment (Pilot Medically Supervised Injecting Centre) Act 2017* at 6.10 pm.[8] It was exactly one year after Coroner Hawkins' inquest into the overdose death of Ms A. Gavin Jennings led the debate in an inclusive, compassionate, but determined fashion: he was getting this job done, at last, with a well-deserved sense of relief and pride. I observed a respectful exchange between Jennings and the shadow minister for health, Mary Wooldridge, as they methodically worked through minor amendments to the bill. Martin Foley slipped quietly into the public gallery to join us in witnessing the final ten minutes of proceedings. It was a very nice touch! A happy contingent — Fiona Patten, Andrew Shears, David Stanley, Emma Greeney, Margot Foster, Michelle Zwagerman, Demos Krouskos, and visiting British drug-safety researcher Fiona Measham — adjourned to the parliamentary dining room to celebrate this historic event. We paid our own way, of course.

I enjoyed two conversations on community radio 3CR at the end of 2017. Nick Wallis and Ash Blackwell invited me to join a discussion on the MSIR in their wrap-up of the year on *Enpsychedelia*, the harm-reduction and drug law–reform program. Emma Hart interviewed me for *Women on the Line*, the national feminist current-affairs program. I love the authenticity and diversity of community radio!

The celebration to thank the friends of RVSDS who had contributed to the success of our campaign was a special occasion. Each person had made an important contribution: letterboxed flyers, catered for community forums, spoken at a forum, contributed items for our friendraising events, interviewed us on radio programs, sung a song for us, blasted *#youtalkwedie* across footpaths in the dead of night, donated much-needed funds with no strings attached, organised *You Talk, We Die* street art, organised the rally, marshalled at the rally, kept us safe at the rally, produced amazing one-minute films of the rally, made banners for the rally, provided wine for our friendraisers, provided professional advice, provided resources including booklets and a film, given us important media tips, provided excellent media coverage, written powerful opinion pieces, taken 'the tour', maintained our website and social-media platforms, worn our T-shirts with pride, and prepared, introduced, and debated a private member's bill. Most importantly, we had shared a simple belief that an MSIC was long overdue and would save lives.

The number of supporters who attended the celebration was beyond our imagination. It was a lovely first outing for Kylie and her baby. As I looked across the crowd, I recalled American anthropologist Margaret Mead's famous quote: 'Never doubt that a small group of thoughtful, committed citizens can change the world; indeed, it's the only thing that ever has.'

—

I had been buoyed throughout this huge year by the support of four elders in my life. Mum's siblings John O'Dwyer, Biddy McNamara OAM, and David O'Dwyer offered encouragement and reinforced the importance of caring for those less fortunate. They had all grown up in the remote community of Savernake, in the Riverina, and knew the benefits and power of volunteering in the community.

I also had several phone calls from social-justice advocate and Catholic nun Sister Maryrose Dennehy FCJ. She had read about our campaign and had heard me interviewed 'on the wireless': 'I have worked in Richmond for many years and am familiar with this sad situation. People with addiction need our love and care, not condemnation. I don't know why they inject themselves, but I know they must be very unwell. I support your work and I am praying for them — and for you.'

13

Help is on the way

JANUARY–APRIL 2018

The new year kicked off with an interview on Bill Pitt's *Living Free* program on 3CR. Melody Patterson and I chatted with him about RVSDS plans in the lead-up to the MSIR opening in July. Melody told Bill and his listeners: 'Events that impacted me last year were building community support and education through the monthly community forums and guest speakers, friendraisers, and, ultimately, the rally. I learnt more about heroin and drug use through RVSDS than I ever imagined I would in my lifetime. I felt a great sense of pride in making a contribution to something so meaningful.'

We anticipated local and political opposition to the trial as was the case when the Sydney MSIC opened in 2001. RVSDS community engagement would continue in 2018, but our forums would be held on an ad hoc basis. The renewal of Victoria Street's shopping strip and general public amenity remained a key objective. We wanted to energise our traders' liaison group with a focus on connecting with local businesswomen.

We had hoped to meet with female traders following a positive conversation I'd had in early December with a long-term Victoria Street businesswoman whose service I had used. Unprompted, she told me how relieved she and other women were about the MSIR opening in North Richmond: 'Our concerns about practical solutions to drug using — like a safe facility near Victoria Street — have been ignored. We are sick of coming to our workplaces alone, afraid of what we might find on the doorstop or on the stairs. Something different needed to happen. We are pleased about the MSIR.'

She was enthusiastic about my suggested meeting of RVSDS women with her colleagues in the new year, signing off with a big hug. When I rang her back the following week to propose a meeting date, she told me that I had been mistaken in thinking she supported the MSIR: 'Businesswomen are unhappy with an injecting room in the area. We won't be discussing this again.'

I knew that I hadn't misinterpreted her warm support, and suspected coercion at play. Regardless, I was disappointed at this lost opportunity (for now) but would not give up on trying to make this meeting of local women a reality.

The immediate focus for RVSDS was our participation in the Victoria Street Lunar Festival in late January. We refreshed our banners and flyers, translating them into Vietnamese and Chinese. DHHS was the state-government department with the oversight of the MSIR trial, so we included its website address and telephone number for clarification of issues arising.[1] Greg Hordacre and I met with Jessie Richardson, NRCH communications director, to discuss collaborative efforts at the festival and beyond. We also met with Meca Ho regarding arrangements for the event. In what was a memorable moment, Meca adjusted his usual attitude and gave an emotional apology for the traders' protest at our rally in August, promising that 'the traders want to work with you'. He also provided me with an invitation to the 'VIP marquee' — and lunch — on festival day.

—

Sunday 28 January was an oppressively hot day. Fortunately, Meca had reserved us the best spot in the precinct — under shady trees in Nicholson Street, opposite Quint Cafe. From 11.00 am to 5.30 pm, our rostered team of volunteers spoke about the MSIR with hundreds of locals and visitors. While most expressed relief that a decision had been made to open a facility, some people had understandable concerns about the impact that it might have on the area. Fortunately, we were able to direct them to the DHHS website and helpline.

Despite the heat, Meca was trussed up in a traditional Vietnamese silk tunic. He clearly revelled in his hosting role and was charming as we arrived at the VIP marquee. He was chuffed that I had worn my Vietnamese conical hat in a show of respect at the community's special event. Other guests in the marquee included Richard Wynne, Yarra councillors Bosler, Stone, Nguyen, Chen Yi Mei, and Fristacky, and federal member for Melbourne Adam Bandt, along with Vietnamese representatives from across the city. Inga Peulich was also there in her capacity as shadow minister for multicultural affairs. A condition of being in the VIP marquee was to contribute to the 90-minute conga line of speeches that launch the festival. I took a 'quality not quantity' approach and, at just 50 words, my speech was unsurprisingly judged 'the best of the lot' by councillors Stone and Fristacky. All VIPs were provided a pair of scissors for a group ribbon-cutting ceremony before heading to a lunch at a restaurant in Victoria Street. Jackie Fristacky congratulated me on the success of the RVSDS campaign: 'Well played!'

Noting that Inga Peulich was standing alone at the restaurant, I decided to say hello. In the spirit of the Lunar Festival and the Year of the Dog — 'dog people have a keen sense of right and wrong and a desire to support the underdog' — I thought it good manners to welcome her visit to our community. Seeing me approaching, however, she turned on her heel and walked away.

—

February was the first clear month our team had had in a long time. We took the opportunity to meet and discuss key issues: upcoming community education forums, the inevitable political and local opposition to the MSIR, and our ongoing role in the community, pre- and post-MSIR. Loraine, Greg, Ciska, Michelle, Tony, Melody, Frank, Dianne, Colin, Liz, John, Kylie, Margot, and I decided RVSDS would maintain a supportive presence in the community, organising barbecues and volunteering at local events and supporting the MSIR team.

I always enjoyed our meetings. These people had become my friends: interesting local people with progressive, 'can-do' attitudes and strong backgrounds in community volunteering. We boasted an eclectic bunch of professions: theatrical production, arts administration, project and people management, education, partnership development in the not-for-profit and university sectors, photography, logistics, small business, engineering, records management, natural-resource management, events management, community activism, communications, strategic thinking, conflict negotiations, business and policy analysis, planning, and, last but definitely not least, hospitality.

Tuesday 20 February marked the first anniversary of Coroner Hawkins' report recommending an MSIC in North Richmond. Heidi Edwards from Liberty Victoria's Rights Advocacy Project had attended the March to Save Lives and had contacted me after the MSIR announcement, requesting my participation on a panel on 'safe injecting rooms and policing — one year on from the coroner's report'. With Fiona Patten as MC, panelists Kate Seear from Monash University, magistrate John Hardy, and I discussed the law-enforcement approaches that would be most effective in ensuring the success of the MSIR trial. I enjoyed meeting with Abbotsford and Richmond residents who also attended the event.

The following evening, our RVSDS team attended a meeting with DHHS officers for an update on the MSIR trial. MSIR project manager Tom Abbott discussed the layout of the interim facility in the refurbished NRCH meeting room and the fitting out of the facility, and answered our questions. I didn't like the name of the facility. I was troubled by the word 'room'. It implied a one-dimensional facility, ergo minimal services, which was inaccurate. A medically supervised injecting *centre* (which we referred to throughout our campaign, to allow an easy comparison to what was offered in Sydney) implies a multidimensional facility with a comprehensive range of allied services, such as AOD counselling, housing services, and mental-health services.

A letter arrived from Martin Foley:

> Thank you for writing to the government last year to express support for a medically supervised injecting facility in Victoria … More Victorians lose their lives because of drug overdoses than do on our roads. The number of overdoses in Victoria has doubled since 2012 … The Andrews Labor Government has listened to these concerns, and we are taking action … The continued advocacy by people like yourself and others who show care and compassion for our community is a huge part of this important decision that will hopefully save many lives.

The minister had personally added a postscript: 'Your leadership has been central to success. Still much more to do! Best wishes, Martin'.

Senior Sergeant Andrew Brick was the keynote speaker at the first community forum of the new year, in March, explaining how the MSIR would be managed from a policing perspective. Questions from the floor focused on the illegality of drug dealing and people being in possession of an illegal substance outside the MSIR versus the legal use of that substance once a person was inside the MSIR. This was a major shift in policing: from the familiar punitive approach to drug use, to a harm-reduction approach to drug use. NSW police had been instrumental in providing input into how this policing 'dilemma' would be managed, legislatively and practically.

Our forum was interesting from another perspective. Two

VOTE

JUDY RYAN
INDEPENDENT CANDIDATE
LANGRIDGE WARD

JUDY SUPPORTS A TRIAL
OF A MEDICALLY SUPERVISED
INJECTING CENTRE
IN VICTORIA STREET

WHY SUPPORT A MEDICALLY SUPERVISED INJECTING CENTRE IN VICTORIA STREET?

STOPS OVERDOSES

SAVES LIVES

REMOVES SYRINGES

CLEAN LANEWAYS

HEALTHY COMMUNITY

SAFE RESIDENTS

HAPPY VISITORS

NO CHAOS

LET'S DO IT!

GOOGLE KINGS CROSS
MEDICALLY SUPERVISED
INJECTING CENTRE

Above: The only photo of the Ryan family with both parents. My second birthday in February 1963 in Wangaratta. Standing: David, Michael, Mary (Mum, holding Gabrielle), Helen, Maurice (Dad). Seated: Judy (me), Louise, Rosemary, Mark.

Left: Independent candidate for Langridge Ward, City of Yarra elections October 2016.

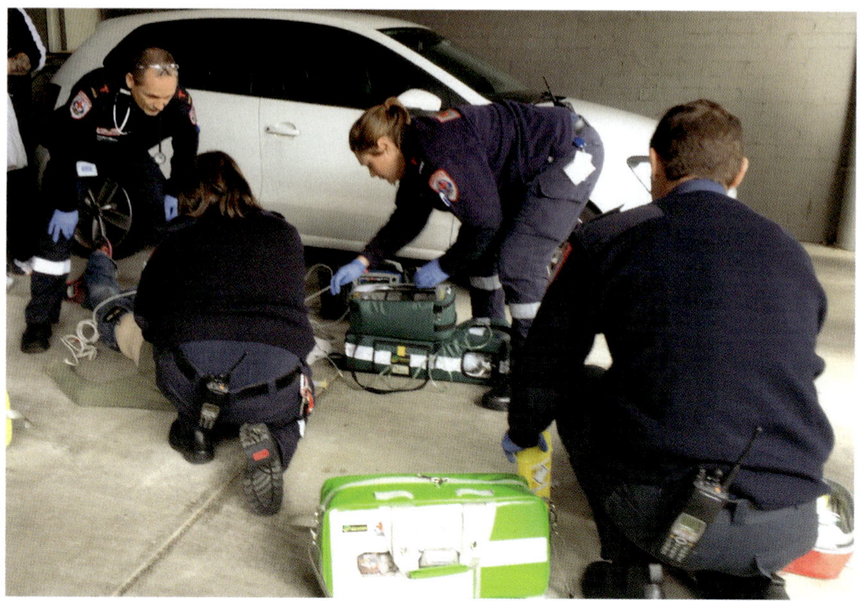

Four paramedics attend to another drug overdose in our carport. When overdoses occur in the MSIR, two nurses manage it with oxygen and naloxone, leaving paramedics free to attend other health emergencies in the community.

A common occurrence before the MSIR opened: three emergency vehicles called out to manage another drug overdose, blocking our laneway and residents' access for hours at a time.

Above: Wurundjeri Elder Aunty Di Kerr OAM conducts the Welcome to Country ceremony at the commencement of the March to Save Lives rally in August 2017.

Left: Me, rallying the marchers. The arctic, wet conditions did not deter hundreds of people from supporting our campaign that day.

Leading the March to Save Lives along Victoria Street. The photo of Sam O'Donnell focused people's minds on why we were campaigning for a life-saving health centre.

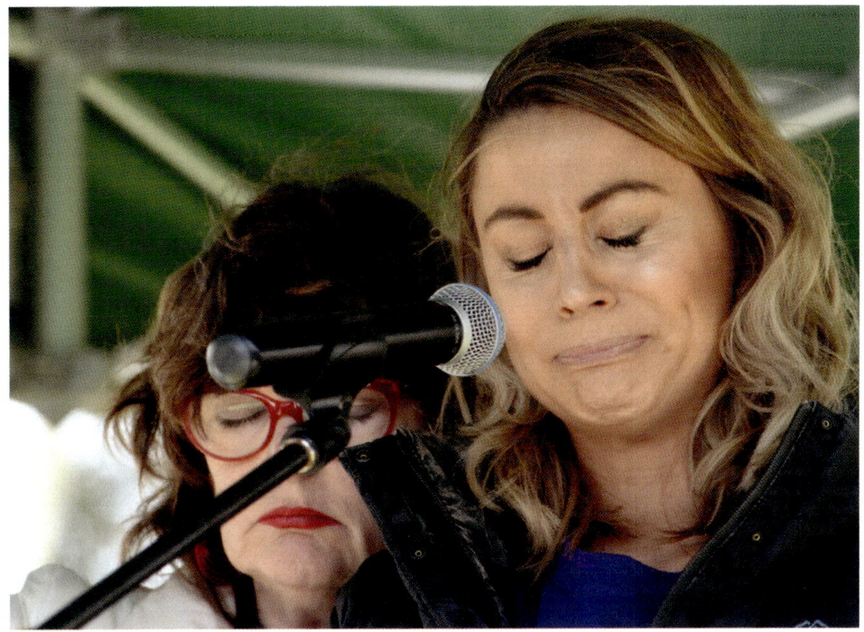

Laura Turner speaking at the March to Save Lives.

Speaking at a press conference outside Victoria's Parliament House in September 2017: 'The government must establish a SIF trial because it is the right thing to do.'

Welcoming the first medical director of the MSIR, Dr Nico Clark, with a tour of the neighbourhood including the street art, 21 May 2018 — five weeks before the MSIR opened.

The Residents for Victoria Street Drug Solutions (RVSDS) team doorknocking the neighbourhood in May 2018.

Victoria's first safe injecting facility: the purpose-built Medically Supervised Injecting Room (MSIR) with the North Richmond Community Health (NRCH) centre behind it. **Photo: Joe Armano/Fairfax**

Ephemeral artwork created to mark the transition from the interim facility in the NRCH centre to the purpose-built facility in July 2019.

MSIR client Hoops and the first painting he ever did, *The Turtle*, at the Victoria Street Alive! inaugural MSIR Artists Exhibition 2022.

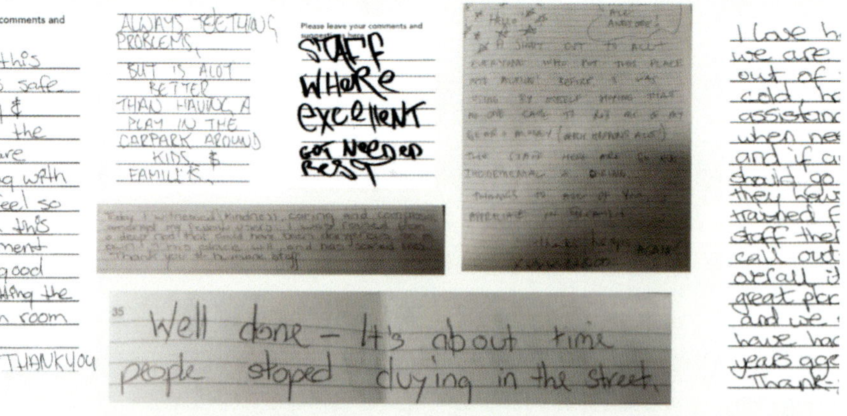

Excerpt from the Visitors Book at the MSIR.

mothers, each sitting beside her primary school–aged son, had contrasting views about the MSIR. 'Charlene' opposed the facility: 'It will attract junkies like those on the corner of Hoddle and Victoria Streets who wash the windscreen of my convertible sportscar.' She described the negative impact that these people had on her young son. 'Laura' spoke quietly about her rehabilitation from addiction and how grateful she was for the introduction of the MSIR trial: 'My son will flourish with a living mother.' It was a thought-provoking discussion, exposing the inevitable contradictions in our community surrounding the MSIR.

On 6 March, DHHS and the City of Yarra convened the second public meeting after the announcement of the MSIR. It was held at the Richmond Bowling Club due to the unavailability of the community meeting room at NRCH. The objective was to discuss issues arising from and the various stages relating to the MSIR's development. As expected, residents who opposed the MSIR were as vocal as those who supported it, amplified by the fact that the club provided liquor services. Mixing alcohol with community information meetings is never a good idea. DHHS was surprisingly unprepared for a shouty debate, and its information got lost in the noise. Various residents approached me with their concerns. I respectfully urged them to submit these issues to Richard Wynne. A few days later, RVSDS met to discuss how we could best assist residents who opposed the MSIR. Explaining issues where appropriate and providing the contact details of elected representatives was considered the best approach. The emphasis was on respectful conversation.

On 27 March, Jeff Kennett resigned as chair of the MSIR's expert review panel in protest at 'the Labor Government's use of taxpayer-funded electoral officers for political purposes in the

2014 election'.[2] The former premier was a convert on the issue of SIFs and had become an outspoken advocate. His appointment was, however, always going to be problematic for the Liberal Party, with its preferred punitive approach to 'managing' people using illegal drugs. Having the former leader in lockstep with the Labor government on such a hot topic would have been a bridge too far for many in the party. Nevertheless, many thought it was a missed opportunity for Kennett.

Happily, the replacement chair of the panel was the eminent Professor Margaret Hamilton AO. With a stellar background in social work and public health, Margaret had decades of experience in the AOD sector and was a champion of the harm-reduction approach to addiction.

—

On 11 April, the government announced a change in policy, allowing the use of methamphetamine (ice) in the MSIR.[3] Ice had been specifically excluded from the list of substances that could be legally consumed in the facility when the trial was first announced. DHHS invited me to attend a press conference outside NRCH at 3.00 pm. I had not been briefed on the matter, so assumed that I would be there to hear the rationale behind the policy shift. When I arrived at Lennox Street, however, there were cameras and reporters with microphones but no one from DHHS. I became the target for requests for a comment on 'the ice backflip'. I deeply resented being put in that position by the department. My support for the MSIR was guaranteed, but I was nobody's stooge.

The community was becoming disgruntled about the poor

communications from DHHS — as was I. After the ice fiasco, I said as much to the DHHS 'community liaison officer', who hadn't attended the media event. He apologised and assured me that it wouldn't happen again.

Meca Ho invited me to speak at the April meeting of the Victoria Street Business Association. There was a positive buzz at the meeting, with excellent feedback from traders about the MSIR. Richard Wynne attended, as did Councillor Daniel Nguyen. The councillor hadn't acknowledged my existence since the 2016 Yarra election, when he had told me that I was 'wasting time with a flawed policy'. Now he refused to hand me the microphone when he'd finished speaking. After some moments had elapsed, I grabbed it from him, which was most unedifying. The traders cheered. Apart from the tangle with Councillor Nguyen, the night was a positive experience that continued to build our relationship with Meca and the traders.

I had a varied and enjoyable end to April. I met with residents from York Street, who lived close to where the MSIR would be located and were strong supporters after years of managing overdoses. They told me about neighbours who had installed expensive automatic security gates to prevent people injecting on their properties. The local police commander, Inspector Rebecca Draper-Schultheiss, invited me for coffee so that she could learn about the motivation behind the residents' campaign for the MSIR. Rebecca had been an experienced communications professional before joining the police force. She understood the importance of community engagement in the lead-up to — and after — the opening of the facility. I also enjoyed another chat on 3CR's *Enpsychedelia*, discussing the anticipated impact of the MSIR trial on the community.

Matt Noffs, author of *Breaking the Ice* and an ardent campaigner for pill testing at music and dance festivals, contacted me. In anticipation of offering Australia's first official pill-testing trial at the Groovin the Moo music festival in Canberra on 29 April, Matt requested the use of the phrase 'You Talk, We Die' for its branding: 'RVSDS has inspired our team.' The trial was successful in reducing harm and drug-related issues at the festival.[4]

Closer to home, drug-related issues in our 'war zone' continued apace. Discarded syringes and overdoses in public and private places were constant. Every time I heard an ambulance siren, I knew help was on the way, but it couldn't come soon enough.

14

Milestone

MAY–JUNE 2018

The first meeting of the local reference group for the MSIR was held on 3 May. Chaired by the parliamentary secretary for health Gabrielle Williams, the purpose of this forum was threefold:

- to keep the community informed on the establishment of the MSIR
- to seek community feedback regarding the ongoing operation of the MSIR
- to identify, discuss, and address any impacts of the MSIR on the local community.

Appointed by the minister, membership consisted of representatives from RVSDS, the Victorian Aboriginal Health Service, the Victoria Street Business Association, the local public-housing estate, community groups, Abbotsford Primary School, Richmond West Primary School, Victoria Police, Ambulance Victoria, the Metropolitan Fire Brigade, the City of Yarra, Harm

Reduction Victoria, NRCH, a local pharmacy, and DHHS. Three key issues raised at the first meeting were improved DHHS communication, the hours of the MSIR's operation, and the recruitment of staff, including a medical director.

I booked an Uber ride in mid-May with a driver who lived in Lennox Street near the NRCH. I asked his views about the MSIR trial: 'I totally support it, as do all my neighbours,' he said. 'We are concerned about the health of drug users.'

While his view was encouraging, RVSDS met to discuss the paucity of accurate information — and the resulting misinformation — regarding the opening of the MSIR in June. We decided that a local doorknocking exercise over the three weekends prior to the MSIR opening would help fill the void. Supported by Colin, Liz, Pat, Greg, Frank and Dianne, Michelle Zwagerman developed a comprehensive community-outreach plan that covered the key neighbourhoods surrounding the MSIR. Donning our purple T-shirts with the orange tick, they were armed with updated materials that included the following statement:

> We care that our community is informed. In order to keep our neighbourhood up to date with factual information and evidence around how existing MSICs operate, we are doorknocking and distributing flyers in the immediate area around the North Richmond Community Health centre, the location of MSIR trial.

A debrief on 19 May confirmed that the first weekend's doorknocking exercise had been successful, with residents appreciating a personal conversation about 'all things MSIR'.

Questions were answered and issues clarified. The second doorknocking weekend, on 26 May, included new community volunteers Mike, Fiona, and Tanya, who were keen to assist. A third doorknocking weekend was held in early June.

A highlight of the month was the official advice from Martin Foley's office that addiction-medicine physician Dr Nico Clark had been appointed medical director of the MSIR. Nico had previously worked for ten years in the management of substance abuse as part of the World Health Organization (WHO) in Geneva. He had been the clinical director of AOD services in South Australia, head of addiction medicine at Southern Health in Melbourne, and head of the WHO Collaborating Centre at the University of Adelaide. His research focused on treatments for heroin, alcohol, and stimulant dependence. Ministerial adviser Trystyn Bowe invited me to meet Nico on 21 May, along with NRCH CEO Demos Krouskos and Kasey Elmore, who would be taking on the role of MSIR operations manager.

I was thrilled to welcome Nico to our community on behalf of RVSDS. To provide context to our role in the MSIR campaign, I suggested a visit to the *You Talk, We Die* mural for a photo to post on our social media. I knew that our 2,000-plus followers would be interested in checking out the medical director of our new facility. The walk would also give me some quiet time to assure him of our ongoing support.

Wanting to share the excitement about his appointment with the rest of the RVSDS team, I invited Nico to meet them the following Saturday after completing their doorknocking efforts. They were pleased to see him, and I was pretty sure the feeling was mutual. Afterwards, he merrily headed home on his preferred mode of transport: his pushbike.

We had a big month coming up, with the opening of the MSIR. We had the facility, an internationally acclaimed medical director, and a generally supportive community. The next challenge was to encourage potential clients to take a leap of faith and inject their illicit substances in the safe, supervised, non-judgemental setting of the MSIR. How difficult would it be to reverse the conditioning of years of running, hiding, injecting, and possibly overdosing alone in our laneways, carports, and gardens? We were about to find out.

—

June started with roadworks at one of the busiest intersections in Richmond. The City of Yarra dug up 60 metres of Lennox Street, from Victoria to Butler Street, for 'beautification' works. Vehicular traffic was diverted, and people — mums with prams, little kids on scooters, elderly folk with trollies, people on bikes, restaurant patrons, shoppers, drug dealers, and people needing to inject — were funnelled through one narrow entrance. Increasing congestion in this already hectic thoroughfare frustrated the community. The timing couldn't have been worse. Some people were already feeling anxious about the impact the MSIR could have. The roadworks, scheduled to last three months, amplified that anxiety.

I was invited by Rebecca Draper-Schultheiss to speak at an MSIR briefing for 30 officers from the Richmond, Collingwood, and Fitzroy police stations on 12 June at Richmond Town Hall. Sydney MSIC operations manager Miranda St Hill headed the list of speakers, explaining the operations and impact of the MSIR based on data from Kings Cross. I was asked to provide a resident's perspective on the community's lived reality before the MSIR opened, and our expectations.

The second local reference group meeting, on 14 June, was a positive occasion, with Gabrielle Williams welcoming Nico Clark as the new medical director. Nico advised that 50 staff — emergency nurses, AOD experts, and social workers — were being trained in time for the opening, and that policies and procedures were being finalised.

Our comrades in Sydney provided critical support to Kasey Elmore and her team in this hectic preparatory stage, generously sharing information and lessons learnt from their years of saving and reforming lives. So generous were their efforts that key staff member Sarah Hiley permanently relocated down south to be part of the MSIR team. RVSDS members and supporters knew Sarah well: she had a starring role in the Sydney MSIC film that we had watched so many times.

Demos Krouskos addressed issues that were swirling around the community. Contrary to local chatter, there had been continued growth in patient numbers at the health centre and no reduction in the use of maternal and child health services. Also addressing local misinformation was the acting principal from Richmond West Primary School. There had been no withdrawal of children in anticipation of the MSIR opening, and there was no decline in school enrolments for 2019. A Melbourne Fire Brigade officer advised that they continued to support the MSIR: their officers preferred attending overdoses in a controlled environment as opposed to tight spaces. Ambulance Victoria's representative advised that most ambulance callouts in the area were for the use of heroin, not ice. The public housing–estate representative advised that her son had died from overdose in

2009 and that she supported the facility. DHHS advised that new communications materials had been distributed to residents, traders, and school parents in response to feedback about the need for more targeted information.

The following week, Nico Clark took Martin Foley, Fiona Patten, DHHS officers, and me on a tour of the new, temporary facility. The community meeting room that had featured Canadian senator Larry Campbell only six months earlier had been transformed into Victoria's first safe injecting facility. Replicating the one-way flow of the Sydney MSIC, its reception area led to a dedicated room with 11 injecting booths and a desk for emergency nurses to oversee the clients. They would exit the facility through the adjacent treatment room, which was overseen by social workers, who would offer access to allied-health services. Operating hours would initially be from 9.00 am to 5.00 pm.

That evening, RVSDS hosted a stall at Melbourne Town Hall for 'Support. Don't Punish', a global initiative calling for drug policies that prioritise public health and human rights. Greg Chipp from Drug Policy Australia chaired a panel of experts discussing various issues surrounding harm reduction. It was humbling to meet with Cherie Short, whose son had died from heroin overdose.

Ahead of the state election on 24 November and before the MSIR trial even began, the Victorian Liberal–National coalition announced that they would 'close the MSIR and tear up the contract for a two-year trial' if they won the election. Even though Richmond was a safe Labor seat and Richard Wynne would fight for the MSIR, I had to make a stand against the conservative parties' ideological opposition to SIFs.[1] I decided that I would also run in Richmond, as a candidate for the Reason Party.

On Thursday 28 June, the eve of the opening of the MSIR, Loretta Gabriel and I were invited to join Nico Clark, Martin Foley, Richard Wynne, Fiona Patten, and members of the emergency-services teams at a media conference in the treatment room at the interim facility. It was a small area, so space was tight, especially with a large media contingent present. Reporters' questions came thick and fast before they fled to file their copy.[2] Richard, who would be recontesting the seat of Richmond, alluded to my candidacy, predicting that he would win. I suggested that he would benefit from huge voter support for the MSIR trial. Loretta spoke about how her son Sam would have welcomed the opening of the MSIR: 'The centre will spare families the trauma of being on high alert every day in fear that their loved one will overdose with nobody to help them. My family suffered that for ten years, to the point where we were alerted to Sam's death in the middle of the night.'[3]

Prior to the commencement of the media conference, I introduced Loretta to Kasey Elmore. When sorting through Sam's chattels, Loretta had found a poem that he had written about his 'angels in North Richmond'. Sam had been a regular client of the needle and syringe exchange at NRCH in the years leading up to his tragic death. He had known the staff (his 'angels') very well, including Kasey, who was then the AOD manager, overseeing the exchange program at the health centre. When regular clients failed to turn up, staff always feared the worst. In Sam's case, their fears were sadly confirmed. Kasey had been shattered to learn of his death after witnessing Loretta's courageous presentation at our rally. Loretta gave a copy of

Sam's poem to Kasey in appreciation of the professional support and kindness she had shown him in those difficult years. Tears flowed ...

The MSIR quietly opened for business on the morning of Saturday 30 June 2018, a day ahead of schedule. The first client was an Indigenous man, an elder in his community. Shortly after 10.00 am, he popped his head into reception and asked whether it was true that he could bring his drugs to inject in that space. After he had injected, he talked with staff about why the centre had opened and performed an impromptu Welcome to Country outside the room. The staff were overwhelmed by the impact and the sincerity of his gesture. I was later told of the significance of the facility to the Indigenous community: 'They view the MSIR as an important health service, protecting their mob. The grounds around North Richmond are important places of spiritual kinship — especially where the eucalypts are abundant.'

I was anxious all morning that day, trying to keep myself occupied at home. I was keen to hear what was going on but was concerned that the MSIR team would think I was obsessed if I turned up onsite. John encouraged me to go. Struggling through the chaotic roadworks, I snuck up Lennox Street at around 2.00 pm and lingered, self-consciously, behind the trunk of one of the majestic native trees in the precinct, the evocative smell of eucalyptus evoking life and hope. The space between the public-housing estate and our embryonic life-saving facility glowed in dappled sunlight, and the sense of calm was palpable. In that brief moment in our hectic inner-city space, I felt totally alone. I was 'in the zone', connecting with my country roots and joyous memories of riverbanks.

My lurking was quickly discovered by Demos, Kasey, and

Jessie Richardson. They understood my desire to check out what was happening — if anything — at the new facility. It was like the primal desire to inhale the smell of vernix on a newborn baby. Demos informed me that 50 clients had registered for injections and that two overdoses had been reversed by nurses: success already!

Upon returning home, I reported in to the RVSDS team and invited them to mark this milestone with a celebration the following afternoon at the Yarra Hotel. There was 100 per cent turnout on that otherwise-bleak winter's day. We sat in front of a huge fireplace with lots of food and wine, enjoying the sweet realisation that the 'military wing' had accomplished its mission, proving an old catchphrase — 'the world is run by those who turn up'.

15

Very early indications of success

JULY–AUGUST 2018

Less than a week after the MSIR opened, Nico Clark publicly announced that, in the first five days of operation, more than 400 clients had accessed the facility. Of these, 95 per cent of clients had injected heroin, 2 per cent had used ice, and 3 per cent had used a mixture of drugs. Crucially, 100 clients had asked for assistance in seeking treatment for their drug use, 'exceeding expectations'. Martin Foley announced that he was 'pleased with the very early indications of success. What we were doing previously was not working. [The MSIR has resulted in] lives saved, fewer ambulance callouts, less incidences in the street.'[1]

The Liberal Party's shadow attorney-general and member for Hawthorn, John Pesutto, was scathing in his criticism of the early report. He claimed that, after six days, the MSIR had not prevented drug use from continuing in public and called for an 'independent analysis'. He would not take the MSIR's or the government's data 'at face value':[2] 'You just can't believe a word that is being said about this facility.'[3]

Reporters from four television networks beat a path to my door that afternoon, requesting an interview about life after the MSIR's opening, and taking footage of my syringe-free laneway. The unanimous assessment of John Pesutto's interview at Parliament House that day was that it had been 'a shocker'. Reporters had questioned his attack on the data provided by the 'so-called doctor': 'Are you saying Dr Nico Clark is lying?'

RVSDS member Loraine Little had called in to Jon Faine on ABC Melbourne radio that morning:

> The MSIR has already made a tangible, immediate, and obvious difference. It's extraordinary. The front bin area of my apartment block has been frequented by people injecting drugs for years. They leave needles, swabs, urine, and sometimes faeces that I would have to clean up on a daily basis. Since the MSIR opened last Saturday, there has not been one person nor one needle in that area.[4]

Victorians would have been forgiven for thinking that two facilities had opened, based on the contrary reports in the daily newspapers. *The Age* reported: 'Melbourne's new safe injecting room has saved twelve drug users' lives and received 400 visits since it opened on Saturday.'[5]

The *Herald Sun*'s front page featured a non-pixelated photo of a man holding a syringe, with the headline 'REjecting Room: Addicts Snub Injecting Facility — Nothing Changed in Heroin Hotspot'.[6]

The tabloid's tone was a stark contrast to articles published prior to the MSIR's opening.[7] Indeed, a more nuanced approach to the *Herald Sun*'s reporting at that time had resulted in Ian Royall being a finalist for a Quill Award for Excellence in Victorian Journalism for his article 'Heroin Scourge: $17 a hit'. Ian credited his editor for the moderate tone:

> We didn't run too hard with opinion pieces. I think [radio 3AW broadcaster] Tom Elliott wrote some, but I don't think there were too many. Most of the responses were in comments or letters to the editor. All credit to my editor, Damon Johnston, for going with it and not doing the normal 'junkie shame on our beautiful streets'.
>
> It was a very *Herald Sun* story in a way, in that we were saying heroin is $17 a hit, which is cheaper than a six-pack [of beer], but I didn't beat it up — I played it fairly straight. In the following days the story was Daniel Andrews saying, 'we're not having safe injecting rooms, it's a very complex issue', and then it rolled on from there.
>
> I don't know if we changed the public's view or the state government's view. If you look at those stories I wrote, the old golden rule of 'don't read the comments', 90 per cent of people were saying 'one bad batch of heroin would solve the problem' or 'take a water cannon down Victoria Street' — those sort of clichés. I've been told by parents [whose children had fatally overdosed] that 'it would be easier if my child had died in a car crash'.[8]

People also recalled that, in February 2017, the *Herald Sun* had published an open letter to the Victorian parliament from 48 key public-health organisations urging the introduction of an MSIC trial.

Alex Wodak reflected on the opening of Australia's second SIF:

> Once again, Australia is experiencing rapidly increasing drug overdose deaths. Why, when the need for MSICs is so great and the evidence is so compelling, has it had to be such an uphill battle to establish a network of such centres in drug hotspots across the country? The answer is inescapable. As long as Australia remains wedded to a failed and futile drug policy reliant on law enforcement to curtail drug availability, pragmatic interventions will be fiercely resisted. This has been the history of harm reduction in Australia, from methadone treatment for heroin dependence, to needle syringe programs and condom promotion to limit the spread of HIV.[9]

—

The City of Yarra's 'beautification' roadworks on the corner of Victoria and Lennox Streets continued to be a major disruption in our lives. For eight weeks, queues of pedestrian traffic merged into one narrow walkway. The broader community bumped up against the frantic drug-using community more than would normally be the case. This strengthened the impression that drug activity had escalated since the opening of the MSIR. The optics gave oxygen to naysayers who suggested the MSIR had negatively impacted the local amenity, creating a honeypot effect. People were frustrated, and we had two more months of roadwork chaos to endure.

The following week, Rebecca Draper-Schultheiss rang me for

a residents' report on how 'things' were going since the MSIR had opened. Anecdotally, there was a reduction in discarded syringes in laneways and fewer ambulance sirens. Residents were encouraging people they found injecting in public and private places to visit the MSIR. We displayed laminated posters in our laneways and carports, and carried 'business cards' — featuring a location map and key information about the MSIR — for distribution to people injecting in public. Residents offered to accompany people to the facility if they were fearful of running the gauntlet of the media pack lurking around Lennox Street.

At the third local reference group meeting, on 19 July, Nico Clark updated the early MSIR data. He reminded us that legislation governing the MSIR prevented some vulnerable people from using the service: if they were under 18 years of age, pregnant, or with bail or parole conditions that prohibited drug use. Opening hours would now run from 8.00 am to 5.00 pm on weekdays, while remaining at 9.00 am to 5.00 pm on weekends. Potential clients required further engagement to encourage them to start using the MSIR — including people who were still injecting publicly, middle-class professionals, and people who erroneously thought they had to show identification to gain admission. Demos Krouskos noted that there had been fewer Code Blue callouts for public injecting overdoses in the NRCH carpark. Penelope Drummond, a resident of the North Richmond public-housing estate for four years and mother of two kids at the school, was a supporter of the MSIR: 'There have been "injecting rooms" on the estate for years: in stairwells, in laundries, in the residents' carpark. Now that the MSIR is open nearby, my children won't be constantly confronted by people injecting.'

I was a panellist at the Drug and Alcohol Nurses Australasia conference at RMIT University, where I was delighted to meet Margaret Hamilton, chair of the MSIR's expert review panel. I also met Dr Erin Lalor, the new CEO of the Alcohol and Drug Foundation, and a Richmond resident. We discussed the decades of drug use and overdoses in the area and the role of the MSIR in saving and rehabilitating lives. I took Erin to view the *You Talk, We Die* mural, which had been partly funded by her organisation.

Four weeks after the opening of the MSIR, staff hosted a barbecue for clients in the courtyard outside NRCH. RVSDS was invited to attend, and Greg, Loraine, and I witnessed the camaraderie of a vulnerable, stigmatised group of people. A staff member reflected:

> The [clients'] tight community is remarkable in the support that they provide each other, given the chaotic nature of their lives. They check on people's whereabouts if they haven't been seen for a while. They carry Naloxone to administer to peers to prevent overdose.[10] They ring 000. They try and keep each other alive. They do an amazing job with very few tools at their disposal. Now, finally, they have the best tool possible: the MSIR.

At the end of July, I was invited to present to legal-studies students about the establishment of the MSIR. It had become a big part of the Victorian Certificate of Education's Legal Studies Unit 4, 'The People, the Parliament, and the Courts', for Year 12 students. Senior legal-studies teacher Peter Farrar told me, 'Teachers and students have found that the contemporary nature of the issue, as well as its focus on social and health issues in the community, is of great interest and relevance to students.'[11]

—

Campaigning for the seat of Richmond was my main focus in August. It was an interesting experience for someone who had run as an independent candidate on a single issue in the 2016 local council election; being a candidate in Fiona Patten's new party required a different mindset. Working alongside other Reason Party candidates while developing joint policies was interesting. Hannah and Maie Gibney agreed to job-share the management of my campaign. Residents, friends, and family members rallied to ensure that it was a lively experience.

Rebecca Draper-Schultheiss encouraged RVSDS to meet with Yarra Street Pastors, a community project aimed at creating a safer night-time experience for people frequenting key districts in the City of Yarra.[12] Her suggestion followed the tragic death of a man on Victoria Street on a bitterly cold night the previous week. While a drug overdose was the likely cause of death, exposure to the elements would have been a contributing factor. It was a tragic situation. Often associated with addiction, homelessness was another complex social issue that needed urgent attention in Victoria. It was significant that Launch Housing, a secular support organisation for the homeless, was a key service provider at the MSIR.[13]

The ongoing roadworks continued to contribute to the degraded state of the North Richmond precinct. The conflation of its disruption with the opening of the MSIR was inevitable but frustrating. In the meantime, we did what we could to improve the local amenity. I escorted the council's street-cleaning officers along Victoria and Lennox Streets, highlighting the problem areas. They committed to regular high-pressure cleaning of the thoroughfares.

At the fourth local reference group meeting, on 16 August, Nico Clark advised that tours of the MSIR were being planned for Tuesday afternoons. Ambulance Victoria's representative reported a decline in both callouts and the administration of naloxone in the area. I raised concerns about the ongoing roadworks and told the group of my meeting with City of Yarra about cleaning the precinct.

On 31 August, Martin Foley used International Overdose Awareness Day to announce that there had been more than 8,000 visits to the MSIR since it opened eight weeks prior. The staff had safely responded to more than 140 overdoses, some of which might have been fatal if not treated directly. The minister and Nico Clark were interviewed by all media outlets. Penelope Drummond rang ABC Melbourne to describe her support of the MSIR, suggesting that it should be open 24/7. ABC television's Richard Willingham filmed my syringe-free laneway for the evening news.

Greg Hordacre submitted the Victoria Street Alive! project for funding consideration in the state government's generous Pick My Project competitive grant scheme. Victoria Street Alive! was overseen by the RVSDS/Victoria Street traders' liaison group. The objective was 'to make Victoria Street a safe, clean and happy place in which to live, work, eat and visit'. A proposed 'community hub' would be a workspace for arts and cultural events, markets, and exhibitions. Festivals, music, and family events would be a feature of our collaborative efforts. We were unsuccessful in securing a grant on this occasion, but RVSDS remained committed to maintaining a practical presence in the community and to developing the project for submission in future funding rounds.

Film producer Dennis Smith from Ruby Entertainment began documenting the story of North Richmond — 'a caring community in difficult times' — to pitch to ABC and SBS. He interviewed RVSDS members, MSIR clients, and councillors among many others as part of his research. There was much to say. The complex layers of life in the area brought out the best in people. I was proud to be part of this inner-city community.

16

The election

SEPTEMBER–DECEMBER 2018

September started with RVSDS cooking halal sausages and mixing with the locals at the iconic Moon Lantern Festival on the North Richmond public-housing estate. We were determined to stay alert to what residents were thinking and saying about life with the MSIR trial in the neighbourhood.

In anticipation of the state election, Luke Henriques-Gomes from *The Guardian Australia* interviewed me and took a local tour for his article 'It's saving lives: community rallies to support Melbourne's drug-injecting room'. In a wide-ranging report based on interviews with traders, residents, a school parent, and a politician, Luke mentioned my candidacy in the seat of Richmond. He reported that a change of government from Labor to the Liberal–National coalition would result in the MSIR trial being cancelled. He also interviewed Greg Hordacre:

> If I'm aware that there are people [in my carport] I always check on them. I always let them know now that there's an injecting

> centre, and I like to find out how come they're in there and not in the injecting centre. There can be different reasons. I've spoken to people who inject each other, they're not allowed to do that in the injecting centre. There's also a guy who's there quite often who smokes, which you're not allowed to do [in the MSIR].

Greg noted that the frequency of sirens in the neighbourhood had dissipated. He shared his feelings about the trial ending if there was a change of government: 'I just can't even imagine that happening. It would be like closing a hospital or a dental service. People are sick. Would you close a hospital just because it suits you to fan the flames?'

Importantly, Henriques-Gomes reported on the traders' change of heart:

> After initial scepticism, the local traders' association also backs the trial. 'I want [the MSIR] to stay open and I want them to continue to save lives,' says Meca Ho.[1]

September's local reference group meeting was my last before the state election. We heard the data that Martin Foley had shared at the end of August: the facility was seeing up to 200 client visits a day — more than 8,000 visits in total — with 140 overdoses safely resuscitated. Dental treatments were now included in a suite of clinical services. It was heartwarming to learn that retired professionals — former dentists, vascular surgeons, and podiatrists — had volunteered to work with these vulnerable clients. NRCH continued to employ outreach staff to engage with people who were not using the MSIR. Public tours of the MSIR were now available on Tuesdays from 1.30 pm to 2.00 pm. Ross Broad from DHHS advised that the construction of the purpose-built facility would commence shortly. We also heard from the City of Yarra that the roadworks on the corner of Victoria and Lennox Streets would be completed at the end of the month. Praise be!

Renowned British author and journalist Johann Hari was guest speaker at Drug Policy Australia's annual Drugs, Depression, Stigma, and Addiction event, at Melbourne Town Hall on 20 September.[2] Greg Hordacre, Michelle Zwagerman, and I were in the audience that night, as we had been invited to host a stall in the wings of our city's historic hall. Johann's presentation to an audience of 800 people focused on 'Why Australia should decriminalise drugs'. We were gobsmacked when he included the following reflection in his presentation:

> In 2012, Judy Ryan returned to live in the Melbourne suburb of Richmond. She saw that there was a lot of chaotic street use of drugs by people with addiction. Everywhere in the world, there's a pattern when this happens. The neighbours band together and demand the police clear out the drug users with force. I've seen it many times.
>
> But Judy thought — what does that solve? So, she started to read about drug policy. She learned that a supervised injection site — where people can use their drugs monitored by nurses, safe from harassment and punishment, and get help — has saved lives wherever it has been tried. So, she set about persuading her neighbours. Others quickly joined her. They went door to door, explaining: these people aren't aliens. They are our friends and neighbours. They need our love and support.
>
> They prevailed. Richmond became the first area — ever

> — where the local people demanded the authorities open a supervised injection site. It has now been open for eleven weeks. It's already saved lives. In Vancouver, the same model has saved 6500 lives in fifteen years. If you feel repelled by the negativity of our politics, do what Judy did. Model a better, loving way. Persuade the people around you.

Johann hadn't hinted that he would be mentioning our team's story when we'd met him fleetingly, just prior to his stage appearance.

We talked to some interesting people at the town hall that night. AOD practitioners from the suburbs of St Kilda, Frankston, and Footscray had followed our campaign in Richmond. They approached us for assistance in lobbying for SIFs in their communities. We were enthusiastic to help any community that recognised the need for an evidence-based health facility for people with addiction. I also met with journalism student Lucy Williams, who interviewed me about the RVSDS campaign for the MSIR and my candidacy in the seat of Richmond. 'Drug reform activist running for Richmond' was published in the University of Melbourne's student newspaper, *Farrago*, in November.[3]

—

In October, I was in full campaign mode. Greg Hordacre was acting RVSDS secretary, which allowed me to focus on defending the MSIR from closure by a Liberal–National government.

To keep myself informed, I managed to squeeze in a day trip to Sydney to hear Richard Branson speak on a panel with

Marianne Jauncey and Khalid Tinasti. It was the launch of the Uniting Church Synod's Fair Treatment campaign, which called on the governments of NSW and the ACT to decriminalise drug use and personal possession.[4] (The Uniting Church is the licensee of the Sydney MSIC.) The panel discussed 'how we can reform lives and reform drug policy for the fair treatment of all people'.[5]

I also enjoyed three days in Canberra in the office of the federal independent member for Indi, Cathy McGowan. I had known Cathy and her extended family for years before her shock defeat of long-term Liberal incumbent Sophie Mirabella in 2013. As a resident of both Wangaratta and Wodonga, I had been an Indi constituent for most of my voting life and was supportive of Cathy's campaign.

I had been keen to participate in Cathy's unique Back of House program for some time:

> The program provides an opportunity for those working — or interested — in public policy and community development to develop skills and build networks, [and] experience a working parliament. At the end of the sitting week, you will have gained a first-hand insight into the mechanics of policy development as well as a better understanding of what it means to be a federal local member.[6]

The empowerment of the community through fostering an understanding of parliamentary processes and building networks is an inspired idea. It is helpful for many community advocates. Indeed, in the unlikely event of me being elected to parliament, I would establish a similar program in my office.

By chance, I bumped into Erin Lalor, CEO of the Alcohol and Drug Foundation, who was meeting MPs in that sitting week, and we had lunch together. Hanging out in Parliament House in Canberra is a great networking opportunity, to be sure.

—

November was huge.

Meca Ho ramped up his support for my candidacy in Richmond. He invited me to share the stage with Richard Wynne and Yarra mayor Daniel Nguyen at the Victoria Street Business Association's launch of the 2019 Lunar Festival program. The association also sponsored a large banner promoting Richard and me as the two candidates who supported the MSIR. It was installed atop the former Quint Cafe on the high-exposure corner of Victoria and Nicholson Streets. Much to our dismay, the sentimental headquarters of RVSDS had shut up shop a few months earlier.

Meca hosted my visit to various businesses in Victoria Street, where he organised the display of my election posters in their windows. He acknowledged that drugs were not the reason why there were For Lease signs in the street:

> There are generational differences with the young Vietnamese people not getting involved in their families' business. Rent and other running costs are higher due to the collapse of the cash economy. Shops are not being renovated when they should be and regulars who prefer clean, maintained premises are taking their business elsewhere. Food trends are changing and there is too much concentration on simple Vietnamese food.

The Liberal–National coalition's election campaign focused on crime, gang violence, and terrorism. During a leaders' debate on ABC Melbourne radio the week prior to the election, Daniel Andrews defended the MSIR trial in North Richmond: 'The local residents have said we had to do something.'[7]

Opposition leader Matthew Guy hit back: 'The opposition will shut down the state's only medically supervised drug injecting room within a week if voted into government in this Saturday's state election.'[8]

Given its determination to close the MSIR, many were bemused by the Liberal Party's decision to not endorse a candidate in Richmond.[9]

Election day came on 24 November. Richard Wynne retained the seat of Richmond in what was a statewide landslide victory for Labor.[10] After experiencing a scare in 2014,[11] Richard was returned with a 3.6 per cent swing in his favour in 2018.[12] This spike was due, in no small way, to voter support for the MSIR trial. When interviewed by Barrie Cassidy on ABC's *Insiders* program the morning after the election, Daniel Andrews conceded as much, saying: 'Labor embraced policies that work … the safe injecting facility saves lives.'[13]

For my part, I polled a respectable 6.57 per cent of the primary vote.[14] I was proud that I had continued my campaign for the MSIR, publicly defending it against the closure threat from a Liberal–National coalition government.

Contrary to the Liberals' ideological stance against the MSIR, socially progressive Liberal voters from the adjacent electorate of Kew who I spoke with on the polling booth supported the MSIR. They were horrified at the prospect of a Liberal–National government closing 'a long-overdue health centre'. Their current

Liberal MP, Tim Smith, was a strident opponent of the MSIR, posting video footage of himself in front of '[Daniel Andrews'] Drug Den'. (It is worth noting that there was an almost 8 per cent swing against Tim Smith.[15]) Sadly, I had become accustomed to people disclosing the struggle they were having with a loved one with drug addiction, or the death of a loved one — a disclosure usually prefaced with 'not many people know this but ...' Drug addiction does not discriminate between party allegiances or electorates. I later discovered that this 'reveal' is referred to in the harm-reduction sector as 'the big secret'. How tragic is stigma?

There were three more noteworthy outcomes from the election. Liberal Party 'rising star' and shadow attorney-general John Pesutto — who had ridiculed Nico Clark's report on the first five days of the MSIR — lost his seat of Hawthorn after only one term in parliament.[16] Inga Peulich lost her seat in the upper house. And, two nail-biting weeks after the election, Fiona Patten was officially declared winner of the highly contested fifth spot for the Northern Metropolitan region.[17]

—

In December, at the final local reference group meeting of the year, members heard from Nico that there had been more than 300 overdoses resuscitated in the MSIR's six months of operation. The facility was becoming busier each month, with more than 1,500 registered clients at the end of November. There was a high demand for dental services, which were provided each Tuesday in the MSIR's consulting room. The GP clinic on Tuesday and Wednesday provided general health care, including treatment for minor skin infections, support for complex mental-health problems, and referrals for other health issues.

There were, of course, the inevitable teething problems. The opening hours were inadequate due to funding constraints, and the prohibition of people under 18 years of age, people who were pregnant, and people who had parole conditions that prohibited drug use were a concern; the possibility of drug-overdose deaths in any of those groups was very real. There were also general deterrents to accessing the facility. The constant media presence in Lennox Street and the prohibition of smoking in the MSIR resulted in continued public injecting. This reality was used by local opponents of the MSIR as evidence that the facility was a failure.

Other topics for discussion were police oversight, community safety and security, and drug dealing. We were all mindful that the MSIR's impact on the public amenity would be a key focus of the expert review panel's report, due in June 2020.

From the RVSDS perspective, the positive early results of the MSIR trial had exceeded our expectations. Loraine Little reflected on a tangible change in her life: 'It took me several months or more to not automatically look into our bin enclosure [in my residential complex] to see if someone was injecting or overdosed there, so ingrained had injecting drug use become part of my daily reality.'

Yet the positive results were a two-edged sword. We could see that the MSIR was struggling with its better-than-expected patronage. There was still much work to do. John Ferguson wrote in *The Australian*:

> Australian Drug Law Reform Foundation's David Stanley cautioned that when the Sydney MSIC was opened nearly

twenty years ago, progress was slow. Shop owners and residents did not warm immediately to the facility's growing pains. 'It took ten years for people to realise people are getting off the street … People are proud of the service now.'[18]

17

Highs and lows

2019

2019 was a roller-coaster ride for RVSDS, the MSIR, and the entire community.

The year started happily with the Lunar Festival launch in January. Lunch was attended by the usual elected officials, including new mayor Danae Bosler. The president of the Bridge Road Traders Association, Herschel Landes, was also there. His family had owned a clothing warehouse in Richmond for many years. I had first met Herschel when we were both independent candidates in the 2016 election: Herschel in Melba Ward, me in Langridge Ward. He was a supporter of the MSIR.

I resigned from my job at the school in February, giving me more time to develop my neglected relocation business and to support the MSIR team and the community. The local reference group resumed its meetings in March. We heard that tours of the facility were providing an important opportunity to engage with the public and were fully booked; Inspector Anne Rudd had replaced Rebecca Draper-Schultheiss (promoted to superintendent) as the local area commander; and the development of the permanent MSIR — on track for completion in the middle of the year — would provide more capacity for allied-health and wellbeing services.

Councillor Stephen Jolly also held a meeting that month. On 5 March, he tweeted:

> I hosted a meeting tonight for residents in my bit of Richmond, the north east section. It was held at the All Nationals [sic] Hotel on Lennox St, which is a sort of DMZ where both public housing tenants and private owners and renters all drink and intermingle ... we moved onto the main debate over the location of the Supervised Injecting Facility and dealing with the ice and heroin industry that's centred in the area. We agreed on [organising] a mass resident meeting in April to get a community agreement on our log of claims to put to the Government prior to the results of the fake inquiry into SIF being tabled in the winter.

I wondered what Professor Margaret Hamilton thought about her inquiry being described as 'fake'.

In April, residents found a flyer in our letterboxes from Stephen: 'RESIDENT PUBLIC MEETING ON THE IMPACT OF THE SUPERVISED INJECTING FACILITY IN THE AREA — What changes need to happen to improve North Richmond and South Abbotsford?' The councillor would be holding a meeting at the All Nations Hotel on 10 April at 7.30 pm.

Due to a prior engagement, I was an apology at that meeting. RVSDS members John, Loraine, Colin, Liz, and Michelle joined other residents at the pub.[1] Michelle's reflection:

> The atmosphere at the All Nations was tense. The beer garden was packed with locals; we were all so close to each other. I think it forced us to be respectful, but I was worried that things could turn nasty. Then people started speaking and I felt relief that there were different opinions that were being heard. When there were mumblings of disagreement, someone shouted that all should be given the chance to speak. So that's what happened, including a man with addiction who spoke. The people who spoke from both sides of the argument were passionate, but there was still a feeling of community and an opportunity to come together to resolve issues.
>
> I had hope after this first meeting.

It was obvious to RVSDS members that many attendees at the pub meeting lacked basic information about the MSIR. They hadn't taken advantage of the 30-minute public tour of the facility, which was a pity. We knew that people who had misgivings about the MSIR had changed their opinion after the tour. I rang Stephen on 17 April to provide that feedback and offer our assistance in planning a follow-up meeting. RVSDS was happy to co-host a community education forum, including tours of the MSIR. He agreed that residents would benefit from such a forum. He forwarded me information about the City of Yarra securing additional funding from the state government for safety and amenity improvements in the Victoria Street precinct, and suggested that he and I should catch up in early May to finalise the agenda for the next residents' meeting, tentatively arranged for 15 May.

On 20 April, Martin Foley publicly announced additional funding of $300,000 for the MSIR and for increased security patrols, lighting, street sweeping, and outreach services. Opening hours would be extended again when the new facility opened. The minister also announced the appointment of retired Victorian police commissioner Ken Lay to the MSIR's expert review panel.

I met with Stephen Jolly on 2 May at the Stingo Hotel in Abbotsford. He was very flattering about RVSDS and asked me to speak at the 15 May meeting about the need for more SIFs in Melbourne. He agreed that a non-pub venue was preferable and that he would finalise the meeting arrangements and get back to me.

I was aware that all City of Yarra councillors had been offered a private tour of the facility as soon as it opened, but when I enquired about this, Stephen admitted that he hadn't booked a tour 'as yet'. I was surprised to hear that, as this would be a minimum requirement for a facilitator, and he had been an outspoken advocate for the trial. His policy was clear, as stated in his election flyer in 2016: 'Fight for a safe injecting facility to minimise drug related harm in Richmond.' It was puzzling, therefore, that he had not found 30 minutes to check out the MSIR for himself. After all, it was just across the street from the All Nations Hotel, where he'd held his 10 April meeting. As I walked home from the Stingo, instead of thinking 'that went well', I should have been hearing alarm bells.

I was exasperated when I found a flyer in my letterbox promoting the second meeting, at the All Nations Hotel on Wednesday 15 May at 7.30 pm. It wasn't to be a community education forum as he had agreed:

> LET'S DISCUSS SOLUTIONS — SECOND RESIDENT MEETING ON THE DRUG SITUATION IN OUR AREA

— On April 10th, locals met at the All Nations Hotel to have their say on the impact of the Supervised Injecting Facility in the area. Many points of view were expressed, and we all agreed that a second meeting was necessary to discuss and vote on potential solutions. This will be it.

In an attempt to salvage the agenda, I joined a small group of North Richmond residents who met with Stephen two nights before the event, but those efforts came to nothing.

The All Nations beer garden was packed on the night of 15 May. I later learnt that members of the expert review panel were at this meeting as observers.[2] Stephen opened the meeting with an intemperate claim: 'What a shitstorm we created last time.'[3]

A second 'shitstorm' was guaranteed as the effect of the booze kicked in. A young woman was booed and jeered when she tearfully spoke about the tragic loss of her friend who had recently overdosed outside the MSIR when it was closed. It was an agonising moment. She was comforted by Nico Clark, who extended an invitation to all present to take a tour of the facility to gain a better understanding of its operations and outcomes. Fiona Patten was heckled when she said that she took responsibility for the MSIR because of her private member's bill. When I got up to speak, the atmosphere was febrile. I decided not to proceed to the microphone after being verbally abused. A neighbour recalled: '[A well-known resident], as she stormed out of the meeting, screamed at Judy Ryan that she "didn't come here to listen to politicians, least of all you" while aggressively pointing and walking up quite close to Judy. I felt extremely uncomfortable.'

Stephen eventually directed the free-for-all towards 'solutions'. Suggestions included the introduction of prescription heroin, opening the facility 24 hours a day, opening other SIFs to take the pressure off Richmond, and supporting police who 'funnel drug users into the MSIR rather than into cells'.[4] Some wanted the MSIR closed or 'relocated' to an unspecified site. One local businessman posited, 'A commando squad with machine guns to clear [drug users] off the street.' This suggestion resulted in applause and laughter from many.[5] Others were aghast.

The meeting concluded with Stephen's desired outcome: people signing up for a new committee that would focus on 'solutions' — which had somehow become a euphemism for 'relocating' the MSIR. It is instructive to read the reflection of 'Rose', who nominated for membership of the new committee that night:

> Jolly's actual intentions were for a socialist-influenced executive committee with two elected positions, chairperson (spokesperson) and secretary (negotiator). In hindsight, this arrangement was probably pre-determined. Three others, including me, put our hands up for the general executive committee. The draft mission statement did not mention that the relocation of the MSIR was a key objective for the committee until afterwards. I probably wouldn't have become involved if I had known that. I just listened in until I was explicitly told at a later date that I wasn't wanted or needed because I had differing views. I supported the MSIR to operate as effectively as it could in its current location.

Another local resident, 'Emily', reflected:

> Having lived with a drug crisis on my doorstep for almost two decades, a night at the pub to discuss the newly instated MSIR

> in the neighbourhood seemed warranted. After all, what could possibly go awry with a celebrity socialist at the helm — apart from everything? The meeting was the catalyst for a divisive rift in Richmond: a circus of raucous and diminishing sensibilities with an overwhelming air of calculated and dangerous hysteria. A night that capsized. It reminded me of how eagerly a society can be led to drink from the waters of fear. The new committee was the result of that environment.

Walking home that night, I felt fearful for the first time in the seven years I had lived in the area. I didn't recognise the behaviour that had been on display in the beer garden. From the ashen faces and muted conversations of people heading off into the night, I wasn't alone, however. It was clear that others, too, had been shaken by the adversarial nature of the meeting, pitting neighbour against neighbour. The disquiet lingers to this day. RVSDS member Michelle reflected: 'Nothing positive came from the May meeting, which is a shame. There was a brief moment of opportunity [after the April meeting] to have pulled "things" together rather than tear them apart.'

I naively expected a phone call from Stephen in the aftermath of his meeting. Having invited me to speak, he might have been concerned about my welfare after witnessing the abuse I copped that night. He might also have explained his change of mind regarding the community education forum. I never heard from him.

—

I represented the Reason Party in the safe seat of Melbourne at the federal election on 18 May, ultimately polling 5.1 per cent of the primary vote.[6] It was another opportunity to promote the MSIR at community events, candidates' forums, and early voting centres. I continued to hear disclosures from people who had experienced the loss of family and friends from drug overdose. A quiet chat with a Liberal Party volunteer was revealing. While recuperating from back surgery, the person had become dependent on prescription painkillers. This had provided the person an insight into the insidious nature of addiction and the importance of professional, non-judgemental support services to manage the situation. The person expressed to me their support for the MSIR, unable to tell anyone else as drug addiction was taboo in their family, social, and political circles.

Another sobering conversation was with 'Nick', a young man who pushed his bike with bulging panniers up the travelator to the early voting booth in The Hive shopping centre. He made a beeline to me to tell his story. He had been released from prison two weeks earlier and was homeless. His bike and his pannier contents were his only possessions. He had been heroin-free for 12 months but was fearful of relapsing due to having nothing — 'no home, no money, no support'. His presence attracted the attention of those around us; there wasn't one person who wasn't moved by his desperation. I wrote my phone number on the back of a flyer and asked Nick to ring me after 6.00 pm. I never heard from him, and I often wonder about him.

—

There were three local reference group meetings in May and June. After 12 months of operation, close to 3,000 people had registered to use the MSIR, and more than 1,100 overdoses had been safely managed at the facility. The secure dispensing unit at NRCH had closed, and the needle and syringe exchange was being transitioned into the new MSIR facility. The City of Yarra was increasing its street-cleaning efforts in the area with the extra funding from the government. DHHS announced a communications strategy to support the changeover to the new MSIR facility, including a community-engagement event in July.

Coroner Jamieson reported in June that 25 fatal heroin overdoses had occurred in the City of Yarra in 2018. The loss of life from drug overdose weighed heavily on the community. Half of the deaths had occurred in the first six months of the MSIR's operation. Jewel Topsfield wrote in *The Age*:

> Jamieson stressed that six months was not long enough to judge the impact of the injecting room on heroin-related harms in the City of Yarra. While advocates might 'understandably be disappointed that deaths did not decline' in the City of Yarra after the injecting room opened in June last year, it was not fair to suggest this meant it was failing to address 'heroin-involved harms'. She also said focusing on harms without also focusing on benefits was misleading. The injecting room had created 'valuable opportunities' for clinicians to engage with vulnerable people and link them with medical treatment and social services they may otherwise not have accessed.[7]

—

DHHS invited a group of people to view the purpose-built MSIR before it opened in early July. Nico Clark led the group, which comprised me, Demos Krouskos, Sam Biondo (Victorian

Alcohol and Drug Association), Frankie Hipkins and Jessie Richardson (DHHS), and Herschel Landes. We were impressed by the enhanced capacity of the new facility: an increase from nine to 20 injecting spaces, additional areas for consulting and treatment, and the relocated needle and syringe exchange. For the first time, people could come in to the MSIR specifically to access health and social services. Housing, mental-health, drug-treatment, oral-health, GP, hepatitis-checking, and legal services would always be available — similar to an outpatients clinic. Nico subsequently narrated a recorded tour of the facility: 'What we saw is that the people using the room had high rates of untreated physical and mental-health issues and that they were open to receiving treatment but they hadn't been able to organise it.'[8]

Herschel had brought along a comprehensive list of questions. If he had been wavering in his support for the facility, it was clear that all concerns had been addressed by the end of the tour. I sensed that the experience confirmed for him the significance of this first-class, life-saving integrated health service. He took a selfie with me and Nico outside the entrance, posted it on social media, and remains to this day a staunch advocate for the facility.

Touring the new MSIR inevitably prompted comparisons with the smaller, interim facility in the NRCH meeting room. How the staff had managed to achieve what they did in such cramped circumstances over 12 months was truly remarkable. As a tribute to their efforts, MSIR clients created an ephemeral mural to mark the transition to the new building. With a nod to *You Talk, We Die,* the words *You Listened, We Lived* were visible on a wall for two days. It was a profound reminder of the lives that had been saved in that time and the non-judgemental care that staff provided to vulnerable people.

The Winter 2019 edition of the literary magazine *Meanjin* featured 'The Visitors Book', an article written by County Court judge Mark E. Dean. It was a report on his visit to the interim MSIR in 2018.

> [I wanted] to see for myself how it operates … I was struck by the life-saving nature of their work and the practical realities of supporting 200 people every day who are injecting themselves with a range of substances … In my thirty-five years as a criminal lawyer and judge, I have not seen a more effective facility: it provides a range of essential services to people suffering from the illness of drug addiction and its complex life impact.
>
> In the relaxation and exit room is a 'visitors' book'. An entry reads as follows: 'Absolutely incredible staff and services. Each time I come here I am greeted with such warm kindness. I feel as though the stigma (that often pervades similar institutions) is the furthest thing away from the place (and as a result my mind and body). My heart goes out to everyone working here, the difficulty of their work, the intelligence and generosity of their minds.'

Another entry:

> 'This is an incredible institution that has already saved my life, and how can I possibly return the favour … I can't, but I have spoken to many people and mentioned the positive aspects, the importance of this place at every opportunity, to encourage anyone who thinks badly or simply wrongly about this to rethink, re-evaluate and support it. Thank you for saving my life.'[9]

Intense media interest surrounded the opening of the new MSIR on 7 July. RVSDS was concerned that the increased surveillance by the media — as well as opponents of the facility photographing MSIR clients coming and going — might continue to deter people from accessing the services. It was a worrying time. RVSDS responded with practical community-engagement activities in the precinct. We observed sage advice from Sun Tzu's *The Art of War*: 'In the midst of chaos, there is also opportunity.'[10]

—

In August, RVSDS gave support to the North Richmond Estate Public Tenant Association (NREPTA), a platform for tenants living in the public-housing estate to have a voice. NREPTA was set up by Penelope Drummond and other residents. These people advocated in relation to their lived experience, apropos issues concerning safety and amenity, service development and delivery, and government policy. The group's first success was securing a supply of sewing machines, and organising sewing sessions for mothers with small children, creating an opportunity for conversation beyond the limitations of their individual apartments.

At local reference group meetings in the months after the opening of the purpose-built MSIR, Nico Clark reported on the recruitment and training of new staff. They were supervising 300 injections each day. The expert review–panel members had been onsite to speak with clients. We were delighted to hear that enrolments for 2020 at Richmond West Primary School had not been negatively impacted by the MSIR. We weren't so happy to hear that MSIR tours, which had been available on Tuesdays at lunchtime, were now scheduled for Friday mornings at 8.00 and 8.30 am. The change to an early-morning timeslot, making it less accessible for the public, was disappointing. The tours had been a practical way of educating people about the facility.

At the meeting we also heard from Richmond pharmacist Perry Moshidis, who reported on buprenorphine, a pharmacotherapy medicine that would be offered to MSIR clients. Pharmacotherapy is the use of medication to assist in the treatment of opioid addiction. It can be used to reduce the intensity of withdrawal symptoms, to manage cravings, and to reduce the likelihood of a lapse or relapse, by blocking a drug or addictive behaviour's effect.[11] There is evidence to support pharmacotherapy, and research is continuing, but medications can only work in conjunction with other treatments, which again points to the importance of offering a suite of services at the MSIR.[12]

The expert review panel — comprising Margaret Hamilton, Ken Lay, and John Ryan (CEO of the Penington Institute) — invited local community groups to meet with them in early August. The panel was keen to hear experiences, perspectives, and suggestions. I had the opportunity to attend two sessions. The first was with Penelope Drummond and members of NREPTA. Penelope led the presentation, outlining the impact of the MSIR on the public-housing tenants. In the evening, I attended with the RVSDS team to present our three key recommendations to the panel:

- open a second licensed facility in the metropolitan area based on overdose figures in local government areas as provided by the Coroners Prevention Unit

- extend the operating hours of the MSIR
- trial the introduction of pharmacotherapy medicine at the new, enhanced facility.

All team members took the opportunity to provide personal reports on their experiences.

International Overdose Awareness Day on 31 August 2019 was memorable. Martin Foley tweeted a poem penned by a talented MSIR client, 'Sammy', who had died of an overdose:

> There is a great place us outcast drug users can go
> A safe room to keep us alive — and everyone should know.
> All are allowed — young, mature, and old,
> as for dedication for my safety, the injecting room is sold.
> Carefully the staff are there so we can safely inject,
> Friendly without judgement for it's our lives they protect.
> Making sure if need be reversing an overdose effect
> All times friendly and helpful, they truly make an effort to connect.
> Those who work here are surely worth much more than their weight in gold.
> I feel warmly treated like family — the reception is never cold.
> Now, three times they have saved my life
> if not for this place, I'd be in great strife.
> So, us users who tend to walk on the edge of a knife,
> I advise you an OD need never end a life.
> My admiration and respect for this caring crew, I cannot portray in words,
> more positive recognition each one of them deserves.

September was a hectic month with the Moon Lantern Festival, a major drawcard in North Richmond. RVSDS cooked halal sausages for the festival volunteers. However, the joy of the festival was tinged with disappointment for me. At the end of a conversation with Victoria Street Business Association president Meca Ho, he told me that he no longer supported the MSIR trial: 'It's politics, Judy Ryan.'

Stephen Jolly's 'move-the-room committee' (MTRC) was garnering support. Its members claimed to approve of the MSIR, 'just not in this location. The facility must be relocated to an industrial site'. There were two glaring deficiencies with this proposition: the absence of any such suitable industrial site, and the absence of a management plan for the hotspot that would remain in the immediate area. Nevertheless, some people were happy, for their own reasons, to rally against 'unsavoury' local elements. When Sky News interviewed the MTRC spokesperson under the banner 'community fight against injecting room', the reporter stated what she thought was the biggest negative of the MSIR: 'It has impacted local property prices.' The interview continued:

> Q: [What is] your view about where [the MSIR] would be located? How on earth did it end up next to a primary school?
>
> A: I can't speak to that [because I didn't live here]. It seems to be a very hastily made decision ... We still have public injecting in the streets — worse than it's ever been [so I've been told].[13]

The lack of an authentic, lived experience in this community was a major credibility problem for the appointed spokesperson of this new committee. He had relocated from Queensland to North Richmond five months after the MSIR had opened.

Property prices weren't the MTRC's only concern. The welfare of local children was another: 'Detractors out there say we shouldn't be bringing the school into the conversation. How can that be the case when our children are subjected to the [MSIR] on a day-to-day basis?'[14] It shocked many, therefore, when the committee produced a massive banner that featured a menacing image of a frightened child peering through opened fingers, with the tagline 'I can't unsee what I just saw — relocate the injecting room'. Draped across the front of a derelict house in Lennox Street — in full view of Richmond West Primary School and a public playground — it enraged the community. If the committee's objective was to win hearts and minds with this visual, it was an own goal.

Residents were constantly affronted by hysterical headlines and crazy images in the pages of the *Herald Sun*, on social media, and on flyers in letterboxes. Resident 'Emily':

> Many of the visuals were deliriously incredulous, portraying vulnerable drug users in the most unbelievable scenarios. This (stigmatised) minority group — who had spent decades seeking obscurity and privacy in our courtyards and finding blind spots in laneways — were suddenly photographed sitting on little mats, arms outstretched as if about to inject and seemingly comfortable with their new-found fame, wearing dark sunglasses in the middle of the street opposite a primary school! It would be hard to find a vein wearing sunglasses.

> The outrage and fury portrayed in the media was not what I encountered walking and cycling daily in North Richmond, using laneways and the public housing estate as I had done for years. As prolific and serial social media magnates, the [move-the-room] committee members managed to compile a visual diary of fake outrage. Residents, traders and folk that I've known for years went along with it, selectively forgetting that moving or closing the room would not eliminate the drug issues. They could, however, feel gratitude in blaming the MSIR for their woes.

The MTRC complained that it wasn't consulted by the authorities, despite reporting numerous meetings with local and state politicians, bureaucrats, and the expert review panel. Maybe the committee thought that consultation equated with getting the outcome they wanted — immediately. When that didn't happen, they blamed a lack of consultation rather than a lack of evidence-based proposals.

A few days after the Sky News interview, I was invited to speak on behalf of RVSDS at a hastily convened gathering, organised by Herschel Landes, outside Richmond Town Hall. I joined Danae Bosler and independent councillor Misha Coleman in a public show of support for the MSIR, its clients, and its staff. We recalled the tragic history of the area before the MSIR trial commenced, encouraging patience in expecting a significant reduction in public drug use in the short term. The MSIR was not the panacea for all the challenges of the last decade: 'Expectations or hopes that the MSIR would solve all problems in the area are unrealistic.'[15]

Immediately following the gathering, there was a council

meeting, where Richmond West Primary School Council president Jim Castles made an impassioned plea: 'The divisive debate around the MSIR is having a deleterious effect on the running of the school. Our view is the politics of this issue should not be inflicted upon children … The school wants the politics out of the school and the school out of politics.'[16]

I received an email from a 'Jonathan Williams' inviting RVSDS to meet with the MTRC: 'We believe we share very similar goals in terms of progressive drug reform, with our only real point of difference seeming to be whether the MSIR should be located in such a high-risk location.' The name of the sender was unfamiliar to me. I made some inquiries and was reliably informed that it was an alias used by a member of the MTRC. Despite my misgivings, I duly disseminated the invitation to RVSDS members for consideration. Thoughtful discussion ensued, with one member positing: 'We may be able to find some common ground from where we could explain our rationale. If you know someone, it's easier to work through issues by building a level of consideration and cooperation.'

While finding common ground was an intrinsic value of RVSDS, members were less enthusiastic on this occasion. The division created by Stephen Jolly continued to ripple through the community. Harassment, stalking, and abuse had become part of everyday life. But in the end, we decided that a delegation of three members — Greg, Michelle, and Frank — would meet with the MTRC at a venue of our choosing.

At the same time, Adam Bandt convened a Greens roundtable in North Richmond to discuss the MSIR. It was well attended by community groups and residents, with Michelle representing RVSDS. Members of the MTRC responded with disbelief to a public housing–estate resident's expressed preference to observe and listen rather than comment at the meeting. Not content with her right to remain silent, they applied pressure, creating an uncomfortable atmosphere. The intimidation became so intense that a concerned resident demanded Adam Bandt's intervention. The housing-estate resident was approached after the meeting by Greens councillor Amanda Stone, who checked on her welfare.

Throughout our campaign for the MSIR, RVSDS members had always engaged in courteous conversations with those who expressed different opinions. However, after hearing about the aggressive behaviour exhibited by MTRC members at the roundtable, we decided, unanimously, to decline their invitation to meet. Jonathan Williams' lengthy response expressed 'surprise and disappointment' at our decision, left a standing invitation to meet, and concluded with 'thank you and take care'.

By this time, known MSIR supporters had been on the receiving end of unpleasant commentary on social media, and had found unused syringes in their letterboxes and dog excrement on their doorsteps. In light of this, the suggestion to 'take care' sounded ominous.

—

Moon Dog Brewery in Abbotsford invited RVSDS to cook the barbecue from 10.00 am to 6.00 pm at its traditional AFL Grand Final event on 28 September. This presented the perfect friendraising opportunity, with locals reporting on their lived experiences, pre- and post-MSIR, while buying our sausages. Many noted that there were fewer syringes, fewer people injecting, and fewer ambulance sirens. We also met Jack Tandy from Abbotsford removalist company Man With A Van. At a subsequent meeting, he and the business owner, Tim Bishop, enthusiastically backed RVSDS and the MSIR and offered their support wherever possible. The event raised much-needed funds for our proposed activities for the kids from the North Richmond public-housing estate over the upcoming summer holidays.

In October, five local women (including me) formed Our Community Leadership Group (OCLG). The purpose of the group was to focus on the positive renewal of our local community in collaboration with an extensive network of local businesses and organisations. Halloween activities in North Richmond in early November kickstarted our accessible, family-friendly events that aimed to unite the community. We also met with Martin Foley to discuss our plans for community renewal.

—

In late October, two outreach workers employed by NRCH (not the MSIR) were arrested and charged with heroin trafficking near the facility.[17] The media had been tipped off and were onsite to capture all the drama of the afternoon. It made for sensational viewing on the evening news bulletins. NRCH CEO Demos Krouskos resigned four days later. The charges against one outreach worker were later dropped. The second was found guilty of trafficking heroin and jailed for 12 months in September 2020.[18]

The outreach workers had been part of the peer-support program. This is where individuals with lived experience of drug use provide support to others by explicitly drawing on their own experiences.[19] It's vital to developing trust and helping people who inject drugs. Peers can watch out for those who may be at risk of overdose, encouraging them to use the MSIR and to seek the professional help they need. But it came with its own risks, it seemed.

The government appointed Dr Joanna Flynn AM to review and update the NRCH policies, including the internal support of peers in the workforce. All recommendations were accepted by management.

> A key finding of this review is that in a high-risk climate, the recent allegations of inappropriate behaviour by NRCH employees have highlighted gaps and shortcomings in governance, leadership, culture, and workforce management that will need to be addressed … Engaging with clients in a harm reduction service may expose a worker with lived experience to situations that may compromise their wellbeing, and this needs to be proactively managed. Several protective factors have been identified as good practice … including ongoing support and debriefing, group supervision and individual supervision, inclusion within a multi-disciplinary team, and access to communities of practice of workers with lived experience.[20]

In the aftermath of these dramatic events and the resulting barrage of negative media, residents rallied in early November in solidarity with each other and the MSIR. They gathered on the grassy knoll outside the facility to share stories and support each other. Two RVSDS members later reflected on the evening's events:

> (Michelle) We stood in a circle, next to the NRCH and MSIR, at the epicentre of the drug scene and public housing, listening

to others share their experiences and waiting our turn to tell our own story.

(Tony) The most memorable experience for me was an impromptu community gathering outside the NRCH with other residents who shared their positive experiences and support for all who were in favour of the MSIR. I'll never forget the words of a local eighty-year-old woman. She said that she had never been afraid to walk her dog late at night and told of her compassion for the addicted who greeted her on those walks. Jewel Topsfield's [subsequent] article in *The Age* was headlined 'No danger: not all residents want the injecting room removed'.[21]

—

On a warm, sunny Saturday afternoon in late November, the MTRC held a rally demanding the MSIR's relocation. A group of around 150 people walked down Victoria Street from North Richmond station and into Lennox Street.[22] A makeshift stage had been set up outside the All Nations Hotel, directly in front of the entrance to the MSIR. The committee spokesperson took to the loudhailer to demand the urgent relocation of the facility.

It must have been a lacklustre event. Stephen Jolly was conspicuously absent and, more significantly, the rally didn't crack a mention in the following day's edition of the *Sunday Herald Sun*. We had anticipated another sensational front-page headline followed by pages of quotes and photos of an angry mob on Victoria Street and outside the MSIR entrance. Nothing. The enduring image for casual observers was the surfeit of billowing

Australian flags overwhelming the makeshift stage.

The Age later published a letter from Richmond resident 'Helen':

> I am perplexed, even horrified, as to the extent of the fuss exhibited by the protesters towards the users of the drug facility in North Richmond.
>
> My grandfather owned a butcher shop in Lennox Street which was used as a soup kitchen during the toughness of the Depression years.
>
> When I downsized … Richmond provided new experiences, plus a grand melting pot of 'the sad, the mad, the bad and the glad'.
>
> Can I presume that the 'enablers' of the gentrification of Richmond should have known there remained untidy and painful aspects of this suburb?
>
> Why then all this scapegoating and marginalisation of addicted and mentally ill persons? Am I being ingenuous in asking where should the facility be? Anywhere but Richmond.

At the end of November, we received the devastating news that a 15-year-old boy had fatally overdosed in North Richmond.[23] As he was under 18 years of age, he was prohibited from accessing support services at the facility just around the corner from his home.

—

I was invited by Nico Clark to present at a professional-development day for MSIR staff in December. RVSDS has huge admiration and respect for the important and difficult work nurses, doctors, and social workers do, so we took this opportunity to organise an oversized 'Thank You' card with many messages of appreciation, including the following:

> Heartfelt thanks to the entire MSIR team for the superb job it does in caring for our marginalised brothers and sisters who would otherwise use our school yards, streets, laneways, carparks, and gardens to inject their drugs with the risk of overdosing. We have known these people over the years. We still care about them but are hugely comforted by the fact that they can receive compassionate and professional assistance at our internationally acclaimed MSIR in North Richmond.
>
> To save lives and refer people to rehabilitation and to allied health, accommodation and personal services is a remarkable legacy of this team, in and of itself. To achieve this outcome under the intense scrutiny of the media, lobby groups and ideological politicians takes that achievement to another level. Many in our community support the MSIR and the life-saving work that is done there. We are proud of it and will continue to work in various ways to ensure that the community amenity continues to improve, with the MSIR and NRCH as its beating heart.

At the presentation, I could sense the team's tension and exhaustion. These professionals had, understandably, developed a siege mentality. Some had been harassed on social media. Others had been treated with hostility by locals when providing outreach services. One reported being tailgated as they drove home from work in the dark; they felt threatened and uncomfortable returning to work. I thanked the staff for inviting me to their session.

After sharing the RVSDS story — including the video of the March to Save Lives — there were tears of relief. One of the nurses, Louise, thanked RVSDS for its campaign and support. It was a cathartic moment. It's outrageous that healthcare workers were subject to harassment and vitriol from people who opposed where — and with whom — they worked.

—

After a joyful, well-attended community twilight picnic on the public-housing estate near Highett Street on 15 December, 'Emily' reflected on the events of 2019:

> Local earnest and reserve prevailed through the goodwill and tenacity of a group of residents who had nothing but the truth to peddle. This comradeship of perseverance and compassion overcame the fabricated move-the-room committee's outrage. No amount of inflammatory rhetoric trumps a story derived from lived experience and wisdom.

At the end of December, Damian Ferrie was appointed interim CEO of NRCH. He had a busy time ahead with the implementation of the 12 recommendations from the Flynn review and anticipating the expert review–panel report and recommendations due in June 2020.

18

A second facility

2020

The Richmond Good Karma Network Facebook page was launched in January, describing itself as 'a safe and positive online group where people are empowered to ask for help and respond to requests for help from others in the Richmond community'. Within 12 months, the page boasted 3,000 members.[1]

Another local advocacy group was launched around that time. Quantities of three flyers promoting 'Supporters of NRCH and MSIR' were distributed throughout North Richmond and South Abbotsford, each featuring a quote from the MSIR Visitors Book: 'Saving lives every day', 'What value do you place on a life?', and 'Thank you for saving my life'. The new advocacy group provided a safe online platform for locals to submit their testimonials and reflections. The administrators were inundated. 'Virginia' was one of the contributors:

> I have lived in South Abbotsford for a generation. In that time, I have made some decisions about how I will educate my

> children about drug use. When my toddler saw a man on the footpath being revived by an ambulance crew, I was determined that he would never see someone die on the street because the community treated them as less than human. One of my proudest times as a parent was witnessing my teenage son giving evidence to a parliamentary inquiry about why a MSIR was needed to save a primary school classmate's life.[2]

During the school holidays, thanks to community efforts led by the North Richmond Estate Public Tenant Association and Our Community Leadership Group, families were treated to pot painting and planting of herbs on the grassed areas on the estate, supported by Bunnings in Collingwood. A twilight movie was shown on a warm Saturday night on the same grassed area, with a screen hung from the top of a huge removalist truck, courtesy of Man With A Van. Kids attending playgroup sessions in the NRCH community meeting room (where the interim MSIR had been located) enjoyed nutritious food provided by food-rescue organisation FareShare. The largesse was extended to grateful MSIR clients next door. Local emergency-services officers popped in with a police car and a fire truck for the kids to crawl over. All of these school-holiday events culminated in an exhibition of the playgroup kids' artwork at The Hive shopping centre.

Volunteers from FareShare commented on the 'surprising calmness and stability' of the NRCH precinct. They confessed to having felt a tad apprehensive about coming to the area following negative media reports about the MSIR, and asked what they could do to improve the reputation of the area: 'Tell your family and friends about your experience here today,' we said. 'Be sceptical when reading — and hearing — the hysteria in the media. Be assured that it will crank up again when school starts in a couple of weeks.' On cue, on 12 February, the *Herald Sun*'s front page featured a pixelated photo of kids with the headline 'Herald Sun photographer captures confronting moment addict overdoses in front of children'.[3] As 'Emily' observed, 'During the January holidays of 2020, a perplexing calm took over North Richmond. Media coverage in all forms ceased and all the shouting and sirens went dead. The number of clients attending the MSIR — approximately 300 daily — didn't falter.'

Friends from the UK, Lyndel and Steve, arrived in Richmond and requested a visit to the 'renowned' precinct 'to see what all the fuss is about'. They had heard about it in the Murdoch media. We headed along Lennox Street towards the MSIR and NRCH. As usual, people were out and about, going to and from both health centres, and to the All Nations Hotel across the road. Orange Sky Laundry — an Australian charity that 'helps to positively connect our friends in need through free laundry, showers and conversation' — was onsite that day. Volunteers were chatting to MSIR clients and to us.[4] They are a regular and welcome feature at the NRCH centre. We wandered around the facilities, the public-housing estate and its carpark, and Richmond West Primary School. It was an ordinary day in the life of a community. While Lyndel and Steve expressed their approval of the precinct, I felt that they were secretly disappointed at the ordinariness of it all: no mayhem to be seen anywhere.

—

As the year progressed, COVID-19 became the centrifugal force in our lives. The local reference group meetings were dominated by the presentation of plans and protocols for managing the pandemic. Damian Ferrie and Nico Clark took advice from Victoria's chief health officer and DHHS to lower the risk of COVID-19 transmission in the local community without disrupting vital services. MSIR staff and clients practised physical distancing and were tested for the virus. There was a new screening process for clients prior to entering, and staff provided clients with the latest information about the virus. Physical distancing meant that the number of active injecting booths had to be halved. Face-to-face health and social services had to be reduced, too. Mental-health and pharmacotherapy (buprenorphine) services were the exception, due to increased demand. Outreach services continued. Some clinics closed altogether, and other services were provided by telehealth. It was a new frontier for everyone.

In view of the extraordinary work being done at both NRCH and the MSIR to protect staff, clients, and the broader community from COVID-19, the lack of positive official communications continued to exasperate. I had a conversation with Quill Award–winning journalist Laura Turner about the life-changing stories coming out of the MSIR. We decided to push for a story that would present this reality to the public in the lead-up to the release of the expert review–panel report, which would determine the facility's future. With cooperation from DHHS, NRCH, and the MSIR, Laura interviewed a former MSIR client and published scientist, 46-year-old 'Saade', who had been injecting heroin for 20 years: 'The week my father died is the same week that I tried heroin. It fixes one thing and wrecks everything else.' While also fighting testicular cancer, Saade had overdosed on heroin four times. He'd turned to the safe injecting room for help. That's when doctors prescribed him buprenorphine, which halted his cravings. At the time of the interview, he had been clean for six months, was no longer injecting, and had reunited with his family. Laura's report received welcome commendation when televised on Channel 9 in late May.

—

The much-anticipated *Review of the Medically Supervised Injecting Room* (the Hamilton report) — detailing the expert review panel's evaluation of the first 18 months of the MSIR trial — was released on 5 June. The report concluded that the trial had succeeded in achieving most of its objectives, noting that 'Implementation remains a work in progress'.[5]

The Hamilton report's key findings:

- 119,223 visits to the facility in 18 months, making it one of the busiest SIFs in the world
- thousands of overdoses safely managed, including 271 that had been 'extremely serious'
- at least 21 lives saved
- no deaths in the facility
- many clients had accessed other health and support services
- clients had received treatment for bloodborne infections
- there had been a reduction in ambulance attendances involving naloxone in the vicinity of the facility during opening hours
- there had been a reduction in reports of public injecting.

The objective that had not been met during the review's assessment period was the improvement of the neighbourhood amenity. Residents' perception was that the volume of discarded injecting equipment had not reduced.

Regarding official communications:

> The expert review panel had observed that the role of NRCH and MSIR in managing the relationship with the local community surrounding the MSIR was at times confusing and apparently compromised ... all their communications [had to be] cleared through DHHS, making timely and direct responses to locals and the media difficult. Going forward ... any licensee must be proactive in engaging with and communicating with the local community and key stakeholders.[6]

The honeypot effect had been explicitly investigated — and disproved — by the expert review panel:

> It does not appear that there has been a direct honeypot effect driven by the MSIR.
>
> Most people using the MSIR (86 per cent) were already coming to North Richmond before the MSIR trial was established to purchase and use heroin. Separately, the Burnet Institute's SuperMIX study (2019) found a shift towards purchasing heroin in Richmond by cohort members in the year before the facility opened, which continued after it opened.[7]

The panel made three recommendations:

- that the MSIR trial should be extended for three years

- that the government should work more closely with the local community to improve the local environment
- that a second SIF should be established 'in the vicinity of a major illicit drug market' outside North Richmond, with the City of Melbourne identified as the desired location.

We were overjoyed. Our key recommendation to the expert review panel — 'opening a second licensed facility in the metropolitan area' — had become the unexpected recommendation in this report.

Another facility would take the pressure off the staff and clients of the MSIR and provide life-saving support in the City of Melbourne. And maybe the relentless media attention in our suburbs would diminish — which would be a good way to improve public amenity.

At an hour-long press conference at Parliament House, Daniel Andrews, Martin Foley, and police commissioner Shane Patton announced the government's response to the report — accepting all recommendations.[8] The MSIR trial would be extended, $9 million would be allocated to improve the amenity in North Richmond, and a second SIF would be established.

After the political announcements, Loretta Gabriel and Nicholas Meadley shared stories of their sons, Sam and Samuel, who had both tragically died from drug overdose before the MSIR opened in June 2018. I spoke about the experience of residents and the need to concentrate on improving the amenity in North Richmond.

Afterwards, a large group gathered for interviews on the grassy knoll outside the MSIR. Residents filled the space, keen to share their thoughts with the media. I stood with Nico Clark, Fiona Patten, two Liberal politicians, and members of the MTRC, one of whom coughed on MSIR supporter Herschel Landes: a vile act in the context of COVID-19. I talked to two nurses and a social worker from the MSIR who were relieved by the news that the trial would be extended.

Dr Yvonne Bonomo, director of the department of addiction medicine at Melbourne's St Vincent's Hospital, penned an opinion piece for *The Age*: 'Opponents of the MSIR have spent the last two years wishing it away without offering an alternative response. But as an addiction medicine specialist, I live in the world as it is, not how others might wish it to be. People are complex. Lives are messy.'[9]

—

By July, new NRCH CEO Trish Collocott advised that MSIR staff were wearing full PPE gear: N95 masks, face shields, gowns, and gloves. They continued to implement measures to further prevent the spread of the virus.

On 2 August, Stage 4 restrictions were put in place across Melbourne, including a curfew from 8.00 pm each night. At his daily press conference on 24 August, Daniel Andrews was asked about whether the MSIR would remain open during Victoria's Stage 4 restrictions:

> It is a health facility. If we closed every hospital or health facility that had a positive case, then people would not get the care they needed, mental health support, alcohol support, trauma, obstetrics, emergency care, right across the board. This is a health

> facility … we're going to do everything we can to not go back to the days when dozens and dozens of people in that part of Melbourne were dying alone in laneways. That facility works. Is it universally popular? No. Do I really care? This is saving lives. We are going to keep it open and build a second one, because it saves lives. We can always debate about how that is done, and whether it can be improved, but this is saving lives.[10]

Inevitably, two MSIR clients were confirmed as COVID-19 cases, with the virus acquired outside the facility.[11] The low number of positive cases in the facility was testimony to the preparedness and professionalism of the NRCH and MSIR teams before and during the pandemic.

—

The City of Yarra council election, on 24 October, was touted by MTRC as 'a referendum on relocating the MSIR'. Despite living in Langridge Ward, the MTRC spokesperson stood as an independent candidate in Melba Ward, where the MSIR is situated, under the 'Richmond First' banner. 'Relocation of the injecting room' was the third-listed policy.

In the event, voters rejected 'Richmond First'.[12] Instead, independent candidate — and public supporter of the MSIR — Herschel Landes was elected in Melba Ward.[13]

Stephen Jolly ran as an independent candidate in Langridge Ward, aligned with 'Richmond First', having parted ways with the Victorian Socialists the previous year. First elected in 2004, Stephen was returned to council despite a negative swing of 4.99 per cent.[14]

Emphatic voter support in 2016 for an MSIR trial had kick-started the RVSDS campaign. Four years on, voters continued to support the MSIR trial, by rejecting the MSIR relocation advocates. The *Herald Sun* published an opinion piece from Victorian Alcohol and Drug Association CEO Sam Biondo: 'What troubles me with those who criticised the MSIR is they forget the expansive public heroin use in North Richmond occurring prior to its implementation … [they] have yet to offer a feasible alternative to the MSIR.'[15]

19

Victoria Street Alive!

2021–2022

Given the Hamilton report's recommendation that the government needed to work more closely with the local community to improve the public amenity in the MSIR precinct, and the allocation of $9 million to achieve that objective, at the end of 2020 Greg Hordacre and I decided to dust off and resubmit the Victoria Street Alive! project, developed in mid-2018, for funding consideration. Second time lucky, perhaps?

In April 2021, we were stunned to learn that our submission had been successful. We were delighted and terrified in equal measure.

Our plan:

- Work with established relationships — council, traders, schools, police, and other community members — to collaborate, create, and deliver inclusive, place-making projects and activities designed to revitalise Victoria Street.

- Bring community together to share, to reflect, and to determine what projects would best enhance our neighbourhood's safety and amenity.
- Create events, activities, and spaces where people could engage, meet, and learn, where ideas could take shape, collaborations be ignited, and partners found.
- Bring our community's ideas to life, turning our streets and empty shops into creative, safe, friendly, and appealing places.

RVSDS was granted $98,500 for 12 months to develop and trial new strategies aimed at renewing our main shopping strip. As we engaged with stakeholders, the overwhelming desire of the community was for the creation of a 'heart' for Victoria Street, identified as the junction where Lennox Street becomes Nicholson Street, Richmond becomes Abbotsford. We knew that securing partnerships with like-minded organisations and businesses would be key to our success.

In agreement with the City of Yarra, event-management company Velodrome Events commenced the transformation of the utilitarian carpark on the north-east corner of Victoria and Nicholson Streets in June 2021. An outdoor beer garden, communal dining hall, and entertainment venue were installed on the erstwhile asphalt blot on the landscape.

In 2022, Velodrome was keen to partner with a community group that could utilise the new venue — known as Abbots Yard — outside of the liquor-licensing restrictions. Victoria Street Alive had two makers' markets on its agenda, a perfect fit for Velodrome and the retro vibe of the new space.[1] The successful markets, held on two Sundays in April and June, showcased the creativity of local makers, artists, designers, upcyclers, and musicians, who had struggled financially throughout the long COVID-19 lockdowns. The community embraced the free, welcoming, and family-friendly environment that reframed Victoria Street as a place of vibrancy and vitality, countering the negative narrative presented in the mainstream media.

Another Victoria Street Alive project was the installation of street-poster art created by local primary- and high-school students.[2] The objective was to amplify young voices through the display of their creative designs. Gustavo Morales, a graphic designer with expertise in inspiring creative poster-making, was contracted by Victoria Street Alive to lead workshops on the Richmond public-housing estate and online, in May. We partnered with Yarra Youth Services, who provided access to the funky Youth Hub for our workshops. Young creatives expressed powerful, poignant views on vexing issues such as climate heating, women's reproductive rights, mental health, and local housing shortages, and these views were amplified when the posters were professionally printed and pasted on walls and buildings along Victoria Street in June. The impact of the posters was immediate, attracting community and broad media interest. Once again, reframing Victoria Street as a place of artistic vitality had been achieved. It was heartening to witness the young artists' pride in seeing their work displayed and celebrated in their neighbourhood.

As a final project in 2022, we planned to green the Victoria Street precinct through the installation of vertical gardens. That turned out to be impossible due to the absence of many commercial property owners in the strip, whose 100 per cent commitment would have been key to ensuring the gardens' durability. A replacement project was urgently required.

Greg and I discussed the possibility of exhibiting photographs that we knew had been taken by clients of the MSIR as part of its art program. A phone conversation with Nico Clark confirmed that some photos were available but not enough for an exhibition. He was nevertheless energised by the prospect of an MSIR exhibition and made a commitment to follow up with the harm-reduction practitioner team leader Sarah Hiley. A letter of agreement was soon signed by NRCH CEO Trish Collocott as licensee of the MSIR, partnering with Victoria Street Alive to stage the 'inaugural MSIR Artists Exhibition 2022'.[3]

We had 12 weeks from the signing of the agreement until our funded program concluded on 30 June — coinciding with the fourth anniversary of the opening of the MSIR. The exhibition was to open on Friday 3 June. There were mighty challenges associated with producing an exhibition at such a short notice. To achieve this, we had to acquire:

- enough finished artwork, photographs, and other items to exhibit, created by people who visited the MSIR and who consented to their work being exhibited — tricky conditions to meet due to the unpredictable lives of the artists
- a suitable and secure exhibition space in Victoria Street for exhibiting an unknown quantity of artworks for a six-week period, with the knowledge that significant preparatory refurbishment would be required
- the services of a professional art curator to install an exhibition in a time frame that was scoffed at by professionals, who suggested that we were 'dreaming'

- the services of a coordinator to liaise with and develop a roster of people who could volunteer as gallery attendants for 96 three-and-a-half-hour shifts across the duration of the exhibition
- the commitment of organisations and businesses to provide practical or financial support to guarantee the success of the exhibition.

What were we thinking to undertake such a huge project in a crazy-tight time frame, counter to the advice of experts in the art-curation field, juggling many moving parts, knowing that if one of them went awry the whole venture would fail — not forgetting that the exhibition was being organised concurrent with two makers' markets and our street-posters project? But we remembered when the 'experts' had sagely advised that there was no hope of securing a SIF in our neighbourhood after decades of political fear. We had proved the naysayers wrong on that occasion; we decided that pushing our luck a second time — and the exhilaration of doing it our way, using the connections we'd fostered — was worth the risk.

We had predetermined deadlines as trigger points for abandoning the project or pivoting to another plan. For example, Friday 13 May was the deadline for the completion of the minimum number of artworks-with-consent required for a viable exhibition. In mid-April, Sarah Hiley and the MSIR staff invited all clients to participate in the '2022 Art Project' workshop: a continuous, seven-days-a-week, 'drop-in' style approach to creating artwork for the exhibition. Interested clients were provided disposable cameras for photographic work or were encouraged to create artwork in the after-care zone at the MSIR: painting acrylic or watercolours on canvas, creating handicrafts, and writing. A painting table and materials were permanently set up across a six-week period in April and May.

The recruitment strategy was successful. Seeing fellow clients at work on their art spurred yet more clients to participate. Many later reflected that, apart from the satisfaction of creating art for the exhibition, it was the mutual support for each other — and the connections they made through creativity and conversation — that was the positive outcome for them. Sarah proudly announced that a decision had been made on the theme for this inaugural exhibition: *My Community*. Perfect!

We had met our deadline: 73 pieces of art were secured for inclusion in the exhibition.

We knew that we needed to engage the services of a professional curator, to contextualise and communicate the purpose of the exhibition, to oversee the installation of the artworks, and to produce the official exhibition catalogue, detailing all artworks and support organisations. This was a tricky manoeuvre, as we lacked both venue and art when we interviewed for the position in early April. Fortunately, Linda Studená, who had experience in 'co-design and community collaboration and development for artists with disability and mental health issues', was happy to take the leap of faith, and unequivocally embraced our crazy plan.

In late April, the owners of The Hive approved a 'casual licence agreement' for our occupation from mid-May of a cavernous, vacant, double-fronted shop on the ground floor of the shopping centre, near the Victoria Street entrance. The occupation of the premises included two weeks for site preparation and art installation, and three days for decommissioning. By securing this space in the acknowledged 'heart' of the community, we felt the gods were on our side.

Contractor Kea Cranko effectively recruited volunteers to work as gallery attendants, and would oversee the roster across the entirety of the exhibition: each day from Friday 3 June to Sunday 26 June, from 11.00 am to 6.00 pm. NRCH guaranteed the availability of a security officer from the MSIR to attend the exhibition space during opening hours.

Finally, Victoria Street Alive proposed an official arrangement with organisations and local businesses whose objectives and values complemented this ambitious project. In exchange for financial donations or in-kind support, logos would be displayed and organisations' support officially recognised in all online and traditional publications, and at the official launch on Thursday 9 June. From major harm-reduction organisations to local business and traders' groups, we were overwhelmed by the generous response to our proposal. The exhibition theme, *My Community*, was appropriate in every respect.

Four weeks after signing the letter of agreement with NRCH, we had a venue, a curator, a volunteer staff coordinator, artists, and support from respected local organisations and businesses. At last, Greg and I could breathe and start to really enjoy the rolling out of this complex initiative.

Nonetheless, the preparation of the site in under two weeks was hectic. Bunnings in Collingwood, a generous business partner, provided labour and materials to paint the walls of the huge space. Linda and my husband, John, and I followed up their efforts with an intense working bee, cleaning and painting the floor and the doors of the space. Carrying out the refurbishment behind black plastic screens draped across the vast expanse of windows fronting the vacant shops created a sense of intrigue for local shoppers. There was always heightened curiosity with the opening of a new enterprise. We decided to keep the screen in situ to prolong the anticipation.

The black plastic didn't deter all interested parties, however, especially the MSIR artists who knew their art was being exhibited behind the screen. In the days before the exhibition opened to the public, the artist Hoops popped his head through a gap in the plastic to see Linda, power drill in hand, hanging a painting, with me as her enthusiastic dogsbody. Hoops exclaimed with delight — and pride — when he spotted his painting of a turtle, which Linda had just installed. He told us that *The Turtle* was the first painting he had ever done and that he was thrilled to see it on the wall. I told him that it was a stunning painting, which it was: 'an amazing first effort'.

Loneliness was sadly a common feature in the lives of the artists. Hoops said how much he enjoyed the art activity at the MSIR because of the interaction with other artists: 'I like to come down here to socialise and be part of the community.' I pointed to a large, powerful painting adjacent to *The Turtle*, called *Not Just Injecting But Connecting* — a collaborative work by MSIR staff and artists: 'Is that what you mean?' I asked him. 'Yes!' was the emphatic response.

Hoops left but returned soon after with two young people from the Vinnies' outreach team to proudly show them his painting. His joy was palpable! It was both memorable and emotional for Linda and me witnessing this moment. Our objective in undertaking this exhibition was already being fulfilled.

The MSIR artists' exhibition *My Community* opened to the public on Friday 3 June.

Two days later, Victoria Street Alive hosted a lunch at the space, catered by FareShare, for MSIR artists, their families, and friends, and for the proud MSIR staff who had overseen the Art Project. Sadly for us, Sarah Hiley was visiting her family in the United Kingdom for four weeks and missed this special event. Moving speeches acknowledged the Indigenous owners of the land, the artists, and the depth of support provided by the staff. It was a true celebration of great partnerships.

The official launch came the following Thursday, 9 June. Final touches were added to the exhibition space. Indoor plants and a stunning native floral arrangement were delivered, along with food and drinks, all donated by local businesses. Amid the flurry of activity, journalist Cara Waters from *The Age* interviewed Greg and me and one of the artists whose work was exhibited.[4] Someone from MSIR asked if staff and the artists were invited to the 'VIP launch' — of course they were invited to the official launch: 'You are the VIPs!'

That night, MSIR staff, partners, supporters, sponsors, volunteers, residents, and artists created an atmosphere charged with excitement, joy, and cheer. Keynote speaker Martin Foley — now the health minister — was a late scratching, due to COVID-19. The 150 guests heard speeches from Greg, Linda, NRCH chair Sally Mitchell, Nico Clark, and Fiona Patten, while I acted as MC. The event was live-streamed so Sarah Hiley could watch it in the UK. Happily, she returned to Melbourne on 20 June, just in time to volunteer as an attendant on a rostered shift, immersing herself in the space that she had been pivotal in creating.

The positive vibe of the stigma-busting launch energised everyone. A decision had been made at the outset of the project that all exhibited artwork listed for sale would be part of a silent auction. Confidential bid sheets were made available to more than 1,000 visitors throughout the duration of the exhibition. Submitted bids were safely secured until the day after the exhibition closed. On Monday 27 June, the highest bidders were telephoned and advised of their successful bids, with arrangements made for payment and collection. To our amazement, every single artwork sold! The entire process was confidential, with all sale proceeds disseminated to the artists. I was the highest bidder for *The Turtle*.

Four Victoria Street Alive events in six months — two markets, the poster design and installation, and the MSIR artists' exhibition — demonstrated how an outdoor event space and two empty shops can be activated to create safe, friendly, and appealing places for those who live near, work in, or visit Victoria Street. RVSDS' authentic community engagement undertaken in prior years profoundly influenced the positive outcomes achieved by June 2022. One can only imagine the long-term benefits that will come of this project and its opportunities for connection in the lives of our most vulnerable community members.

On Thursday 30 June, Greg and I attended an informal lunch on the sun-drenched grassed area outside NRCH to celebrate four years of the MSIR. There were food trucks, fire pits, musicians, storytelling, laughter, and people playing cricket and kicking the footy, evoking memories of country gatherings. There was a buzz in the air, with many of the exhibition artists in attendance; they spoke of their pride at having participated in *My Community*. That evening, we hosted a party at the now vacant exhibition space to thank everyone who had worked with us to ensure the success of our Victoria Street Alive projects:

a last hurrah. We heralded the start of the fifth year of our MSIR saving and rehabilitating lives.

Evidence shows that arts and culture build communities, ultimately contributing to safety and amenity. The plan is to repeat the markets and the street-posters project, and to host a second MSIR artists' exhibition in 2023. Our community loves it, and our key stakeholders are demanding it.

How hard could it possibly be?

Afterword

Janet McCalman was born and raised in Richmond. An esteemed Australian social historian and academic, she remains a keen observer of her birthplace and a commentator on its evolution. Her 2021 preface for the third edition of her book *Struggletown* — addressing 'the politics of gentrification' — is instructive:

> [W]hile modern Richmond may now appear homogenously affluent, renovated and smart, the underlying problems of class, poverty and exclusion have not gone away: rather they are now focused on residents in public housing and on the lost souls of the streets …
>
> One brave reform and a local flashpoint has been the medically supervised injecting room (MSIR) operating out of the North Richmond Community Health (NRCH) service. Lives are being saved and the streets are being cleaned up, but while a privileged, noisy minority wants the clinic to move to someone else's patch, others, including families from the adjoining primary school, have been strongly supportive. These are the class tensions of the twenty-first century in the inner city.[1]

—

Amid these tensions, any tragedy or antisocial behaviour in the community is readily attributed to the MSIR. This conflation was writ large in March 2021. Sadly, a young man was found deceased, on the grassy knoll near the SIF, at 7.00 am, before it opened for the day.[2] A few days later, an intruder at Richmond West Primary School triggered a whole-of-school lockdown. The man was charged with 'trespassing, resisting police, possession of a controlled weapon and being drunk in a public place'.[3] Significantly, the charge of 'being drunk in a public place' was omitted from the *Herald Sun* report on the intrusion: 'He was charged with trespass, possessing a controlled weapon and breach of bail. One parent said her son had seen drug users injecting themselves in the school grounds.'[4]

Once again, calls came for the centre to be 'relocated'. A garish flyer appeared in letterboxes announcing another All Nations Hotel 'community meeting'. It was dutifully attended by the media,[5] but even ahead of the meeting, veteran 3AW shock jock Neil Mitchell was touting its conclusions:

> Nasty events there over the past week. A man found dead. A man with a knife. New security at the school. Urgent meetings with the education department. Community meeting at 7.00 pm there tonight. I think even if you support the injecting room, it is in the wrong place. Pause the trial. It's starting to impact on lives — too much — on residents. It's been a rough couple of weeks in the area with the MSIR. I spoke to a school mother and her nine-year-old daughter ...[6]

Exasperated, I wrote a letter, published by the *Herald Sun*, who titled it 'Injection of Sense':

The intruder at the local primary school is charged with being drunk.

Move the nearby pub?

A man tragically died near the supervised injecting facility (SIF) when it was closed.

Extend its opening hours?

For decades, parents, children and teachers witnessed injecting and overdosing in the Health Centre's carpark next door to the school.

Code Blue alerts meant the Centre's staff abandoned their patients to resuscitate overdoses in that carpark. Bodies under sheets, ambulances and syringes were viewed from the school.

The life-saving facility is situated on that carpark because it was an overdosing hotspot. Overdoses and addictions are now successfully managed inside that facility.

This community desperately needs the second injecting facility in the city — and then some more.

ABC Melbourne's Ali Moore interviewed Salvation Army major Brendan Nottle about that organisation's support for the opening of the second SIF in the city.[7] Ali's emphatic reference to the 'horrific recent events in North Richmond' associated with the MSIR frustrated me, so I rang the talkback line to update Ali and her thousands of listeners: 'Facts and language matter, Ali. What is "horrific" is the community's memory of the overdoses, deaths, and ambulance sirens and callouts in the years before the MSIR opened. That situation is much improved.'

A gaudy eyesore appeared on Lennox Street during the dark winter months of Melbourne's long COVID-19 lockdown. The Department of Education replaced Richmond West Primary School's cyclone fences with a patchwork of opaque, coloured screens attached to two-metre metal poles. The justification for the fortification was 'to better protect students' safety and privacy'. It was interesting to note, therefore, that only Lennox Street and a short section on the southern boundary received the prison treatment. The east side fence remained without opaque screens.

Residents hate it. Parents hate it. Kids hate it: 'We can't get people's attention when we need our balls thrown back to us.' 'I miss patting people's dogs when they walk past the fence.' 'I can't see out.' 'Being at school is like being in a prison.' Discreet childish scribble on the fence on the southern border indicates the strength of the kids' views: 'I hate the fence. FUCK THE FENCE.'

—

Next door to the school is the MSIR. Across the street is the All Nations Hotel. Each requires a government licence to operate, but compare the two.

The All Nations Hotel, established 1870:

Enterprise:	for profit
Drugs:	legal — alcohol

Staff:	unqualified, they welcome and engage clients walking in off the street, and sell alcohol under Responsible Service of Alcohol guidelines
Patrons:	people aged 18 years and over
Prohibited:	people under the age of 18; smoking tobacco
Services:	sale of a central nervous system–depressant drug; no onsite health services for intoxication or addiction
Controversial?	no — despite neighbours occasionally reporting urination and vomiting in gardens, smoking, congregating on the street after hours, aggressive behaviour, and damage to property

The MSIR, established 2018:

Enterprise:	not for profit
Drugs:	sourced by clients, prior to entry, through illegal, unregulated suppliers: heroin (95 per cent), methamphetamine (2 per cent), other drugs (3 per cent)
Staff:	highly trained, they welcome and engage clients walking in off the street, ensure people don't die from overdose, provide access to health services
Patrons:	people aged 18 years and over; generally marginalised, long-term drug users with many associated health problems; stigmatised, often homeless, and mentally unwell; poorly linked in with treatment and care

Prohibited:	people under the age of 18; smoking tobacco; first-time injecting drug users; people with parole conditions that prohibit drug use; pregnant women
Services:	provision of clean drug-use equipment (not drugs); ensuring people don't die from overdose; improving health and social functioning of clients; facilitating greater voluntary access to a network of treatment and care by reducing barriers to that access
Controversial?	very — evidenced by *Herald Sun* newspaper headlines: 'REjecting Room', 'Drug room ghetto', 'The horror movie: Richmond or Detroit?', 'Residents fear creation of "ghetto"', 'ONE STOP DRUG SHOP', 'The residential Chernobyl' …

I recall daily life in the contested triangle of the hotel, NRCH, and the primary school in the years before the MSIR opened. Kids leaving school at 3.00 pm could have witnessed:

- people leaving the pub under the influence of alcohol
- people injecting — sometimes overdosed — in the NRCH carpark; bodies alone or surrounded by the centre's medical staff or emergency services attempting resuscitation.

Two case studies demonstrate the contradictions in community attitudes and ongoing hypocrisy of our approach to people who use one substance — good, licit drugs — versus those who use another — bad, illicit drugs.

The first case study, February 2021: 'Kings Cross businesses are calling for the removal of the Medically Supervised Injecting

Centre from the downtrodden strip if the area is to thrive from the removal of the lockout laws.'[8]

As the Sydney MSIC prepared to celebrate 20 years of continuous operations without losing a single client to overdose death in the facility, Doug Grand from the Kings Cross Liquor Accord wanted to kick the MSIC out of Darlinghurst Road. His was one of many calls by some in the rapidly gentrifying community of Kings Cross and Potts Point to see it either closed or 'relocated'.[9] Former MSIC medical director Ingrid van Beek responded:

> You can perhaps understand my dismay at this week's [*Sydney Morning*] *Herald* headline 'Kings Cross businesses want removal of injecting centre to revive strip.' In the article, Kings Cross Liquor Accord's coordinator, Doug Grand … says of [MSIC clients]: 'Some of them get abusive, some of them get aggressive.' He needs to speak to his members about just how abusive and aggressive their alcohol-affected clientele can be. Has he forgotten why the lockout laws were introduced in the first place?
>
> Kings Cross had become nightmarish on weekend nights, with hundreds of drunken revellers spilling out onto the streets — plastic glasses required to reduce the 'glassings', which had become common … The hospital emergency and police data for violent incidents, including the tragic deaths of two young men, told the story.[10]

The second case study, October 2021: 'The [Victorian Liberal] MP for Kew, Tim Smith, resigned as shadow attorney-general yesterday and released a statement saying he had made a "serious error of judgment" after he collided with a car and then the wall of a Hawthorn home where there were children inside.'[11]

A strident opponent of the MSIR, Smith resigned from shadow cabinet after crashing his car into a private house: he had recorded a blood-alcohol reading of 0.131 — almost three times the legal limit of 0.05. His response when asked if he had taken a drug test after the crash: 'I've never taken a drug in my life.' Journalist from *The Age* Kate Halfpenny called him out: 'Let me be the one to break it to you, Tim Smith, alcohol is a drug … Along with nicotine, it's the most commonly used drug in Australia. In 2019–20, alcohol accounted for 74,500 (53 per cent) of our drug-related hospitalisations.'[12]

Smith had previously called for another state MP with drug problems to resign. In October 2019, when Labor Party MP Will Fowles revealed his struggle with drugs, alcohol, and mental-health issues, Smith tweeted: 'Will Fowles should resign. He clearly isn't up to being a member of parliament. The people of Burwood deserve much better.'[13]

When it comes to alcohol, business owners and legislators don't consider their own behaviour — or their businesses — as being 'drug'-related. This may provide an explanation as to why legislators feel free to judge other drug users, hence anomalies in legislation.

Marianne Jauncey noted:

> How utterly dreadful it is that one drug is celebrated and sold with the government getting taxes, while users of other drugs are demonised and criminalised. All drugs can be harmful and those with dependence issues deserve treatment and support — no matter what the substance happens to be.[14]

The medical terminology is AOD: alcohol and other drugs. The reader will note what goes first.

Alcohol is the most harmful drug.

It is the most widely used psychoactive drug in Australia. It causes more chronic diseases and is linked to more deaths than many illicit drugs.[15]

The Australian Institute of Criminology reports that it's alcohol, more than illicit drugs, that is involved in both domestic and non-domestic homicides.

One in ten workers report usually drinking alcohol at work. This is ten times more than those who report drug use at work.[16]

According to the Australian Drug Harms Ranking Study, the 'overall relative harm score', which combines 'prevalence weighted harm to users and harm to others', for alcohol is 100.00. Tobacco scores 37.1, ice 32.0, cannabis 17.3, heroin 16.9, prescription opioids 13.6, and so on.[17]

We've heard from the media that we're in the middle of an 'ice epidemic' because of the huge harm the drug is causing individuals, loved ones, and others. Ice is an issue in Australia, that's true — but the media is not reporting an 'alcohol epidemic', when alcohol is the drug causing the highest level of harm to our society.

I am not advocating for the stigmatisation of 'drinking'. I am saying that drug dependence of any kind is a health issue, a treatable condition, and treating it as such may contribute to improved understanding among the public who are accustomed to unhelpful media stereotypes.

—

Heroin use and overdose led to the need for the MSIR, and heroin is the main drug used in the facility. Among other health services, the MSIR offers chances at rehabilitation. The success of pharmacotherapy — slow-release injections of buprenorphine — offered from September 2019 to April 2020 — has been labelled a '"Game changer" treatment [that] cuts heroin use'.[18] Anthony Weeks, Nico Clark, and Shelley Cogger co-authored a paper published in *Drug and Alcohol Review*:

> Opioid agonist treatment is offered to those who are opioid dependent and who wish to reduce or cease heroin use … Of the forty-one clients commencing depot buprenorphine … 59 per cent did not return to the facility to inject heroin.[19]
>
> Some people that were previously using the facility ten times a month stopped visiting altogether while on the injection. The average person that uses our injecting room has been using heroin for twenty-five years, or as long as fifty-five years, and they're telling us they're feeling that it's easy for them not to use.
>
> What this has shown is no matter how challenging people's life experiences have been to date, no matter how long they have been using heroin for, they can really do well in a short period of time with the right support.
>
> It shows us that an injecting room is not just a place for people to inject but also for people to access the services that they've otherwise struggled to access.[20]

Buprenorphine is available to take once a week, once a month, or once every six weeks. The injection produces stable levels of the drug, so most patients experience few or no side effects, as reported by 'Summer': 'Having an injection that removes the daily struggle, that daily choice, is quite freeing for people … they can get on with their normal lives … It's completely given my life back.'[21]

This was much-needed good news and a real boon for clients, staff, and the community. It prompted me to write a letter to *The Age*:

> Mindful of the current pressure on our ambulance services, I was heartened to read 'Dramatic cut in heroin use under new drug therapy'.
>
> Ambulance callouts to overdoses in our area have decreased since the supervised injecting facility opened and the success of the new drug therapy, which 'reduces and stops heroin use' for some clients, will continue to reduce that demand.
>
> I applaud the 'game-changing' work of this essential health service. It is positively impacting the lives of people with addiction and the broader community.[22]

At the same time, Paul Dietze from the Burnet Institute released the results of its longstanding Melbourne Injecting Drug User Cohort Study (SuperMIX), the largest cohort study of people who inject drugs ever conducted in Australia:

> The [MSIR] is being sought and used by vulnerable populations including: a high proportion of young people; people who identify as Aboriginal and/or Torres Strait Islander, and people who live locally.
>
> It's attracting people who experience the most trying conditions and who are most at risk — the homeless, the unemployed and people who are struggling the most. It's also

> being used by younger people, and that's important to link this group with treatment, education, and support early on in their injecting experience.
>
> The study also found that those who use the service frequently are much less likely to inject in public, pointing to a wider community benefit.[23]

Lisa Townsend, who had lived with heroin addiction for years, credited the MSIR for turning her life around:

> Had I not been able to access the support there, I'd either be dead or still in the throes of my addiction … I'm living proof that the whole injecting room set-up, with all the wraparound services, do work to help people on their recovery and aren't just there to make drug use an easy thing.

Lisa accessed services offered by both the MSIR and NRCH, including housing, oral, and mental-health services. The non-judgemental staff helped motivate her to recover.[24]

It's important to remember that a SIF is of greatest benefit in an existing drug-use and overdose hotspot:

> Living distant from a SIF is a known barrier to use, so [the SuperMIX] findings underscore the limited geographic coverage of a single SIF site in a city as large as Melbourne.
>
> Although 58.3 per cent of frequent users lived more than two suburbs away, they still lived in suburbs that were relatively close, such as Fitzroy. There's a relatively small number of people who are coming from other places.[25]

It is a full-time job calling out dodgy media reports about the MSIR. An article in the *Herald Sun* required such a response. Shadow minister for health Georgie Crozier was quoted as saying, 'Frontline police, residents, traders and families are all saying the North Richmond centre is making things worse ...'[26] Her claim that these groups 'are all saying' was misleading. Knowing it was a waste of energy, I left a voicemail message for the reporter, John Masanauskas, requesting an opportunity to provide an alternative view. I also invited Georgie Crozier and shadow minister for mental health Emma Kealy to meet with residents who live near the MSIR, parents from the school, and a client from the MSIR. A respectful hearing took place a month later in the NRCH community meeting room, with lived experiences shared with the two politicians. Nevertheless, the Liberal–National coalition vowed to relocate the MSIR to a suitable, undisclosed location if it won the state election in November.

The second MSIR expert review panel was established in 2021, 'to hear from people who visit, live or work near or at the service about their experiences and perspectives of the trial'. I hope they interviewed the senior fire brigade officer stationed at Richmond who rang ABC Melbourne radio on 29 August 2022 during another discussion about a second SIF in the City of Melbourne:

> [Richmond] is the epicentre of heroin in Melbourne. We respond to all unconscious and/or non-breathing patients to support Ambulance Victoria. This includes drug overdose. Calls for ODs are down roughly 75 per cent since the MSIR opened.

> With this many lives being saved, my crew and I cannot fathom the cold-hearted attitude of the people who think the continued gentrification of their suburb is more important than the many lives that are being saved. Also the politicians who use this topic to score points to win votes — simply disgusting.

Expert review panel chair John Ryan (a member of the first panel), Christine Kotur, and Rob Knowles must deliver their final report and recommendations in December 2022. The report will affect the future of the MSIR beyond its trial period, ending June 2023, and the future of the second SIF, in the City of Melbourne. This book will have gone to press before that happens. Whether the report is positive or negative, however, there will always be more battles to be fought, new opponents to established SIFs, and new SIFs that need to be established in other 'war zones'.

When I reflect on my life since that Sunday in July 2016 when I found the young man overdosed at my back gate, I recall the despair and sense of helplessness I felt that afternoon. '*They* should do something' was my pathetic reaction to the crisis at hand. If anyone had told me that day that 'in four years, you will hear that a second SIF will be planned for Melbourne — and in six years, the first SIF will start its fifth year of providing support and dignity to people with addiction' — I would have said, 'You're dreaming.'

I thought about Mum — again. What would she say to me? I

ached to talk with her, to tell her about everything. But I knew that she knew! And she would have said — with an air of self-assuredness: 'I told you. You should never die wondering.'

Acknowledgements

You Talk, We Die would not have happened without Melbourne's long COVID-19 lockdowns in 2020 and 2021. Throughout the RVSDS campaign, I often thought that I would write a book about this wild ride 'one day'. I had an eclectic collection of notes, media articles, flyers, spreadsheets, and photos that would help tell our story. With the lockdowns, I had no excuse to defer any longer. Gratitude and huge thanks to John for his gentle encouragement and patience in reading and commenting on each chapter of my first-ever manuscript with diplomacy and thoughtfulness: 'Judes — I don't think this will get past legal!'

Thanks to other people who were happy to be involved in the creative process: Jackie Yowell, Marianne Jauncey, David Stanley, Mark Sheehan, Greg Hordacre, Loraine Little, Michelle Zwagerman, Veronica McGowan, and Ruth McGowan. Eternal gratitude to all of you for your professional advice and for adding colour and movement to this story.

This book is my first encounter with the publishing process. I expected to self-publish *You Talk, We Die* due to the 'controversial' nature of SIFs: what publisher would touch it? However, following a kind referral from Matthew Kelly, I was shocked when Scribe publisher Henry Rosenbloom rang me to advise that he had 'read the manuscript completely and am prepared to take it on. I have shared it with staff, who believe that it is an important story that deserves to be told.' I was speechless. Huge thanks, Henry, for taking a leap of faith in pursuing my 'messy' manuscript.

Senior editor David Golding has been reassuring and so easy to work with. He has provided thoughtful advice on everything from the copyediting and cover design to the rearrangement of parts of the manuscript to ensure the story flows. His encouragement was welcome: 'you know what you are doing, and it's your manuscript, so please consider all of my changes in the document to be suggestions … I'm happy to discuss anything.' Thank you so much, David. I would like to also thank the cover designer, Guy Ivison, the design and production manager, Mick Pilkington, the proofreader, Julian Welch, and my publicist, Cora Roberts.

I have always loved maps in books that ensure my full immersion in any story: thanks to Daniel Riddiford for designing the best map I have ever seen in a book.

Photographs bring the community's story to life: huge thanks to Ciska Burrie from RVSDS (March to Save Lives) and Paul Dunn Photographs (MSIR Art Exhibition).

Huge gratitude to the first supporters of my crazy idea to campaign for an MSIR trial: you backed my gamble, door-knocking and handing out flyers and answering questions at the polling booth on a bitterly cold council election day in October 2016. My eternal gratitude to all of you, starting with my campaign team of two: John Riddiford and Loraine Little, Christine Robinson, Dan Riddiford, Declan Mitchell, Gabrielle Gibney, Hannah Gibney, Helen Gibson, Jane Elms, Josephine Camilleri, Liz Ryan, Lou Ryan, Maie Gibney, Margaret Ryan, Meg Gorman, Meg Quinn, Michael Ryan, Rosemary Denton,

Sue McNamara, Tara Whitehead, and Trish Ryan.

Nothing would have happened without the Residents for Victoria Street Drug Solutions core team: 'If not us, who? If not now, when?' The coming together of compassionate residents with diverse skill sets is absolute proof that the universe provides in abundance: Ciska Burrie, Colin Gomm, Dianne McCulloch, Frank McCulloch, Greg Hordacre, John Riddiford, Kylie Troy-West, Liz Gomm, Loraine Little, Margot Foster, Melody Patterson, Michelle Zwagerman, and Tony Worsteling.

The generosity and support of the Kings Cross MSIC team enabled our campaign to gain momentum, most notably by allowing us access to the film that taught our community so much and made us cry and kept us positive. Thank you to Marianne Jauncey, Miranda St Hill, Sarah Hiley, Jennifer Jones, Julie Latimer, and Rohan Glasgow.

Grieving families courageously spoke out so we could learn about lives that are burdened by addiction and its trauma, and kept us focused: Cherie Short, Laura Turner, and Loretta Gabriel.

Drug-law reformists and harm-reduction trailblazers taught us all so much: Alex Wodak, David Stanley, Demos Krouskos, Greg Denham, Fiona Patten, Kasey Elmore, Larry Campbell, Marianne Jauncey, Miranda St Hill, Nico Clark, Paul Dietz, Penny Francis, Peter Wearne, and Tony Parsons.

Journalists, film producers, and street artists helped to tell our story: Alice Wilson, Andrew Kavanagh, Anthony Zielke, Ash Blackwell, Bill Pitt, Brendan Donohoe, Caleb Walmsley, Charlotte Grieve, Daniel Riddiford, Dean Sunshine, Dennis Smith, Emma Hart, Jayne Dullard, Lucy Williams, Matt Thompson, and Nick Wallis.

People who said yes without hesitation: Annie Ryan, Ash

Blackwell, David Stanley, Hannah Bretherton, Ian Gibson, Kate McNamara, Laura Turner, Loretta Gabriel, and Sue McNamara.

My extended family: elders John, Biddy, and David; siblings Ro, Helen, David, Michael, Mark, Lou, and Gabrielle; their partners, nieces, nephews, and cousins — too many to name here. Your support and encouragement from the outset is recorded with love and gratitude.

My immediate family who have been on this journey with me from the very beginning: John, Dan, Louie, Charlie, Nadia, Tom, and Katie — I love you all heaps for supporting my obsession and contributing in countless ways to our community. Especially to John for his honest feedback on the very first draft which kept me going. Eternal love and gratitude.

Last but not least: so many people were involved with the RVSDS campaign for the MSIR. I started listing all the names but was fearful about omitting someone. While I will not be able to do justice to all the ideas, work, efforts, and support that individuals and organisations contributed to our campaign, I do want to acknowledge that there would be no story without all of you, so please consider this a genuine, grateful acknowledgement of your support.

> 'There is no power for change greater than a community discovering what it cares about.'
>
> **Margaret J. Wheatley**

APPENDIX 1

Not all school parents

The location of the MSIR, adjacent to the northern boundary of Richmond West Primary School (RWPS), is an oft-reported 'vexed' issue. The media has portrayed opposition to the MSIR's location as being widespread among school parents. This is not the case. Parents who support the MSIR, its staff, and the clients do so quietly for fear of repercussions.

North Richmond resident and school parent 'Emily' captures the essence of the culture and values of the school — and the local community — in the following snapshot of an important feature on the school calendar: the annual 'welcome to new parents' barbecue.

> In February each year, there is a 'welcome to new parents' BBQ. It's a simple buffet-style affair, held in the school grounds. The tradition is for long-term parents to cook up a storm, provide salads galore, invite people to grab a plate, to mingle and to greet the new members of our school community.
>
> In 2017, our invitation went to everyone in North Richmond — including those beyond the school gates, doing it

tough and struggling with addiction. Back then, our community acknowledged and accepted where we lived: we understood that our privilege came with the responsibility to look after everyone.

No eyebrows were raised, therefore, when a few hungry folk — swaying gently under the influence of something — rocked up for a feed. A small group of three — one woman and two men — entered the school grounds, lured by the irresistible smell of onions on the grill and the sounds of laughter. They placed their bags down and joined the queue for a snag and a chat. This is how things rolled at RWPS and in North Richmond itself: an unspoken understanding of those less fortunate. Naturally, there were always a few cheerful misunderstandings or, as the locals called it, 'opportunities' for parents who came to the school from outside the area to learn a few things. It's important to remember that the school was built to cater for families from Richmond's public housing estate.

On this particular day, it was parents from affluent Malvern — drawn to the school for its famous Mandarin immersion program — who missed the mark completely. They thought that the 'swaying' visitors were school parents. They diligently welcomed them (as per our BBQ policy) with conversations about parenting and information on the language program that shot right over our guests' heads like a full-throttle 747. However, there was no sense of alarm or outrage from anyone in the school community on this day in 2017.

In my mind, this event is a constant reminder of why acceptance and understanding will always triumph over fences, fear, and privilege within a community, and how much we have to learn at a BBQ in North Richmond if we simply give it a chance.

As the location of the MSIR next to the school is a flashpoint in any discussion around its existence, I have compiled the thoughts of some past and present school parents to provide the reader with an understanding of their thoughts about the issue. All comments are anonymous. Some have been sourced from media publications listed in the Notes. Others are available on savinglivesnrch.org. Some are private comments and reports that I have received, including one from a teacher who was at the school when the Mandarin bilingual program was established in the 1980s.

School parents who support the MSIR location

School parent 1 — April 2020: Drugs have always been around North Richmond. In the eight years since my kids have gone to RWPS, I have not experienced an increase in drug use. I've always spoken to my kids about what's going on for drug users and my kids have never had trouble negotiating their way to and from school.[1]

School parent 2 — April 2020: Our daughter commenced at RWPS in 2012. The drug culture was well established next to the school and throughout the streets of North Richmond. Drug paraphernalia, public injections and overdoses were, sadly, a common occurrence. After it opened in June 2018, the MSIR trial was supported by parents and residents who had experienced the nightmare of death in our streets. They understood its importance and place in a neighbourhood entrenched in decades of complex drug torment.[2]

School parent 3 — June 2020: As residents of Highett Street since early 2015, and parents of two children at RWPS, we strongly support the MSIR. A key to the amenity of the neighbourhood being improved for us since the MSIR trial began is that the longstanding issue of drug use in the area has been publicly acknowledged and now actively managed by government services. Since the 1990s, we have lived in a number of suburbs with illicit drug use. We think that this is the first time we have seen a bold government policy implemented that has proven to be successful in other locations, like Kings Cross.

The fact that we know there are clear support services for people in our community is another way that amenity of the neighbourhood has been improved. Having direct and practical action for connecting and supporting people, harm minimisation and saving lives means that our neighbourhood is a positive place. Treating all people with respect, providing opportunities for support and connection is something we should invest in; we are pleased that this is what is happening in our local community.

The presence of the MSIR and Yarra Council has also been valuable in terms of collecting needles that are left in public places. We have government-department land behind our house and, in the past, there were many used needles left there. This is a rare occurrence now. We are very happy that the state government has created and invested in this facility. We hope that the trial will be extended and developed further.[3]

School parent 4 — June 2020: As I reflect on the impact of the MSIR, for me that mostly revolves around my two daughters going to RWPS. My older daughter is now in high school so the timing of my story would be around five years ago when she was in second grade. We were walking north up Lennox Street from school towards Victoria Street, past a man passed out on the footpath. She asked,'Why do they do that?' to which I answered something like 'they prefer to being like that than where they were before taking drugs'. She took that answer in and moved on. Context is key here.

My kids were educated in the school yard as well as in the classroom to be alert but not alarmed by local drug behaviour. There are well-established protocols and practices, and healthy norms in the cohort. My kids are more inquisitive than scared by the street experience just described. My observation over recent times is that there is less street depravity than there was prior to the MSIR trial. Similarly, there is less routine anti-social/violent behaviour in the multi-level carpark.[4]

School parent 5 — August 2020: My oldest daughter is in her fourth year at RWPS; my youngest daughter has just begun there. We live a distance from the school and commute, so the impact of Richmond's drug and homelessness problems is not as visible to me. But we have no intention of leaving the school and, if anything, the existence of the injecting room has increased my happiness with — and security in — the school.

From day one of attending the school, Richmond's issues were evident. I've found three needles walking from the train station or car which is not a lot but three more than satisfactory. More visible are the many homeless and/or strung-out individuals along Lennox Street and at the corner of Victoria Street.

The nature of the area makes me watchful as a parent and

has involved some education of my children: caution, but more importantly, the teaching of empathy and to learn not to be judgmental. I have never felt threatened, nor have I been concerned for the safety of my children. We sometimes go to a bakery on Victoria Street, followed by a walk along Lennox Street to school which typically means passing individuals who are drug affected or in withdrawal. These individuals are clearly in bad shape, but they have never done anything remotely threatening to me or my children. Most of them clearly understand that other people are wary, and they are intent on not causing trouble to others.

From my perspective, I have noticed little change since the opening of the injecting room. I have not found any needles on the streets — and I look for them. I have not noticed an increase in drug-affected individuals. I do not know if the improved fencing around RWPS was necessary but may be prudent. I have met with representatives of Richmond West, North Richmond Community Health centre, and local and state government representatives. I have complete faith in their expertise and their wisdom.[5]

School parent 6 — March 2021: A school parent, who did not want to be identified for her children's sake, said she understood drug use [near the school] could be confronting. But she said she had not been scared or threatened, and the debate was creating unnecessary fear. 'We should talk about it … but I don't think we should be scared. And if we're scared of people, I think that creates a horrible atmosphere to think that people are inherently dangerous,' said the mother, who has [two children] at the school.[6]

School parent 7 — November 2021: Parents from outside the neighbourhood enrolled their child at the school despite being fully aware of its 'controversial' neighbour, the MSIR. The facility and its clients prompted many conversations with their child regarding social justice, support for those less fortunate and how the teachers keep the kids safe. The lockdown response to the intruder incident in March 2021 was not a big deal for their child. The parents could see that the staff were under pressure from the media focus and the opponents' onslaught at the time. The parents delivered flowers and a note expressing gratitude and ongoing support for the professionalism and care of the staff for all of the children.

School parent 8 — November 2021: We have lived in North Richmond continuously since 2006. Our children have been at RWPS since 2016. At first, we chose RWPS ahead of other local options because of its bi-lingual Mandarin program, but, really, it is the culture of the school that makes our family proudest to belong. Successive principals have known every child by first name — and the children address all their teachers by first name in return. School assemblies are run by the children, reminding us who the school is really working for. The education and the care at this open-intake state school are stronger by far than the most exclusive schools that our parents could have sent us to 30+ years ago.

The partnership between RWPS and the North Richmond Community Health (NRCH) centre has been a great blessing, especially since the MSIR opened. Their collaboration has been very helpful in bringing dental care programs to our children and their classmates. We cheered when NRCH staff liaised with the school to ensure its teachers could get vaccinated against COVID-19 as quickly as possible during 2021. When there have been important events around the health centre (security concerns, drug overdoses, changes to programs), NRCH and RWPS have been loyal neighbours to each other. This has undoubtedly put the school's families in a better position to know what is going on. The community is safer and better informed because of this partnership, and a better environment for bringing up our children.

By contrast, we remember the streets around RWPS in those last few years before the injecting room opened. North Richmond has long been an area where drug education is a daily matter — where children can see that drugs are a problem and want parents and carers to help them understand it. Like many households, we were already coping with drug use by trespassers in our backyard, dodging used needles seemingly on every street and footpath, taking the kids on detours to avoid psychotic behaviour or the distress of overdose victims. Those downsides have generally improved since the MSIR's arrival. Meanwhile, drug users in the area now have a safe place to go, in a neighbourhood that cares to help them stay alive.

School parents who oppose the MSIR location

School parent 1 — August 2018: Thanks for making contact again and the invitation to share. My reflections have been influenced on personal experiences living close by and sending my children to RWPS. I am still waiting to see any positives from the MSIC being placed in the NRCH [two months ago] and still feel a more appropriate location should be considered.

We often have to go a longer way home when my children feel unsafe on that particular pathway running adjacent to the MSIR on Lennox Street. The drug-related activity was bad before, but it is just as bad now. Although, given the needle dispensing machine is still accessible 24/7 it is no surprise (it has since been relocated inside the MSIR). As much as I had been against the location, I had been hopeful and optimistic that it was going to help the situation in North Richmond. However, it does not seem to have made much difference but rather, left more of a feeling of uneasiness within the community.

School parent 2 — August 2018: I vividly remember the night I first learned about the reasons why an MSIR was so important but equally how uncomfortable I felt with the idea that it might be set up next door to the school. Personally, I'd not ever witnessed drug-taking on the streets before the MSIR opened and I still haven't (thankfully) but I still feel incredibly uncomfortable with the decision to build the permanent facility next to the school. We tend to approach the school from the south, so we have no need to walk past the MSIR. So my reflections are bittersweet — happy that lives are more likely to be saved but not at all happy that our children's needs have been put below everyone else's.

School parent 3 — March 2021: A father felt a level of 'unknown risk' for his two sons at the school: 'they [people with drug addiction] are seen fornicating, defecating, urinating, drug taking, swearing, fighting, abuse, oral sex being performed, needles, vomit, in no particular order, on no particular day …

and now it culminates with a dead body.' He said it was wrong to argue the facility saved lives because it could have achieved that elsewhere in North Richmond.[7]

School parent 4 — March 2021: RWPS is brilliant. Parents do go to the school because of the bi-lingual program. The teachers are incredible. That's why I won't be removing my daughter from the school even though she sees things no kids should be allowed to see. I absolutely love the school so I think I will keep the kids there.[8]

School parent 5 — March 2021: The problem has grown since the injecting room has been established. It does support a very vulnerable part of the community and they do need it but don't put it next to our kids' school. Our 10-year-old son can walk down the street saying, 'that one's taken ice, that one's taken heroin because he's sleepy, that one's got his shirt off because he's hot because he's taken ice'. It's not fair on our little kids who are living this.[9]

School parent 6 — March 2021: A parent who has lived nearby for six years and has two daughters at the school said her girls seemed safe once they were inside school grounds — past a security guard who has been monitoring the gates in recent weeks. But she said incidents inside the school crossed a line and had 'really stoked a lot of fear'. She worried about what her children saw outside while they were at school. 'I know that's one of my concerns … I can't control what they're seeing out of that fence because I'm at work.' She had not been planning to enrol her children at RWPS but was 'blown away' by its bi-lingual Mandarin immersion program. 'It is the best school in the area. It is offering what other schools aren't offering in the state.'[10]

School parent 7 — June 2021: A nearby resident and school parent disputed [the Burnet Institute's research findings in June 2021] that many of the users were local, saying she regularly saw 'users arrive in taxis and cars. Yes, the area's had a drug problem for years, but it is so much more active now. There are so many people around'.[11]

Past teacher who supports the MSIR location

'Death prompts injecting room debate' (*The Age,* 29 March 2021) confuses the issue and is misleading. It has been clearly stated that the men involved (in the tragic death outside the MSIR when it was closed and the intruder at RWPS) were NOT clients of the injecting room. So, who is making all the fuss and calling for the removal of the centre?

I was a teacher at RWPS for 12 years from 1980. It was — and still is — an amazingly vibrant, rich, diverse, and rewarding multicultural community. Teaching there involved many and varied challenges, the community drug problem being one of them. Drugs were an issue then in the community as they are today. The only difference is that today the issue is being tackled with the introduction of the safe injecting centre.

In forty-five years of teaching in the city, in farming communities, and in private and state schools, I have dealt with many children dealing with many issues. Children who suffer anxiety. Children who have lost family members, experienced domestic abuse, family breakdowns; children with debilitating disabilities; children who suffer myriad health issues, some fatal.

The most distressing, though, were the refugees, arriving weekly at RWPS in the 1980s, fleeing war-torn countries — traumatised children who had seen and experienced the worst of life. The bi-lingual programs were created to assist these new arrivals with the maintenance of their mother tongue. The programs were not intended to be a drawcard for parents who are now 'blown away' by the program.

I am tired of reading about the attitude of many current RWPS parents wanting the site closed or 'moved' because of the anxiety levels of their children. [Their] children may have had a range of unsavoury experiences but probably not as life changing as the atrocities and trauma experienced by our new arrivals from war-torn countries who flooded into RWPS. They enrol their children at the school because it continues to offer the excellent Mandarin bi-lingual program with the knowledge that RWPS is in a drug overdose hotspot and where the supervised injecting facility is located. These parents then vigorously and relentlessly campaign to close the facility. They are lucky they can change the situation for their children unlike the cases I cited above. Simple — just remove their kids from the school. They can find another excellent bi-lingual program in a 'safe' area.

It's no surprise that RWPS is still an outstanding school, attracting attention for its brilliant programs. Parents wanting their children to attend RWPS, however, should be aware that it is next to a safe injecting centre. If this is too confronting for them, go elsewhere. Let the centre continue its life-saving work. The needs of this caring, inner-city community with a long, tragic history of drug overdoses and deaths should be the priority — not individual parents.

—

My School data shows that Richmond West Primary School's NAPLAN (National Assessment Program — Literacy and Numeracy) results, 'when compared to students with a similar background', consistently rated 'close to', 'above' or 'well above' in the requisite areas. NAPLAN is the only national assessment that all Australian children undertake. It provides comparable data about student performance in reading, writing, spelling, grammar, punctuation, and numeracy, nationally and over time.[12]

Student enrolments at the school have increased steadily across the past six years: from 231 in 2015 to 307 in 2021.[13] Healthy enrolments at RWPS — due to the positive culture and the bilingual immersion program — seem assured: 'Mandarin has cemented its position as the most popular language at Victorian government schools and is now studied by almost one in five foreign-language students. The language has surged in popularity over the past decade to account for 19.6 per cent of total languages enrolments.'[14]

APPENDIX 2

MSIR clients speak

Clients of the MSIR are encouraged to leave messages in a visitors' book. Here is a sample.

I find this place is safe, friendly, and helpful. The staff are amazing with help. I feel so safe in this environment.

It was a good idea putting in the injecting room. A BIG THANK YOU.

I love how we are kept out of the cold, have assistance when needed and if anything should go wrong, they have well trained friendly staff there to call out to. Overall, it's a great place and we should have had it years ago. Thank-you.

Always teething problems but is a lot better than having a play in the carpark around kids and families.

Well done — It's about time people stopped dying in the streets.

Hello. A shout out to all and everyone who put this place into action. Before I was using by myself hoping that no one came to rob me of my gear and money (which happens a lot!) The staff here are so non-judgemental and caring. Thanks to all of you. Appreciate greatly. Thanks heaps again.

Staff were excellent. Got needed rest.

Today I witnessed kindness, caring and compassion amongst my fellow users. I was roused from a deep nod that could have been dangerous on my own. This place will and has saved lives! Thank you to humane staff.

Me the Customer! I say thank you to the people who lobbied 4 the money to make this all possible. I thought total surrender & us, the consumer, would be on the losing side on the war on drugs, but this centre is a win. So, thank you to the staff who put themselves on the front line, for us. Their time, their skills for a cause that you would have to fully believe in & to put yourselves on the front line, for us. These words are not enough. I will support you, stand up for you, respect you! Thank you!

—

'Georgia' introduced herself to me after the formalities of the March to Save Lives rally in August 2017. We have kept in touch over the years. This is her personal reflection:

My journey starts in suburban Brisbane. I feel I am, or want to be, me but nature's been cruel to me.

Later we're in country Queensland. I'm bullied in a new school. I never manage to put down roots. I've come to think all my old dreams are impossible. I'll drift from one thing to another until, at twenty-one, I return to live in a city again.

It's not long until I start to show the world around me and my family who I am and how I see my place. It's at once exciting and alternatively frightening. Despite their prosperity, I face lots of hardships and do so at times alone.

I try multiple ways to find my calling, or what others call 'getting a job' or career. I move about a lot and spend months at times in emergency accommodation. Of course — and it's almost inevitable for girls like us — much of that effort fails to bear fruit.

With only myself left to sell if I have nothing, an inevitable but then well-worn path unfolds before me. There's much to see that the comfort of my early life hasn't prepared me for.

I might have thought I'm stepping up from $40 a day in today's terms to ten or twenty times that but my need to get by in hardship — and the trauma of my loss — was blinding me to a life-changing course I'd embarked upon.

Twenty years later — I'll find myself estranged from parents who've become multi-millionaires. Time, I think, has taught us no amount of money buys happiness or a perfect life. In spite of this I don't know if I'll have a home before I'm old.

I was to first see Melbourne from its bayside streets in a week of cold nights — I don't know how I ever did it. Somehow along the way I'd get used to seeing so much it'd be unremarkable that I'd follow. And so, I did. OMG — my grief, loss and hurt of hardship, persecution and being shunned was gone. I'd never felt as calm in years. I came to later know I made a Faustian bargain that I'd return to regularly. Somehow, I took a break and years later my world — rocked by trauma once again — sent me back there.

I come here for what's almost killed me twice, but Pavlovian conditioning has me seeking out the chimera of my Faustian bargain.

On social media I'm energised for a while as there's proposed a room to keep us safe. There is a small nasty mob that says we are an inconvenience, nuisance, pest, like that we are rats or cockroaches, that saving us is no good because we'll 'use again' and that's all we are.

If a life's priceless, the cost is worth it even if we save just a few, because any easily preventable death in a country as rich as ours is one too many. This has been me, once in a friend's house and another time in a restaurant bathroom — a young worker possibly who'll never know if they didn't stumble upon me in time, I wouldn't be telling my story now.

I come to see the vision realised — to see us live another day — and become touched by learning that the small, nasty mob is very small, and more people support what's right.

I've been supporting the fight because I feel the privilege of my voice comes with a duty to fight for what's right. Knowing what I've been through, and the stories and experiences shared to me by others on this part of my life's journey.

Others avert their gaze or whisper 'there's one' or 'it's a junkie' but they'll never know the whole of my story: its hardships, traumas, and times I found stuff to do I loved. They didn't see me on the Overland Track, or the mischief and adventure of the snow, or the kindness shown by 'one of those people' who took me into a home out in the shed of an abandoned house.

I'm a human being who is transgender. I'm not ashamed nor ever will be.

I live for the day and the month. The ship's sailed for anything else.

In 2018, when Lisa Townsend walked into the MSIR, she had been addicted to heroin, on and off, for 25 years. She clearly remembers when she first heard about the MSIR opening:

> I went into the [NRCH] centre to dispose of some syringes and to get some clean ones. And there was all this buzz in the area, everyone talking about the injecting room. About how great it was and to go in there. It was safe.
>
> It just changed how I even viewed myself: they've done this for people like me, so maybe we do matter. You know, maybe we're not something that needs to be swept under the rug and forgotten. I thought, the next time I'm down there [in North Richmond], I'm going to go in there and see what this was all about.[1]

Science writer and interviewer Donna Lu asked Lisa how that facility — and its staff — saved her life.

> When you're withdrawing from heroin, there's nothing more painful … It gave me a warm, welcome environment, no matter what time of day, no matter what I needed help or support with. They saw me as a person, not a drug addict. They gave me back my self-worth. They made me feel like I mattered. Even if I tripped up, they never made me feel like a failure. That was the main thing that helped get me back on track.
>
> A lot of people think of the injecting room as a drug den. The reality is that once you go in there, you're under the eye of nurses and other staff. They help you stay safe and use in a clean

environment. Takes pressure off ambos and hospital admissions. Drugs are in the community, no matter where you live. People struggle with addiction and suffer in silence.[2]

What's Lisa's message to people who are opposed to the second SIF, in the CBD?

I want to say what if it was one of your loved ones who came to you and said they were an addict. Wouldn't they want to know there is help and support for them no matter what their situation, no matter who or what they are, or how they got there?

Wouldn't they want to know that they feel safe and supported while they tackle the reasons that they became an addict. It's an issue that isn't going away any time soon. [We] as a community need to tackle it head-on.[3]

APPENDIX 3

Decriminalisation and legalisation

Drug decriminalisation — mentioned a few times herein — refers to a reduction of legal penalties for someone possessing a small amount of illicit drugs for personal use. This can be done either by changing the penalties to civil penalties, such as fines, or by diverting drug-use offenders away from a criminal conviction and into education or treatment options (also known as 'diversion').[1]

> In 2001, Portugal decriminalised the personal possession of all drugs as part of a wider re-orientation of policy towards a health-led approach. Possessing drugs for personal use is instead treated as an administrative offence, meaning it is no longer punishable by imprisonment and does not result in a criminal record and associated stigma. Drugs are, however, still confiscated and possession may result in administrative penalties such as fines or community service.[2]

Prevent, Disrupt, Connect, Care: Victoria Police drug strategy 2020–2025 is an interesting read. Taking a similar approach to the Portuguese, Victoria Police will 'divert and refer [people who use drugs] to treatment and [will] intervene early to prevent offence escalation'.[3]

> In addition to more traditional law enforcement approaches, the strategy emphasises the need for strong, collaborative relationships between Victoria Police and its partners and community. These connections are vital to divert and refer people who need help into appropriate services and embed prevention approaches specific to local needs and harms. Under the strategy, police will continue to trial different ways of supporting programs and services which are effective in reducing the harmful effects of drugs and related problems.[4]

Fiona Patten introduced a bill into the Victorian parliament in March 2022 to decriminalise the possession and use of small quantities of drugs, and to treat addiction as a health issue, not a criminal matter. International evidence shows that removing criminal sanctions and treating drug use like a health issue:

- reduces the costs to society, especially to the criminal justice system
- reduces social costs to individuals, including improving employment prospects
- does not increase drug use
- does not increase other crime
- reduces the damaging stigma attached to people who use drugs.

Drug *legalisation*, by comparison, would move to treat currently illicit drugs in the same way alcohol and tobacco are treated, as legal, regulated products. This would further move the problem away from police and the criminal justice system and concentrate responses within health. Furthermore, governments could accrue taxation revenue from legalised drugs, as they currently do from gambling, alcohol, and tobacco: 'A regulated government monopoly could secure direct income … research suggests this may be as high as $600 million a year for a regulated cannabis market in New South Wales.'[5]

I thought about drug legalisation when speaking with a long-term resident of the North Richmond public-housing estate and supporter of the MSIR. She shared the experience of daily life in her tower. With CCTVs installed outside and incompetent security officers installed inside, drug dealing occurs unabated in the hallways and stairwells.

Listening to this description of her lived experience, I briefly imagined how that would change immediately if all illicit drugs were legalised, smashing organised crime, destroying the black market. I imagined if these drugs were regulated to ensure user safety, increasing tax income for governments for expenditure on health services — rather than funnelling existing tax money into more jails. And life for my friend would improve overnight. Just imagine.

References and resources

The titles below provide further insight into addiction, treatment, and harm reduction.

Carl Erik Fisher, *The Urge: our history of addiction*, Scribe, 2022

Matt Noffs, *Breaking the Ice: how we will get through Australia's methamphetamine crisis*, HarperCollins, 2016

Johann Hari, *Chasing the Scream: the first and last days of the war on drugs*, Bloomsbury, 2015

David Nutt, *Drugs — Without the Hot Air: minimising the harms of legal and illegal drugs*, UIT Cambridge, 2012

Ingrid van Beek, *In the Eye of the Needle: diary of a medically supervised injecting centre*, Allen & Unwin, 2004

Coronial reports

Coroner Jacqui Hawkins, *Finding into Death with Inquest: Ms A*, 20 February 2017, coronerscourt.vic.gov.au

Coroner Audrey Jamieson, *Finding into Death Without Inquest: David Leslie Chapman*, 8 May 2017, coronerscourt.vic.gov.au

Coroner Gregory McNamara, *Finding into Death Without Inquest: SO*, 7 July 2017, coronerscourt.vic.gov.au

Legislation

Drugs, Poisons and Controlled Substances Amendment (Pilot Medically Supervised Injecting Centre) Act 2017 (No. 66 of 2017), Victorian Parliament, 19 December 2017, legislation.vic.gov.au

Professional publications

Medically Supervised Injecting Room Trial: review panel summary (Hamilton report), June 2020, www2.health.vic.gov.au/about/publications/researchandreports/med-supervised-injecting-room-trial-summary

Review of the Medically Supervised Injecting Room (Hamilton report), June 2020, parliament.vic.gov.au/file_uploads/Review_of_the_Medically_Supervised_Injecting_Room_June_2020_WsP785dN.pdf

Prevent, Disrupt, Connect, Care: Victoria Police drug strategy 2020–2025, police.vic.gov.au/drug-strategy

Alison Ritter, 'Decriminalisation or Legalisation: injecting evidence in the drug law reform debate', 2021, ndarc.med.unsw.edu.au/blog/decriminalisation-or-legalisation-injecting-evidence-drug-law-reform-debate

Susana Ferreira, 'Portugal's radical drugs policy is working. Why hasn't the world copied it?', 5 December 2017, theguardian.com/news/2017/dec/05/portugals-radical-drugs-policy-is-working-why-hasnt-the-world-copied-it

Harvey Slade, 'Drug Decriminalisation in Portugal: setting the record straight', 13 May 2021, transformdrugs.org/assets/files/PDFs/Drug-decriminalisation-in-Portugal-setting-the-record-straight.pdf

Videos

Marianne Jauncey, 'Uniting Medically Supervised Injecting Centre', 2014, youtube.com/watch?v=tX_TPH8x0XU

Daniel Riddiford, 'March to Save Lives', 27 August 2017, youtube.com/watch?v=lyFNQqTuL9s

Anthony Zielke, 'March to Save Lives: rally for a medically supervised injecting centre in North Richmond', Alcohol and Drug Foundation, 27 August 2017, youtube.com/watch?v=qANj3nLGAMU

Anthony Zielke, 'RVSDS Street Art Time Lapse', Alcohol and Drug Foundation, 21 August 2017, youtube.com/watch?v=TdvUa7ZDqZE

Notes

I started writing a personal diary at the outset of the campaign. It formed the first draft of this book. I used an Excel spreadsheet to record dates, names, key events, and personal reflections. Most quotes in this book come from that source: correspondence and conversations with residents, NRCH and MSIR clients, school parents, past teachers, politicians, and journalists. I also took copious notes at meetings, at our community forums, and at the coronial inquest in December 2016. I have also drawn on the many sources listed below.

Introduction

1 Wurundjeri Woi Wurrung Cultural Heritage Aboriginal Corporation, 2021, aboriginalheritagecouncil.vic.gov.au

2 Michael Cannon, *Old Melbourne Town Before the Gold Rush*, Loch Haven Books, 1991, p. 180

3 'Meet the Australian children fluent in Mandarin', 29 October 2013, bbc.com/news/world-asia-24672295

4 Frances Adamson, 'Speech at the ACBC/Asialink Luncheon, Victoria and China at 40, in Melbourne', 9 November 2012, china.embassy.gov.au/bjng/121109HOMspeechmelbourne.html

5 Janet McCalman, *Struggletown: private and public life in Richmond 1900–1965*, Melbourne University Publishing, 1984, p. 283

6 Coroner Jacqui Hawkins, *Finding into Death with Inquest: Ms A*, 20 February 2017, coronerscourt.vic.gov.au; Coroner Audrey Jamieson,

Finding into Death Without Inquest: David Leslie Chapman, 8 May 2017, coronerscourt.vic.gov.au

7 Nico Clark, 'International Overdose Awareness Day 2021 with the Yarra Drug and Health Forum', 6 September 2021, ydhf.org.au/events/international-overdose-awareness-day-2021/

8 Richard Willingham, 'Premier Daniel Andrews rejects coroner's call for a safe injecting room', 21 February 2017, theage.com.au

9 'Uniting Medically Supervised Injecting Centre', 2014, uniting.org/community-impact/uniting-medically-supervised-injecting-centre--msic

10 Sally Finlay, 'For users, writing is on the wall', 27 April 2000, theage.com.au

1. They should do something

1 Mark Mordue, 'Down by the River: Nick Cave's boyhood in Wangaratta (1959–70)', 19 August 2019, sydneyreviewofbooks.com

2 Benjamin Preiss, '"I love this place": Andrews boards big red bus for trip to his roots', 29 October 2018, theage.com.au

3 Danny Hill, general secretary, Victorian Ambulance Union, vicambounion.org

4 Victoria Drug Policy Expert Committee, *Drugs: responding to the issues, engaging the community: stage one report*, April 2000

5 Legal and Social Issues Committee, *Inquiry into the Drugs, Poisons and Controlled Substances Amendment (Pilot Medically Supervised Injecting Centre) Bill 2017*, 7 September 2017, parliament.vic.gov.au

6 John Fitzgerald, 'Supervised Injecting Facilities: a case study of contrasting narratives in a contested health policy arena', *Critical Public Health* 23(1), 2012, pp. 77–94

7 'History of the Uniting MSIC', www.uniting.org/community-

impact/uniting-medically-supervised-injecting-centre--msic/history-of-uniting-msic

8 Ann Hill, *Clonpett to Bylands and Beyond: history of the descendants of Michael and Bridget O'Dwyer (nee Leahy)*, private family collection, 1997

9 'Ray O'Dwyer — father of the scheme', *Border Morning Mail* (Albury), 11 April 1969; corurgan.com.au

10 WAW Credit Union Co-operative Limited, wawcu.com.au/About-Us/History

11 Mark Ryan, *Mary T and MJ: 1922–2003*, private family collection, 2012

2. There's only one poll that counts

1 'History of the Uniting MSIC', www.uniting.org/community-impact/uniting-medically-supervised-injecting-centre--msic/history-of-uniting-msic

2 Paul Dietze, Rebecca J. Winter, Alisa Pedrana, and Astrid Leicht, 'Mobile Safe Injecting Facilities in Barcelona and Berlin', *International Journal of Drug Policy* 23(4), 2012, pp. 257–60

3 'Council Election Results: Yarra 2016', October 2016, vec.vic.gov.au

3. Getting on with it, starting in Sydney

1 UnitingCare NSW ACT, *Cross Currents: the story behind Australia's first and only Medically Supervised Injecting Centre*, February 2014, uniting.org/content/dam/uniting/documents/community-impact/uniting-msic/MSIC-Cross-Currents.pdf

2 'Community Impact', https://www.uniting.org/community-impact/uniting-medically-supervised-injecting-centre--msic

3 teens.drugabuse.gov; 'Fact Sheet: illicit opioids including heroin', 2021, aihw.gov.au
4 UnitingCare NSW ACT, op. cit.
5 drugabuse.gov/publications/drugfacts/heroin
6 UnitingCare NSW ACT, op. cit.
7 Benjamin Law, 'Dicey topics: Bob Carr talks politics, death and religion', 23 June 2018, theage.com.au
8 'History of the Uniting MSIC', www.uniting.org/community-impact/uniting-medically-supervised-injecting-centre--msic/history-of-uniting-msic
9 UnitingCare NSW ACT, op. cit.
10 Law Reform, Road, and Community Safety Committee, 'Transcript: Inquiry into Drug Law Reform Melbourne', 5 June 2017, pp. 188–9, parliament.vic.gov.au

4. The coronial inquest

1 Richard Wynne, 'CCTV to boost public safety in the heart of Richmond', 2 December 2016, richardwynne.com.au/media-centre/media-releases/
2 Nino Bucci, 'Melbourne's deadly "heroin rectangle": within these seven blocks, 20 people die each year', 6 December 2016, theage.com.au
3 Alex Wodak, 'The long fight for safe injecting rooms', 7 July 2018, thesaturdaypaper.com.au
4 Tony Wright, 'Change from Sex Party to Reason Party', 21 September 2017, theage.com.au

5. If not us, who? If not now, when?

1 Johann Hari, *Chasing the Scream: the first and last days of the war on drugs*, Bloomsbury, 2015

2 Matt Noffs, *Breaking the Ice: how we will get through Australia's methamphetamine crisis*, HarperCollins, 2016

3 Ingrid van Beek, *In the Eye of the Needle: diary of a medically supervised injecting centre*, Allen & Unwin, 2004

4 Allan Clear, 'Review of *In the Eye of the Needle: diary of a medically supervised injecting centre*', 15 September 2005, harmreductionjournal.biomedcentral.com

5 Laura Turner, 'It could have saved my sister's life', 19 June 2017, 3aw.com.au

6 Denham Sadler, 'Australia is lagging behind on safe injecting rooms and it's killing people', 6 June 2017, junkee.com

7 Coroner Jacqui Hawkins, *Finding into Death with Inquest: Ms A*, 20 February 2017, coronerscourt.vic.gov.au

8 Law Reform, Road, and Community Safety Committee, 'Transcript: Inquiry into Drug Law Reform Melbourne', 5 June 2017, parliament.vic.gov.au

9 Nino Bucci and Benjamin Preiss, 'Coroner recommends trial of safe injecting room in North Richmond', 20 February 2017, theage.com.au

10 Richard Willingham, 'Safe injecting room trial wins backing of influential officer Ron Iddles', 23 February 2017, theage.com.au

6. It's a marathon, not a sprint

1 'Residents for Victoria Street Drug Solutions Incorporated Association', 9 March 2017, consumer.vic.gov.au

2 *Australia21: shaping the future*, 20 March 2017, australia21.org.au

3 Marianne Jauncey, 'Uniting Medically Supervised Injecting Centre', 2014, youtube.com/watch?v=tX_TPH8x0XU

4 Harm Reduction International, www.hri.global/what-is-harm-reduction

7. Location, location, location

1 Law Reform, Road, and Community Safety Committee, 'Transcript: Inquiry into Drug Law Reform Melbourne', 5 June 2017, parliament.vic.gov.au

2 Coroner Audrey Jamieson, *Finding into Death Without Inquest: David Leslie Chapman*, 8 May 2017, coronerscourt.vic.gov.au

3 Law Reform, Road, and Community Safety Committee, op. cit.

4 Ibid.

5 Legal and Social Issues Committee, *Inquiry into the Drugs, Poisons and Controlled Substances Amendment (Pilot Medically Supervised Injecting Centre) Bill 2017*

8. The 'military wing'

1 Brendan Wrigley, 'Howard to lead drug law reform study trip to Europe and North America', 5 July 2017, thecourier.com.au

2 Goya Dmytryshchak, '"We probably weren't brave enough on injecting rooms," says Victoria's former police chief Ken Lay', 22 July 2017, theage.com.au

3 Jenny Valentish, 'The *Herald Sun*'s Ian Royall on the campaign for Richmond's safe-injecting centre', 16 January 2018, aodmediawatch.com.au

4 Coroner Gregory McNamara, *Finding into Death Without Inquest: SO*,

7 July 2017, coronerscourt.vic.gov.au

5 Charlotte Grieve, 'New Richmond alliance pushes for safe injecting room', 7 July 2017, theage.com.au

6 Ian Royall, '$17 a hit of heroin: evil drug now cheaper than a six-pack', 12 July 2017, heraldsun.com.au

7 Judy Ryan, 'How injecting rooms will save lives in Richmond and Abbotsford', 13 July 2017, heraldsun.com.au

8 Jenny Valentish, op. cit.

9 Dean Sunshine, 'Ling — 2016–2018', *Land of Sunshine: documenting street art and graffiti in Melbourne and beyond*, 20 August 2017, deansunshine.com

10 Mayonaize, mayonaize.com

11 Jean-François Mary, Jordan Westfall, Marilou Gagnon, and Zoë Dodd, 'They Talk, We Die: silent protest at the international harm reduction conference — Montreal', 14 May 2017, volteface.me

12 Alice Wilson, 'Neighbourhood watcher: Judy Ryan's war on drugs', 3 August 2017, wordpresscomauyarrareporter.wordpress.com

13 Dr Alex Wodak AM, 'The long fight for safe injecting rooms', 7 July 2018, thesaturdaypaper.com.au

9. March to Save Lives

1 Anthony Zielke, 'RVSDS Street Art Time Lapse', Alcohol and Drug Foundation, 21 August 2017, youtube.com/watch?v=TdvUa7ZDqZE

2 Dean Sunshine, *Land of Sunshine: documenting street art and graffiti in Melbourne and beyond*, 20 August 2017, deansunshine.com

3 Emily Bowden, '"You Talk We Die": Abbotsford mural calls for action on safe injecting rooms', 22 August 2017, theage.com.au

4 Ross Stevenson and John Burns, *Rumour File* interview with Judy

Ryan, 22 August 2017, 3aw.com.au
5 Ian Royall, 'Traders association president Meca Ho said traders had not been consulted by the protest', 22 August 2017, heraldsun.com.au
6 Daniel Riddiford, 'March to Save Lives', 27 August 2017, youtube.com/watch?v=lyFNQqTuL9s; Anthony Zielke, 'March to Save Lives: rally for a medically supervised injecting centre in North Richmond', Alcohol and Drug Foundation, 27 August 2017, youtube.com/watch?v=qANj3nLGAMU
7 Cameron Houston and Benjamin Preiss, 'Protesters demand safe injecting rooms in Richmond', 27 August 2017, theage.com.au
8 Jo Lauder, 'Is it time for Melbourne to get its first safe injecting room?', 1 September 2017, abc.net.au

10. 'You better come in'

1 John Ferguson, 'Heroin centres "favoured" but Victorian MPs neutral', 7 September 2017, theaustralian.com.au
2 Ian Royall, 'Bid for safe injection room denied', 7 September 2017, heraldsun.com.au
3 Legal and Social Issues Committee, *Inquiry into the Drugs, Poisons and Controlled Substances Amendment (Pilot Medically Supervised Injecting Centre) Bill 2017*
4 Richard Wynne, 'Inaugural speech to Victorian Parliament', *Hansard*, 9 November 1999, pp. 175–8, parliament.vic.gov.au
5 'Seat of Richmond Results — October 2014', 12 December 2014, abc.net.au
6 Cameron Houston and Benjamin Preiss, 'Protesters demand safe injecting rooms in Richmond', 27 August 2017, theage.com.au
7 Judy Ryan, 'Living in a government-sanctioned drug ghetto in 2017',

VAADA News, September 2017, p. 3, vaada.org.au

8 Daniel Piotrowski, 'Welcome to Australia's most liveable city: inside the heroin hellhole behind the trendy cafes', 17 September 2017, dailymail.co.uk

11. The press conference

1 Anonymous (name provided), 'Testimonials — Past Teachers — Richmond West Primary School', May 2020, savinglivesnrch.org

2 Anonymous (name provided), 'Testimonials — Residents of North Richmond and South Abbotsford', May 2020, savinglivesnrch.org

3 'Larry Campbell', en.wikipedia.org

4 Matt Johnston, Cassie Zervos, and Ian Royall, 'Safe drug injecting room trial in Melbourne's inner north', 31 October 2017, fionapatten.com.au/news/safe-drug-injecting-room-trial-melbournes-inner-north/

5 Noel Towell, 'Woman collapses from suspected overdose as premier announces injecting room trial', 31 October 2107, theage.com.au

6 Richard Wynne, *Hansard*, 10 November 1999, p. 245, parliament.vic.gov.au

7 Ally Foster, 'Victoria to trial supervised drug injection room amid heroin crisis', 31 October 2017, news.com.au

8 Jane Lee, 'Richmond residents hopeful injecting room will improve community', *AM*, 1 November 2017, abc.net.au

9 Gareth Boreham, 'Woman who lost nephews to drug overdoses welcomes safe injecting room', 31 October 2017, sbs.com.au

10 David Johnston, 'Judy Ryan celebrates safe heroin injection trial in North Richmond announcement by Victorian Premier Daniel Andrews', 31 October 2017, bordermail.com.au

12. The MSIC Act

1 Coroner Jacqui Hawkins, *Finding into Death Without Inquest: Skye Suzanne Turner*, 16 October 2017, coronerscourt.vic.gov.au

2 Richard Wynne and Judy Ryan, '"The loss has been devastating": Labor's case for safe injecting rooms', 8 November 2017, stitcher.com/show/pod-on-the-hill

3 Jane Armstrong, 'Safe injection site opens in Vancouver', 15 September 2003, theglobeandmail.com

4 drugabuse.gov/publications/drugfacts/naloxone

5 Shana Morgan, 'Tilley's fears for smack mums' kids', 18 November 2017, bordermail.com.au

6 Bill Tilley, 'Drugs, Poisons and Controlled Substances Amendment (Pilot Medically Supervised Injecting Centre) Bill 2017', second reading, 15 November 2017, parliament.vic.gov.au

7 Judy Ryan, '"Offensive" comments by Tilley are way out of step', 21 November 2017, bordermail.com.au

8 *Drugs, Poisons and Controlled Substances Amendment (Pilot Medically Supervised Injecting Centre) Act 2017 (No. 66 of 2017)*, Victorian Parliament, 19 December 2017, legislation.vic.gov.au

13. Help is on the way

1 'Info on Medically Supervised Injecting Room Trial', 1 January 2018, www2.health.vic.gov.au

2 Joe Hinchcliffe and Benjamin Preiss, 'Jeff Kennett quits key role with safe injecting rooms over ALP rorts', 27 March 2018, theage.com.au

3 Anthony Colangelo, Matilda Boseley, and Adam Carey, 'New safe injecting room to accept ice users', 11 April 2018, theage.com.au

4 Martin Heyman, 'Pill testing first at Groovin' the Moo a success', 30 April 2018, themusicnetwork.com

14. Milestone

1 Philip Mendes, 'Why does the Victorian Liberal-National Coalition remain opposed to supervised injecting facilities?', 29 November 2018, abc.net.au
2 Stephanie Anderson, 'Melbourne's first safe injecting room, clean, sterile and "will save lives"', 29 June 2018, abc.net.au
3 Benjamin Preiss, 'Up to 300 a day to use Melbourne's first safe injecting rooms', 29 June 2018, theage.com.au

15. Very early indications of success

1 Chloe Booker, '"12 lives saved" in Richmond safe drug injecting room's first week', 6 July 2018, theage.com.au
2 Luke Henriques-Gomes, 'Victorian government rejects criticism of drug-injecting room saying it is saving lives', 6 July 2018, theguardian.com
3 'Division over success of new supervised drug injecting centre', 6 July 2018, yahoo.com
4 Carlo Sands, 'New injecting room is good news: no wonder the Herald Sun hates it', 19 July 2018, greenleft.org.au
5 Chloe Booker, op. cit.
6 Genevieve Alison, 'Rejecting room — addicts snub injecting facility; nothing changed in heroin hotspot', 6 July 2018, heraldsun.com.au
7 Nicole Lee, 'A tale of two stories on Melbourne's injecting room', 9 July 2018, aodmediawatch.com.au

8 Jenny Valentish, 'The *Herald Sun*'s Ian Royall on the campaign for Richmond's safe-injecting centre', 16 January 2018, aodmediawatch.com.au
9 Alex Wodak, 'The long fight for safe injecting rooms', 7 July 2018, thesaturdaypaper.com.au
10 Bridget Hanson, Rebecca Porter, Amanda Zold, and Heather Terhorst-Miller, 'Preventing Opioid Overdose with Peer-Administered Naloxone', 9 January 2020, harmreductionjournal.biomedcentral.com
11 *VCE Legal Studies Unit 4 — The People, the Parliament and the Courts*, 30 October 2019, parliament.vic.gov.au/images/Unit_4_AOS_2_Module_5_-_Student_Learning_Activities.pdf
12 'Welcome to Yarra Street Pastors', streetpastors.org
13 Launch Housing, launchhousing.org.au

16. The election

1 Luke Henriques-Gomes, 'It's saving lives: community rallies to support Melbourne's drug injecting room', 16 September 2018, theguardian.com/australia-news/
2 Johann Hari at Melbourne Town Hall, 20 September 2018, www.drugpolicy.org.au/johann_hari
3 Lucy Williams, 'Drug reform activist running for Richmond', 24 November 2018, farragomagazine.com/2018/11/24/drug-reform-activist-running-for-richmond/
4 Fair Treatment campaign launch, 12 October 2018, www.fairtreatment.org
5 'Uniting's Fair Treatment Campaign Launch with Sir Richard Branson', 12 October 2018, www.insights.uca.org.au/events/unitings-fair-treatment-campaign-launch-with-sir-richard-branson/

6 Cathy McGowan, Back of House program, 12–14 October 2018

7 Jon Faine, 'Premier Andrews: "the local residents have said we had to do something"', 22 November 2018, abc.net.au

8 Adam Carey and Aisha Dow, 'Victorian Liberals to shut down injecting room in a week if elected', 21 November 2018, theage.com.au

9 Richard Willingham and Stephanie Anderson, 'Liberal Party won't run in Richmond, dealing blow to Labor's Richard Wynne in fight against Greens', 8 November 2018, abc.net.au

10 'An Analysis of the Victorian State Election', June 2019, parliament.vic.gov.au

11 '2014 Election Results: Richmond', vec.vic.gov.au

12 '2018 Election Results: Richmond', vec.vic.gov.au

13 Barrie Cassidy, *Insiders* interview with Daniel Andrews, 25 November 2018, facebook.com/InsidersABC/videos/503816973465697

14 '2018 Election Results: Richmond', vec.vic.gov.au

15 '2018 Election Results: Kew', vec.vic.gov.au

16 Ben Potter, 'Liberal's John Pesutto loses seat of Hawthorn', 4 December 2018, afr.com

17 Benjamin Preiss, 'Fiona Patten wins back upper house seat after nervous two-week wait', 11 December 2018, theage.com.au

18 John Ferguson, 'Locals up in arms against needle exchange facility', 25 May 2019, theaustralian.com.au

17. Highs and lows

1 Paul Sakkal, 'Public heroin use spurs calls for change at Richmond injecting room', 10 April 2019, theage.com.au

2 Margaret Hamilton, 3 August 2020, ydhf.org.au/professor-margaret-hamilton-presents-on-the-msir-review-to-the-community/

3 Michael Fowler, '"It's not fair": residents vote in favour of moving safe injecting room out of Richmond', 15 May 2019, theage.com.au

4 Law Enforcement Assistant Diversion (LEAD) program in Seattle, kingcounty.gov/depts/community-human-services/mental-health-substance-abuse/diversion-reentry-services/lead.aspx

5 Michael Fowler, op. cit.

6 Federal election results, 2019: 'Melbourne, VIC', results.aec.gov.au/24310/Website/HouseDivisionPage-24310-228.htm

7 Jewel Topsfield, 'Coroner backs injecting room despite no drop in local heroin deaths', 19 June 2019, theage.com.au

8 Nico Clark, 'Medically Supervised Injecting Room Video Tour', 26 September 2019, nrch.com.au/msir-tour/

9 Mark E. Dean, 'The Visitors Book', *Meanjin*, Winter 2019, search.informit.org/doi/10.3316/INFORMIT.510176457866102

10 Sun Tzu, *The Art of War: the ancient classic*, Capstone Publishing, 2010

11 www2.health.vic.gov.au/alcohol-and-drugs/aod-treatment-services/pharmacotherapy-for-aod-treatment

12 www.turningpoint.org.au/treatment/about-addiction/treating-addiction/pharmacotherapy

13 Peta Credlin, 'North Richmond Injecting Room must be "urgently relocated"', 13 September 2019, www.skynews.com.au

14 Ibid.

15 *Review of the Medically Supervised Injecting Room* (Hamilton report), June 2020, parliament.vic.gov.au/file_uploads/Review_of_the_Medically_Supervised_Injecting_Room_June_2020_WsP785dN.pdf

16 Jewel Topsfield, 'Divisive injecting room debate having "deleterious effect" on local school', 18 September 2019, theage.com.au

17 Rachel Eddie, Jewel Topsfield, and Benjamin Preiss, 'Drug trafficking charges for outreach workers linked to safe injecting room',

24 October 2019, theage.com.au

18 Adam Cooper, 'Drug outreach worker guilty of trafficking heroin appeals jail term', 28 September 2020, theage.com.au

19 Joanna Miler, Hannah Carver, Rebecca Foster, and Tessa Parkes, 'Provision of peer support at the intersection of homelessness and problem substance use services', *BMC Public Health* 20, article no. 641, 7 May 2020

20 Joanna Flynn, 'Statement on the Independent Review', 19 December 2019, nrch.com.au

21 Jewel Topsfield, 'Not all residents want injecting room moved', 19 November 2019, theage.com.au

22 Monique Hore, 'Safe injecting room "destroying the community"', 25 November 2019, heraldsun.com.au

23 Marnie Banger, 'Push for perspective on Vic injecting room', 25 November 2019, canberratimes.com.au

18. A second facility

1 Richmond Good Karma Network, facebook.com

2 'Testimonials', savinglivesnrch.org

3 Rohan Smith, '*Herald Sun* photographer captures confronting moment addict overdoses in front of children', 12 February 2020, news.com.au

4 Orange Sky Australia, charity that offers free laundry, showers, and conversation to homeless people, orangesky.org.au

5 *Medically Supervised Injecting Room Trial: review panel summary* (Hamilton report), June 2020, www2.health.vic.gov.au/about/publications/researchandreports/med-supervised-injecting-room-trial-summary; *Review of the Medically Supervised Injecting Room* (Hamilton report), June 2020, parliament.vic.gov.au/file_uploads/

Review_of_the_Medically_Supervised_Injecting_Room_June_2020_WsP785dN.pdf
6 Ibid.
7 Ibid.
8 'Second safe injecting facility announced for Melbourne', 5 June 2020, abc.net.au
9 Yvonne Bonomo, 'It may not be pretty, but it works', 7 June 2020, theage.com.au
10 www.theguardian.com/australia-news/live/2020/aug/24/coronavirus-australia-latest-updates-health-economy-business-queensland-hotspots-victoria-hotel-inquiry-parliament-scott-morrison-josh-frydenberg-jobkeeper-follow-live?page=with:block-5f431f248f08f9fdc758c715#block-5f431f248f08f9fdc758c715
11 Monique Hore, 'COVID-19 cases reported at North Richmond safe-injecting room', 23 August 2020, heraldsun.com.au
12 'Council Election Results — Yarra 2020 — Melba Ward', 23 October 2020, vec.vic.gov.au
13 Ibid.
14 'Council Election Results — Yarra 2020 — Langridge Ward', 23 October 2020, vec.vic.gov.au
15 Sam Biondo, 'Demand for injecting room can't be denied', 11 January 2021, heraldsun.com.au

19. Victoria Street Alive!

1 victoriastreetalive.com.au/maker-s-market
2 victoriastreetalive.com.au/street-posters
3 victoriastreetalive.com.au/artexhibition
4 Cara Waters, 'Art brings residents and safe injecting room users together', 20 June 2022, theage.com.au

Afterword

1 Janet McCalman, *Struggletown: private and public life in Richmond 1900–1965*, Melbourne University Publishing, 2021, pp. x–xii
2 Alex Chapman, 'Dead body found just outside Melbourne primary school as drop-off time set to begin', 18 March 2021, 7news.com.au
3 David Estcourt, 'Man who allegedly entered school armed with knife, homemade knuckle dusters faces court', 18 March 2021, theage.com.au
4 Suzan Delibasic and Shannon Deery, 'We're living in constant fear', 19 March 2021, heraldsun.com.au
5 Tom Cowie and David Estcourt, 'Parents warn of "damaging" injecting site', 25 March 2021, theage.com.au
6 Neil Mitchell, 'The comment from nine-year-old Richmond girl that left Neil Mitchell shaken', 24 March 2021, 3aw.com.au
7 Brendan Nottle, 'CBD safe injecting site makes sense for city's recovery', 8 July 2021, theage.com.au
8 Angus Thompson and Lucy Cormack, 'Kings Cross businesses want removal of injecting centre to revive strip', 9 February 2021, smh.com.au
9 John Moyle, 'Kings Cross injecting centre celebrates 20 years', 12 May 2021, sydneysentinel.com.au
10 Ingrid van Beek, 'Alcohol not injecting room the real worry for the revival of Kings Cross', 14 February 2021, smh.com.au
11 Sumeyya Ilanbey and Ashleigh McMillan, 'Push to oust Lib MP over drink-driving', 1 November 2021, theage.com.au
12 Kate Halfpenny, 'Let me be the one to break it to you, Tim Smith — alcohol is a drug', 5 November 2021, theage.com.au; 'Alcohol, Tobacco and Other Drugs in Australia', 24 September 2021, aihw.gov.au

13 Tim Smith, twitter.com/timsmithmp/status/1182201873006125056

14 Marianne Jauncey, online response to 'Death of Sydney man puts alcohol home deliveries in spotlight', 1 November 2021, 9now.nine.com.au/a-current-affair/

15 adf.org.au/reducing-risk/alcohol/

16 adf.org.au/insights/alcohol-epidemic/

17 Yvonne Bonomo, Sam Biondo, John Ryan, et al., 'The Australian Drug Harms Ranking Study', *Journal of Psychopharmacology* 33(7), 2019, pp. 759–68

18 Rachel Eddie, '"Game changer" treatment cuts heroin use', 10 May 2021, theage.com.au

19 Anthony Weeks, Shelley Cogger, and Nico Clark, 'Initial experience with subcutaneous depot buprenorphine in a medically supervised injecting facility', *Drug and Alcohol Review* 40(7), 2021, pp. 1,354–5

20 Erin Cooper, 'New heroin treatment option yielding positive results among patients at Melbourne injecting rooms', 15 June 2021, abc.net.au

21 Ibid.

22 'Callouts have fallen', *The Age*, 10 May 2021

23 Paul Dietze, 'North Richmond SIF supporting the most vulnerable, new study shows', 11 June 2021, www.burnet.edu.au

24 Donna Lu, '"I'm living proof": how Melbourne's drug-injecting room has changed — and saved — lives', 19 June 2021, theguardian.com

25 Paul Dietze, op. cit.; Rachel Eddie, 'Melbourne's first safe injecting room "fulfilling its purpose" research finds', 11 June 2021, theage.com.au

26 John Masanauskas, 'Melbourne CBD supervised injecting room plans stall', 4 January 2022, heraldsun.com.au

Appendix 1. Not all school parents

1 'Testimonials', savinglivesnrch.org
2 Ibid.
3 Ibid.
4 Ibid.
5 Ibid.
6 Rachel Eddie, 'Death prompts injecting room debate', 29 March 2021, theage.com.au
7 Ibid.
8 Neil Mitchell, 'The comment from nine-year-old Richmond girl that left Neil Mitchell shaken', 24 March 2021, 3aw.com.au
9 Tom Cowie and David Estcourt, 'Parents warn of 'damaging' injecting site', 25 March 2021, theage.com.au
10 Rachel Eddie, op. cit.
11 Rachel Eddie, 'Injecting room "on course"', 11 June 2021, theage.com.au
12 myschool.edu.au/naplan-explained
13 myschool.edu.au/school/44988
14 Madeleine Heffernan, 'Mandarin takes top spot at schools', 8 November 2021, theage.com.au

Appendix 2. MSIR clients speak

1 Donna Lu, 'The injecting centre that saved Lisa's life — interview with Lisa Townsend', *The Full Story*, 8 July 2021, podcasts.apple.com/au/podcast/full-story/id1482061243
2 Ibid.
3 Ibid.

Appendix 3. Decriminalisation and Legalisation

1 Alison Ritter, 'Decriminalisation or Legalisation: injecting evidence in the drug law reform debate', 2021, ndarc.med.unsw.edu.au/blog/decriminalisation-or-legalisation-injecting-evidence-drug-law-reform-debate

2 Harvey Slade, 'Drug Decriminalisation in Portugal: setting the record straight', 13 May 2021, transformdrugs.org/assets/files/PDFs/Drug-decriminalisation-in-Portugal-setting-the-record-straight.pdf; Susana Ferreira, 'Portugal's radical drugs policy is working. Why hasn't the world copied it?', 5 December 2017, theguardian.com/news/2017/dec/05/portugals-radical-drugs-policy-is-working-why-hasnt-the-world-copied-it

3 *Prevent, Disrupt, Connect, Care: Victoria Police drug strategy 2020–2025*, police.vic.gov.au/drug-strategy; Simone Fox Koob, 'Police take health-focused approach to tackle rising drug use', 16 December 2020, theage.com.au

4 'Victoria Police launch five-year strategy to tackle drug related harm', 17 December 2020, miragenews.com

5 Alison Ritter, op. cit.